BEING A TEACHER EDUCATOR

This collection offers a timely and wide-ranging contribution to the research-informed improvement of the work of teacher educators. Drawing on original research studies conducted across a range of European countries, Canada, and Israel, contributors offer insight into not only questions of curriculum and programme development, research, and professional development, but also their day-to-day experience as teacher educators, student teachers, and mentors in schools.

Themes explored include teaching and working with students, teacher educators as researchers, the partnership work of teacher educators, the professional development needs of teacher educators, professional development approaches for improving teacher education, and teacher educator empowerment.

Arising from the international community of the Association for Teacher Educators in Europe (ATEE), and drawing together theory and practice, this book offers a unique survey of the contributions of teacher educators and charts a path for future directions of the field.

Anja Swennen has retired from the Vrije Universiteit in Amsterdam, the Netherlands, where she was a teacher educator and researcher. She is currently co-editor of the *European Journal of Teacher Education*.

Elizabeth White is Principal Lecturer at the Centre for Research in Professional and Work-Related Learning, University of Hertfordshire, UK.

BEING A TEACHER EDUCATOR

Research-Informed Methods for Improving Practice

*Edited by Anja Swennen
and Elizabeth White*

Routledge
Taylor & Francis Group

LONDON AND NEW YORK

First published 2021
by Routledge
2 Park Square, Milton Park, Abingdon, Oxon OX14 4RN

and by Routledge
52 Vanderbilt Avenue, New York, NY 10017

Routledge is an imprint of the Taylor & Francis Group, an informa business

British Library Cataloguing-in-Publication Data
A catalogue record for this book is available from the British Library

Library of Congress Cataloging-in-Publication Data
Names: Swennen, Anja, editor. | White, Elizabeth, editor.
Title: Being a teacher educator : research-informed methods for improving practice / Edited by Anja Swennen and Elizabeth White.
Description: Abingdon, Oxon ; New York, NY : Routledge, 2021. | Includes bibliographical references and index.
Identifiers: LCCN 2020019615 (print) | LCCN 2020019616 (ebook) | ISBN 9780367518585 (hardback) | ISBN 9780367518592 (paperback) | ISBN 9781003055457 (ebook)
Subjects: LCSH: Teachers—Training of. | Teachers—In-service training. | Teacher educators. | Educational change.
Classification: LCC LB1707 .B46 2021 (print) | LCC LB1707 (ebook) | DDC 370.71/1—dc23
LC record available at https://lccn.loc.gov/2020019615
LC ebook record available at https://lccn.loc.gov/2020019616

ISBN: 978-0-367-51858-5 (hbk)
ISBN: 978-0-367-51859-2 (pbk)
ISBN: 978-1-003-05545-7 (ebk)

Typeset in Bembo
by Apex CoVantage, LLC

CONTENTS

FIGURES

TABLES

EDITORS

Anja Swennen has retired from the Vrije Universiteit in Amsterdam, the Netherlands, where she was a researcher and teacher educator. Her research focussed on teacher education, the professional development of teacher educators, and the history and policy of teacher education. Lately, she is thinking and writing about the concept of Brave Research – research that encourages communities of enquiry that include and benefit students, teachers, teacher educators, and researchers. Anja published several academic books, articles, and book chapters about policy, practice, and research in teacher education as well as on identity and autonomy of teacher educators. She also disseminated her work in professional publications and at national and international conferences. Anja is co-editor of the *European Journal of Teacher Education*.

Elizabeth White is Principal Lecturer at the University of Hertfordshire, UK. Her responsibilities include research lead in teacher education and professional lead for the School Direct Route into teaching. She currently co-chairs the Association for Teacher Education in Europe's Research and Development Community for the Professional Development of Teacher Educators. Her research focuses on teacher educators, especially those who are based in their workplace, alongside their learners. She is interested in their pedagogical choices, their professional development needs, and how they can be nurtured in a professional learning community to support their emerging identity.

CONTRIBUTORS

Karl Attard is Senior Lecturer at the University of Malta. Karl obtained a Bachelor of Education (Honours) degree from the University of Malta in 2000, a Master of Science from Loughborough University in 2001, a PhD from Loughborough University in 2006 focussing on ongoing learning in the teaching profession, and a Master in Education with distinction focussing on educational leadership of the University of Malta in 2008. Karl's research interests are career-long professional development of teachers and teacher educators, in-service and pre-service teacher education, reflective practice, teacher-led research, informal workplace learning, collaborative learning communities, narrative enquiry, and self-study methods.

Smadar Bar-Tal is a lecturer and techno-pedagogical consultant of the Center for Innovation and Excellence in Teaching at Levinsky College, Israel. Smadar has a PhD from Anglia Ruskin University. She served as head of the high school teacher training programme at Levinsky College and as head of the department of online teaching and online teaching environments at the MOFET Institute in Tel Aviv. She is a researcher and curriculum designer of technology-mediated teaching and learning, particularly online discussions and social networks. Smadar teaches courses on digital pedagogy and leads online workshops for novice teachers.

Mhairi C. Beaton joined the School of Education at the University of Aberdeen, UK, working with both student teachers and qualified teachers, following many years teaching in the Highlands of Scotland. Mhairi is currently Senior Lecturer at the Carnegie School of Education at Leeds Beckett University, in the north of England. She works with qualified teachers who are seeking to make their classroom practice more inclusive through master's- and doctoral-level study. Mhairi's research interests lie at the intersection of inclusion, student voice, and teacher education.

Claire Dickerson is a research fellow in the School of Education at the University of Hertfordshire, UK. Her research interests include teacher education, professional learning, and changing practices in learning and teaching. Recent studies have involved documenting the views and experiences of student teachers, teachers, and teacher educators in schools and higher education institutions. The research findings contribute to learning about the value of articulating pedagogy as a means of developing practice and to understanding teacher education and teacher development.

Maria Assunção Flores works at the University of Minho, Portugal. She received her PhD at the University of Nottingham, UK, in 2002. She was a visiting scholar at the University of Cambridge, UK, in 2008 and 2009 and at the University of Glasgow, UK, in 2016 and 2017. Her research interests include teacher professionalism and identity, teacher education and professional development, curriculum, assessment, leadership, and higher education. She has published extensively on these topics both nationally and internationally. She was the Chair of the International Study Association on Teachers and Teaching (2013–2019) and is Past Chair of the Board of Directors of the International Council on Education for Teaching. She is executive editor of the journal *Teachers and Teaching Theory and Practice* and co-editor of the *European Journal of Teacher Education*.

Paul Holdsworth studied Romance Languages at Cambridge University, UK, after which he qualified in Public Administration. For several years, he led the European Commission's work in the field of school education policy, working alongside academics and other professionals from across Europe. He developed a particular interest in the initial and continuing education of teachers, and of those who educate them. This led him to study for a master's degree in Education at the University of Bath, UK, as part of which he undertook research amongst the teacher educator community. He was awarded a Master of Arts with distinction in Education.

Monique Leijgraaf is currently working as a teacher educator and educational researcher at the University of Applied Sciences iPabo in Amsterdam, a Dutch college of teacher education for primary education. Both her teaching and research focus on diversity and critical citizenship, in particular on issues related to teacher education for social justice, power and power relations, privilege, and pluralism. She is one of the chairs of the Research and Development Community for Social Justice, Equity and Diversity of the Association for Teacher Education in Europe.

Ann MacPhail is a physical education teacher educator in the Department of Physical Education and Sport Sciences, and Assistant Dean, Research in the Faculty of Education and Health Sciences at the University of Limerick, Ireland. Her teaching and research interests focus on (physical education) teacher education, professional learning needs of teacher educators, curriculum and assessment, curriculum and instruction models, ethnography, and self-study.

Jean Murray (PhD) is Professor of Education in the Cass School of Education and Communities at the University of East London in England. Her research focuses on the sociological analysis of teacher education policies, research, and practices internationally. Jean has written well over 200 books, chapters, journal articles, and official reports on these issues and has also run a large number of educational research projects. Jean is a National Teaching Fellow for Advance HE in the UK. She has taught at all levels of higher education and in schools, as well as being an educational consultant on professional learning for governments, NGOs, and universities across the world. She has been an active member of the academic community in the UK and internationally for more than 20 years.

David Powell started his teaching career as a part-time lecturer in Travel and Tourism at Stafford College, UK, in 1986. He became a senior manager and moved from there, via staff development, into initial teacher education (ITE) in 2005. He is presently Director of the Education and Training Consortium, an ITE partnership between 20 further-education colleges and the University of Huddersfield. His research interests include further education–based teacher educators' use of modelling and how student teachers learn how to teach. David is the editor of *Teaching in Lifelong Learning*, a journal to inform and improve practice, aimed at the further education sector.

Tom Russell is Professor in the Faculty of Education at Queen's University, Canada, where he taught from 1977 to 2019. His research focussed on how people learn to teach and how teachers improve their teaching, with special reference to learning from experience and the epistemology of practice. He is particularly interested in how beginning teachers develop professional craft knowledge from practicum experiences and their first year of teaching. He has edited a number of books with international colleagues, and he was co-editor of *Studying Teacher Education: A Journal of Self-Study of Teacher Education Practices* in its first 15 years of publication.

Tami Seifert is currently Senior Lecturer at Kibbutzim College of Education, Tel Aviv, Israel. She has a PhD in Instructional Design and Technology from Old Dominion University (Virginia, USA). She served as Head of the Department of Educational Computing, Head of Academic ICT, and Vice Director of the Teacher Training for Graduates Program at Kibbutzim College of Education. At present, she also instructs teacher educators specialising in learning design in the information age at the MOFET Institute. The curriculum contains theoretical and practical elements and is meant to prepare teacher educators to serve as role models for their own students.

Leah Shagrir is a teacher educator and a researcher. She is the Academic Head of the Eilat Campus, Levinsky College of Education, Israel. For the last few years she has served as the elected chair of the research and development community called the Professional Development of Teacher Educators, part of the Association for Teacher Education in Europe. For 15 years Leah has headed the MOFET Institute – a national intercollegiate research centre for professional development of teacher educators. In 2009 Leah was awarded a Distinguished Fulbright Award in Teaching to conduct research at Vanderbilt University in Tennessee, USA.

Miranda Timmermans is working as Applied Professor at Avans University of Applied Sciences, Breda, the Netherlands. Her PhD was on the quality of professional development schools. In addition to this quality issue, her research and work is also focussed on workplace learning and teaching and school-based teacher education – trying to find critical characteristics of a workplace pedagogy. Miranda is the chair of Velon, the Dutch Association of Teacher Educators. The aim of Velon is to contribute to the quality of the professional development of teacher educators and of the profession as a whole.

ACKNOWLEDGEMENTS

We would like to thank the teacher educator community of the Association for Teacher Education in Europe (ATEE) who have contributed in so many ways to this book: as individual participants in the research projects and as discussants at the annual conferences, enabling us to develop our ideas; and to the Professional Development of Teacher Educators Research and Development Community whose members contributed to *Becoming a Teacher Educator* and collaborative research project initiatives. Thank you to Åsa Morberg, chair of ATEE, for her encouragement.

A special thanks to our colleagues who reviewed the chapters: Fatma Bikmaz, Pete Boyd, Alaster Douglas, Ellen Beate Hellne-Halvorsen, Marcel van der Klink, Quinta Kools, Joana Maria Mas Mestre, David Powell, Jeanny Prat, Miranda Timmermans, and Corinne van Velzen.

Thank you all very much for your constructive reviews.

Anja Swennen
Elizabeth White

PREFACE TO *BEING A TEACHER EDUCATOR: RESEARCH-INFORMED METHODS FOR IMPROVING PRACTICE*

In 2004 I attended my first Association of Teacher Education in Europe (ATEE) conference in Agrigento, Sicily. I had finished my PhD on teacher educators in England a few years earlier, and was seeking international collaboration to extend my research and to develop my practice, both as a teacher educator working with pre-service teachers and as a mentor involved in the induction of new colleagues joining my university. I was so lucky in my timing, as that conference saw the first meeting of the Research and Development Community (RDC) on the professional development of teacher educators (PDTE), started by Anja Swennen and Marcel van der Klink. That conference was astonishing for me; through interacting with colleagues from across the world, I felt my knowledge about being a teacher educator expanding day by day.

During the past 15 years, this highly active RDC has become a major source of my professional learning, and many of its members have been important influences on my research and practice. Those positive influences have also affected in similar ways the work of many other teacher educators. Since its inception, the group has always produced and exchanged research-informed knowledge about the professional development of teacher educators, often by engaging in joint studies and activities. It was a great pleasure, for example, to see the publication of the group's first ATEE book – *Becoming a Teacher Educator* – edited by Anja and Marcel in 2009. On behalf of the RDC, I was also able to co-edit, with Jenny Harrison, a Special Issue of the *European Journal of Teacher Education* (volume 31, issue 2) on induction and further professional development for teacher educators. Importantly, through these and many other collective projects and publications, the work of the RDC has had an impact by helping to improve the professional development of teacher educators in Europe and beyond, strengthening the position of our occupational group in the fast-changing field of teacher education.

I was delighted, then, to receive an invitation last year from Anja and Elizabeth White (the current RDC co-chair) to write this preface for a second ATEE book, this time focussing on *being a teacher educator* and research-informed methods for improving practice. I gladly accepted the invitation, feeling that the book was a timely one and welcoming its emphases on research to improve practice and to value teacher educators' voices. These things seem vital because, as those of us who work in the field know only too well, pre-service teacher education is now widely seen as a policy lever for bringing about changes in the teaching profession and subsequent overall improvement in the quality of schooling systems. This emphasis is not new, of course: historical analyses (see, for example, Larabee 2004; Swennen 2012) show that teacher education has long been a focus of policy makers' attention when teachers and teaching are deemed to be inadequate by governments. What is new is the *systematic* politicisation of teacher education internationally, with increasing levels of government intervention and regulation and resultant 'reform' agendas in many countries across the developed and developing worlds (Trippestad, Swennen, and Werler 2017).

Furthermore, as Chapter 1 of this book identifies, in recent years teacher educators themselves have come under the policy microscope with their centrality to teacher education recognised in pan-European policy documents, including a detailed report from the European Commission (2013). At this level of European policy, the recognition has been positive in the main, but in other contexts, teacher educators have been the systematic targets of denigration as educational policy makers, seeking to 'reform' teacher education and play a 'blame game' (see, for example, Gove 2013; Cochran-Smith, Piazza, and Power 2013). These recognitions – and mis-recognitions – of teacher educators bring mixed blessings; as Goodwin (2019, v) states, the occupational group is "simultaneously blamed for the failures of schools and teachers, at the same time that we are perceived to be essential instruments – linchpins – of reform, change and innovation". Certainly then, teacher educators are "a profession increasingly in the public eye" (European Commission 2013, 6).

Two further factors add further complexity to considering teacher educators' positions in the field: first, the shifting and ill-defined nature of the occupational group itself; and second, the many and often contested discourses and practices around research in and on teacher education. The first factor informs the context for this book; the second is central to its validity and its contribution to research-informed practice in the field.

Undeniably, teacher educators belong to a heterogeneous and fast-changing occupational group. As long ago as the 1990s, Ducharme identified a 'problem of definition' (1993, 2) in its membership criteria, due in part, to the differing roles and types of work undertaken within the academy, and in part due to self and communal ownership of, or resistance to, the label of 'teacher educator'. Certainly, in some European countries – for example, Ireland and Norway, where teacher education has taken 'a university turn' (Murray 2015) by increasing the academic levels of pre-service programmes – similar debates about being, or not being, a teacher educator continue to burn.

Other policy changes have also triggered shifts in who can be defined as a teacher educator. Highly significant here is 'the practice turn' (Mattsson, Eilertson, and Rorrison 2011; Reid 2011). Across Europe, this has led to schools and serving teachers becoming more active in teacher education (European Commission 2015; Murray 2015); in England and parts of the USA it has even resulted in schools taking the lead in pre-service programmes. This has resulted in more inclusive definitions of teacher educators as "all of those [who] actively facilitate the (formal) learning of student teachers and teachers" (European Commission 2013, 8).

There have long been divisive – and sometimes contradictory – concepts, discourses, and practices about research within teacher educators' work (Ellis et al. 2014; Murray and Kosnik 2013). Teacher education is usually stated to be research informed or research based, and teaching and research tend to be routinely portrayed as synergistic in teacher educators' work and identities. But, at one and the same time, research and teaching may also be positioned as competing activities, separated from one another by academic norms and working practices and having different significance for teacher educators, according to their positions in academic hierarchies. This is a familiar dualism which has its roots in the history of teacher education, but in contemporary versions of teacher educators' work, it is common to find such tensions even in national contexts where research is widely acknowledged as a key element of professional learning.

The BERA RSA report (2014) on research *in* and *on* teacher education across the UK usefully identified three ways in which schools and teacher education institutions engage with research: to inform programme design; as content for programmes; and as the active production of new knowledge. This admirable report emphasised the importance of all these types of research in developing practice across the continuum of teacher education, but, regrettably, it did not voice a clear opinion on how all teacher educators could engage in the *production* of research; nor did it analyse how such activity could contribute to their practice, identities, and professional development.

This book clearly helps to redress that gap, focussing as it does on research designed to improve teaching, inform reflective practice, and contribute to professional development. Focuses here are on four themes: research about and by teacher educators; teacher education in partnership between schools and higher education institutions; knowledge of the work of teacher educators; and the professional development of this occupational group. All of these themes are very timely, given that the book is written at a time when teacher educators in many countries are facing such significant changes in how their work is conceptualised and enacted.

Collections like this book provide a model of how well-framed and authentic research by practitioners can support the development of individual teacher educators as scholars and researchers. Each chapter also helps to understand 'insider perspectives' (Sikes and Potts 2008), a factor which, as Chapter 1 rightly argues, is important in offering significant 'insider' insights into broader changes in the field of teacher education; these are essential to consider as they form a further part of the contexts which have shaped and driven the production of this book.

As I indicated previously, the research reported here is not only of individual benefit to the teacher educators producing it and to their students; rather, supported by the ATEE RDC, it will benefit a much larger professional community. It thus has the potential to further strengthen knowledge of practice, policy, and identity in the field and to empower teacher educators as an occupational group. In the words of Vanassche and Kelchtermans (2015, 15), it meets, then, the double agenda of contributing to the development of practice, and to "the development of a publicly accessible and grounded knowledge base on teacher education".

This is certainly an interesting and highly relevant time to be researching in the field of teacher education. This book reminds us that, whilst teacher educators may be under increasing pressure to meet global reform agendas, with their active engagement in research often a struggle and the demographics of their occupational group changing, it is still possible for individuals and collectives to find new, creative, and research-informed insights into our field. Long may this space for such creativity and high-quality research continue, and long may research and development groups such as this RDC continue to flourish.

Jean Murray, The Cass School,
The University of East London, UK

References

BERA-RSA. 2014. *Research and the Teaching Profession: Building the Capacity for a Self-Improving Education System*. London: RSA.

Cochran-Smith, M., P. Piazza, and C. Power. 2013. "The Politics of Accountability: Assessing Teacher Education in the United States." *The Educational Forum* 77 (1): 6–27.

Ducharme, E. 1993. *The Lives of Teacher Educators*. New York: Teachers College Press.

Ellis, V., J. McNicholl, A. Blake, and J. McNally. 2014. "Academic Work and Proletarianisation: A Study of Higher Education-Based Teacher Educators." *Teaching and Teacher Education* 40: 33–43.

European Commission. 2013. "Supporting Teacher Educators for Better Learning Outcomes." http://ec.europa.eu/education/policy/school/doc/support-teacher-educators_en.pdf.

European Commission. 2015. "Strengthening Teaching in Europe: New Evidence ROR Teachers Compiled by Eurydice and CRELL." http://ec.europa.eu./education/library/policy/teaching-profession-practices.en.pdf.

Goodwin, L. 2019. "Preface." In *International Research, Policy and Practice in Teacher Education: Insider Perspectives*, edited by J. Murray, A. Swennen, and C. Kosnik, V–VII. Switzerland: Springer Nature.

Gove, M., 2013, March 23. "I Refuse To Surrender to the Marxist Teachers Hell-Bent on Destroying our Schools." *The Daily Mail.* www.dailymail.co.uk/debate/article-2298146/I-refuse-surrender-Marxist-teachers-hell-bent-destroying-schools-Education-Secretary-berates-new-enemies-promise-opposing-plans.html.

Larabee, D. 2004. *The Trouble with Ed Schools*. New York: Yale University Press.

Mattsson, M., T. Eilertson, and D. Rorrison, eds. 2011. *A Practicum Turn in Teacher Education*. Rotterdam: Sense.

Murray, J. 2015. "Teacher Education and Higher Education." In *Teacher Education in Times of Change*, edited by G. Beauchamp, L. Clarke, M. Hulme, M. Jephcote, A. Kennedy,

G. Magennis, I. Menter, J. Murray, T. Mutton, T. O'Doherty, and G. Peiser, 180–200, Bristol: Policy Press.

Murray, J., and C. Kosnik, eds. 2013. *Academic Lives and Identities in Teacher Education*. London: Routledge.

Reid, J. 2011. "A Practice Turn for Teacher Education?" *Asia-Pacific Journal of Teacher Education* 39 (3): 293–310.

Sikes, P., and A. Potts, eds. 2008. *Researching Education from the Inside: Investigating Institutions from Within*. London: Routledge/Falmer.

Swennen, A. 2012. *Van Oppermeesters tot Docenten Hoger Onderwijs: De Ontwikkeling van het Beroep en de Identiteit van Lerarenopleiders* [The Development of the Profession and Identity of Teacher Educators]. Amsterdam: VU University Amsterdam. http://dare.ubvu.vu.nl/handle/1871/38045.

Trippestad, T., A. Swennen, and T. Werler. 2017. *The Struggle for Teacher Education; International Perspectives on Governance and Reforms*. London: Bloomsbury Academic.

Vanassche, E., and G. Kelchtermans. 2015. "Facilitating Self-Study of Teacher Education Practices: Toward a Pedagogy of Teacher Educator Professional Development." *Professional Development in Education* 42 (1): 100–122.

1

INTRODUCTION TO *BEING A TEACHER EDUCATOR*

Research-Informed Methods for Improving Practice

Elizabeth White and Anja Swennen

In this edited volume we have brought together research-based illustrations from the lives and professional development of teacher educators. The aim of this book is to add to our understanding of teacher education and the lives and work of teacher educators. Research-informed understanding of teacher education supports the work of teacher educators with students and in curriculum and programme development, research and their own professional development. We hope this book will also support policy makers in making better decisions for teacher education and to take into account those who have to implement these policies and innovations: the teacher educators.

The book is grounded in the international community of teacher educators in the Association of Teacher Educators in Europe (ATEE) and succeeds the ATEE book *Becoming a Teacher Educator*, published in 2009, edited by Anja Swennen and Marcel van der Klink. The title of this first book was *Becoming a Teacher Educator,* and it seemed fitting to call the second one *Being a Teacher Educator.* The titles reflect the themes of the books – moving from the challenge of being a novice teacher educator to the experiences of those who have developed their professional identity as teacher educators over years of practice. *Becoming a Teacher Educator* was for the larger part about the transition, the changes in identity and induction of teacher educators. The first title also conveys the state of the profession now and the position of teacher educators ten years ago. The profession of teacher educators at the time could be characterised as an emerging profession (http://ec.europa.eu/assets/eac/education/policy/school/doc/support-teacher-educators_en.pdf; Swennen and van der Klink 2009), with research about, for, and of teacher educators in an early stage (Murray and Male 2005).

Over the past decade most of the themes in *Becoming a Teacher Educator* have matured, but one of the topics that has remained the same is that of the influence of politics and policy on teacher education and thereby on the work of teacher educators. Teacher education is subject to constant change as a result of the ongoing interventions of governments, and this governmental interference often leads to increased standardisation and testing in education and in teacher education (Cochran-Smith 2016; Sahlberg 2016). This is true of many so-called Western countries and has been subject to research and other publications over the past ten years (Musset 2010; European Commission 2015). Whilst numerous reports have been published about teachers, education, and teacher education on national and international levels, there is still, after all these years, little increase in the attention paid to those who time after time must put these ever-changing policies into practice: the teacher educators. As far as we know, there is just one positive exception. In 2013 the European Commission published a report with the title 'Supporting Teacher Educators – for Better Learning Outcomes' (European Commission 2013). This seems to be the only policy report with a focus on the work and professional development of teacher educators, and in ten years no national or regional government has produced documents on teacher educators. However, in response to this report, the International Forum for Teacher Educator Development (InFo-TED) project was funded by Erasmus+ from 2016 to 2019 with the goal of strengthening European teacher educators' professional development through an interactive network of European teacher educators learning from each other via a virtual learning platform and face to face meetings; creating resources to support the professional development of teacher educators, and fostering knowledge creation and a shared European vision for teacher educator development and teacher educator leadership (https://info-ted.eu/wp-content/uploads/2016/04/Summary-E-InFo-TED-project.pdf). Evidence from InFo-TED continues to indicate a need for teacher educator professional development to be addressed in European educational policy (https://info-ted.eu/).

Four themes have clearly developed over the past decade – and not only in this book: research about and by teacher educators; teacher education in partnership between schools and higher education institutions; knowledge of the work of teacher educators; and the professional development of teacher educators.

Being a teacher educator in the current era means that research is becoming an increasingly important part of the work – so much so that the current book is subtitled 'Research-Informed Methods for Improving Practice'. It is now far more often the teacher educators themselves doing research to improve their own understanding and practice, and desiring to share that research with others. This provides the valuable perspective of insiders on policy, research, and practice in teacher education, and contributes to a better understanding of the fast-changing contexts of the field of teacher education (Murray, Swennen, and Kosnik 2019). Each chapter in this book arises from the contributors' research, including individual and collaborative self-studies, qualitative studies in their own context, and international studies, case studies, and action research.

The second theme, which has become much more normal after ten years, at least in many western European countries, is educating teachers in partnerships. The large group of specialists in primary and secondary education who are situated in school and are explicitly involved in educating teachers are increasingly referred to as school-based teacher educators and as a result, the profession of teacher educators has increased in a quantitative sense.

Teacher educators have also developed in a more qualitative sense as individuals and as a professional group. This is reflected in the third and fourth themes, knowledge of the work of teacher educators and the professional development of teacher educators, which are expanding as a result of both research and the growing voice of teacher educators (Robinson 2010; Hadar and Brody 2017; van der Klink et al. 2017). The chapters in this current book include the voices of teacher educators from a range of European countries, Canada, and Israel. A spectrum of routes into teaching exist in these countries, from academic pathways in Portugal, to academic and semi-academic pathways involving Teacher Education Institutions in the Netherlands, to academic and school-led pathways in England. The complexity of initial teacher education pathways leads to less common language and nuances, significant between different contexts, and teacher educators need to be cognisant of these in their work and research. The contributions in this book provide different international perspectives on what is fundamentally the same role, and provide an opportunity for learning from the diversity of approaches.

In bringing together these chapters, our aim was to foster the voice of teacher educators and support teacher educators to strive towards a greater visibility of their contributions to high-quality teacher education and education in general. Most chapters support the research-informed improvement of various aspects of teacher educators' work with student teachers, such as pedagogy, mentoring, and teacher educators' supervision of research. They contribute to the improvement of teacher educators' work, including curriculum development, research, and professional development of themselves and their colleagues. The chapters address a broad audience that includes not only the teacher educators themselves, but also researchers in teacher education and their managers. There are, therefore, strong links between research and practice in each chapter. In this book, teacher educators through their work as researchers are:

- Improving teaching and working with student teachers;
- Providing for the professional development needs of teacher educators;
- Providing professional development that fosters reflection, teachers' self-direction and self-assessment, and/or supports collaborative processes for improving teacher education;
- Empowering and increasing teacher educators' voice and participation in national and international initiatives to improve teacher education.

In the chapter 'Being a reflective teacher educator: professionalism or pipe dream?', Holdsworth challenges the teacher educator profession to find ways to arrive at a shared understanding of the concept of 'reflective practice' to inform both their own professional development and initial teacher education curricula across institutions. Holdsworth draws evidence from a small-scale research project designed to discover the extent to which teacher educators are attached to the concept of reflective practice, how they conceptualise reflective practice, how their beliefs and conceptualisations inform their practice, and what underlying factors influence their conceptualisations, beliefs, and practice. Using mixed methods, his findings draw on data from 48 questionnaires and nine semi-structured interviews with a self-selected sample of teacher educators who are members of ATEE. His findings suggest that the teacher educators in this sample promote reflective practice for student teachers and themselves. However, their conceptualisations of reflective practice are ambiguous and their personal and professional belief system have more influence on their conceptualisation and operationalisation of reflective practice than does empirical evidence of the value of reflective practice. He highlights the need for empirical research on the impact of reflective practice on developing the effective professional practice of student teachers, teachers, and teacher educators. Initial teacher education courses regularly espouse the importance of reflective practice in their institutions, yet do not provide guidance in reflective practice to those who teach it. Holdsworth's research emphasises a professional development need for teacher educators around how to reflect and how to teach student teachers to reflect.

This leads us into an example of the professional development of teacher educators in developing their own reflective practice and learning how to teach reflective practice to student teachers. In 'Understanding the reflective process through self-study: a teacher educator's journey towards continuous professional development', Attard shares his learning journey as a teacher educator who was provoked into action by student teachers' lack of reflection,. As Attard sought to develop prospective teachers' reflective skills, he realised the need to model reflection and of having reflective conversations with the student teachers. Through the methodology of self-study, collecting his own systematic reflections over an 11-year period and carrying out a thematic analysis, Attard learned more deeply about the reflective process in order to support the learning of student teachers, simultaneously providing for his own continuous professional development. His findings indicate that reflection-on-action happens when there is a felt need, and when the learning from reflection is relevant to those needs. This increases through self-questioning and conversing with other teacher educators. Attard draws our attention to the fact that teacher educators who can tolerate uncertainty are better at analysing practice and learning from it. As his practical theory shifted from being the expert about teaching situations to being able to analyse professional practice, his own practice has become better informed. This reflective process has been iterative and on-going and has affected the learning and development of student teachers.

The value of self-study is highlighted in the chapter titled 'Developing as teacher educators: lessons learned from student voices during practice and research', where Russell and Flores explicitly model reflection through their self-study to develop their practice. Russell and Flores share their self-studies listening to student teachers' perceptions of the teaching and learning taking place in their courses, and the use of tickets-out-of-class. They make a strong argument for teacher educators doing self-study to research their own practice, for their own professional development and to improve teacher education from within. They illustrate the importance of the pedagogy of teacher education for those learning to teach, because student teachers are considering how they themselves will teach. The authors believe it is important to make their pedagogy transparent, so self-study was a way to explicitly model reflection as a key part of teacher educator practice. The impact that their engagement in self-study had on their student teachers demonstrates the value that student-teachers placed on this approach, and provides a strong motivational force for other teacher educators to develop this practice.

Focussing on a localised collaboration between teacher educators in two institutions, the next chapter, 'Teacher educator collaboration and a pedagogy of teacher education: practice architectures, professional learning, praxis, and production', by Powell, considers the pedagogy of the teacher educators. The research became more participatory, democratic, collaborative, and emancipatory as relationships built between the teacher educators, and the research lead was able to open up opportunities for conversations that helped to develop the research further. Powell writes about the collaboration between a university-based teacher educator and a team of six teacher educators from further-education colleges in England, using a participatory action research approach, considered what happens when teacher educators work together to explore modelling and develop their own pedagogy of teacher education. A Viewing Frame was produced as a new teaching resource for student teachers to focus on the practice of the teacher educators whilst they are teaching. This also provided a tool to enable the teacher educators to examine the layered nature of their pedagogy. Practice architectures (Kemmis et al. 2014) are introduced as a lens to study the practice of teaching student teachers, and the practice of researching teaching. Through this chapter, Powell contributes to an understanding of the sayings, doings, and relatings of practice and the languages, resources, and relationships of practice architectures that shape the work of a group of teacher educators and are rarely studied. The Viewing Frame is available for all teacher educators on the For Learning in Teacher Education website (www. go.herts.ac.uk/FLiTE).

Continuing to focus on improving teaching and working with student teachers, we move from one aspect of the curriculum to consider the risks of opening up the curriculum to allow student teachers more freedom to find their own routes. In '"Are we doing the right thing?" Challenges teacher educators face when taking the risk of opening up possibilities for students', Leijgraaf challenges teacher educators to risk opening up possibilities for student teachers. In response to government control, competency-based checklists, and standardised, structured lesson planning by teacher educators, the teacher educators at a college of primary-teacher education decided to take a risky initiative by opening up their taught sessions so that students could follow their own interests and routes. Leijgraaf shares the findings of her small-scale research project, carried out over three years, exploring the meanings that teacher educators and student teachers gave to this redesigned curriculum for primary teacher education. Data was collected through individual and focus group interviews with teacher educators and student teachers, observations, programme evaluations, and journaling. The result of the change was enthusiasm from teacher educators and student teachers; however, teacher educators expressed some insecurity about the quality of the programme, the balance between what they held important, and what the student teachers wanted to know. They had concerns about how the student teachers would handle the uncertainty, and related this to issues of trust and confidence. The student teachers expressed a sense of freedom, yet also insecurity, and reported incidents of unexpected learning from the insecurity they experienced. Leijgraaf recommends discussion in the teacher educator community around providing a space and trusting relationships for student teachers to experience freedom and the existential dimensions of education, and leading the public debate about what education really is.

Following from brave teacher educators who are opening up the curriculum for their learners, the next chapter considers listening to the beneficiaries of the education process, being open to learn from pupils themselves. In 'Old learning, new learning: Teacher educators as enquiring professionals', Beaton carried out research within the Scottish education system, listening to the voice of pupils as to how teacher educators might better prepare student teachers for 21st-century classrooms. The researcher critically reflects on the espoused theory of pupils as partners in the process of learning and assessment, and the perceptions of the pupils, surfacing ambiguity in understanding and practice. The chapter explores the benefits and challenges for university- and school-based teacher educators of becoming 'enquiring professionals', open to learn, including learning from pupil voices.

The work of teacher educators extends beyond teaching and working with student teachers. The next chapter shifts the focus from teaching to teacher educators networking to support their professional development. In 'A professional social network as a platform for teacher educators' professional development', Seifert and Bar-Tal share their research findings about a professional social network for teacher educators in Israel, called Shluvim (meaning 'integrated' in Hebrew).

Another significant role of teacher educators is carrying out collaborative research. The next chapter, 'International semi-collaborative research initiative: a critical reflection of the research process', by Shagrir, provides a model for semi-collaborative research and opens up the learning from the research process to inform teacher educators who may choose to carry out collaborative research in the future. The research initiative, carried out by the Research and Development Community (RDC) called the Professional Development of Teacher Educators (PDTE), which operates within ATEE, was designed to investigate the professional characteristics of expert teacher educators. The collaboration provided the opportunity for active involvement of all participants, enabling them to contribute from their knowledge and expertise. An advantage of carrying out collaborative research is the opportunity that it provides for the professional development of the collaborators at any stage of their career. This chapter looks in depth at the steps involved in the initiative to consider critically the process from the perspective of the group chair who led the research. The clear and comprehensive picture of the steps involved in the initiative provides a helpful model for those considering semi-collaborative research. The critical reflection on the process and its contribution to the professional development of the collaborating teacher educators highlights the challenges and benefits to be considered at each stage.

The following chapter, 'Learning from stories about the practice of teacher educators in partnerships between schools and higher education institutions', by White, Timmermans, and Dickerson, considers the strengths and weaknesses of a specific international collaborative research project with the output of tools to support the professional development of teacher educators. There is little opportunity for teacher educators' (formal) professional development. This is often an even greater problem for school-based teacher educators (White, Dickerson, and Weston 2015), providing an imperative to develop resources for the professional development of teacher educators that is directly related to the activities they engage in. This chapter reports on an international collaborative research project between two teacher educators from England and the Netherlands, respectively, who collected stories about challenges in practice from school-based and institute-based teacher educators working in partnerships. The stories were developed into a tool for professional learning and development, and were used with groups of school-based and institute-based teacher educators in workshops to support boundary crossing. These stories are available to all teacher educators on the **For Learning in Teacher Education** website (www.go.herts.ac.uk/FLiTE).

The last two chapters focus on the value of commitment to active international engagement in order to contribute to local, national, and international policy and practice in the field.

In 'Teacher educator as researcher: striving towards a greater visibility for teacher education', MacPhail strongly argues the case for teacher educator involvement in research, demonstrated through her own involvement in research at different levels, in Irish and international contexts. The reflection of this teacher educator focusses on the importance of the researcher role in raising the visibility of teacher education. MacPhail first shares her experiences on researching her own practices with pre-service teachers, using self-study that captures her ongoing journey as a teacher educator. The second level is her exposure as a credible teacher educator who connects with the university's strategic position, and the third level is contributing to multidisciplinary research. This is the voice of a teacher educator calling on teacher educators to conduct sustained and systematic research that informs the development of teacher education policy in individual jurisdictions and then formalising teacher education connections across all jurisdictions to produce coherent teacher education policies in the European Union.

Finally we consider the concept of teacher educators doing 'Brave Research', moving beyond self-study to develop our practice individually and as a profession to more ambitious projects where the impact of the research may lead to the transformation of education, striving to ensure that the learning and life chances of individuals and communities are not limited by social or economic factors. In

'Brave Research as a means to transform teacher education', Swennen and Powell bring the book to a fitting conclusion, calling on teacher educators to be 'braver' in their choice of research topic, research design, and research partners. Swennen and Powell have used discussions carried out at the ReimagineFE event, June 2018, and at the ATEE Annual Conference, August 2018, to consider the idea of Brave Research. They share a conceptual framework for Brave Research that embraces and champions diversity and inclusion; has an insider perspective; seeks to do research with diverse and excluded groups; occurs in a third space; is methodologically multilateral, with researchers that are bricoleurs, modelling Brave Research and bravery in their research; focusses on practice; and accepts there may be more than one interpretation. We extend the invitation to you to join this discussion about Brave Research, what it means, and how together, as teacher educators, we can build it and make it happen.

Teacher educators responding to this call to bravely focus their research towards social justice and transformation of practices and systems will be using their professional voices and research to have a positive impact on education and the communities they serve. Starting from *Becoming a Teacher Educator* to *Being a Teacher Educator*, we hope that the next book in this series will be 'Bravely Researching as Teacher Educators'.

References

Cochran-Smith, M. 2016. "Foreword." In *Teacher Education in Times of Change*, edited by G. Beauchamp, and L. Clarke, x–xvi, Bristol: Policy Press.

European Commission. 2013. "Supporting Teacher Educators for Better Learning Outcomes." Accessed on 6 August 2019 at http://ec.europa.eu/assets/eac/education/policy/school/doc/support-teacher-educators_en.pdf.

European Commission. 2015. "Shaping Career-Long Perspectives on Teaching. A Guide on Policies to Improve Initial Teacher Education." Accessed on 6 August 2019 at http://ec.europa.eu/dgs/education_culture/repository/education/library/reports/initial-teacher-education_en.pdf.

Hadar, L., and D. Brody. 2017. "Professional Learning and Development of Teacher Educators." In *The SAGE Handbook of Research on Teacher Education*, edited by J. Clandinin, and J. Husu, 1049–1064. London: Sage.

Kemmis, S., J. Wilkinson, C. Edwards-Groves, I. Hardy, P. Grootenboer, and L. Bristol. 2014. *Changing Practices, Changing Education*. London: Springer.

Murray, J., and T. Male, 2005. "Becoming a Teacher Educator: Evidence From the Field." *Teaching and Teacher Education* 21 (2): 125–142. doi: 10.1016/j.tate.2004.12.006.

Murray, J., A. Swennen, and C. Kosnik. 2019. "International Policy Perspectives on Change in Teacher Education." In *International Research, Policy and Practice in Teacher Education: Insider Perspectives*, edited by J. Murray, A. Swennen, and C. Kosnik, 1–14. Switzerland: Springer Nature.

Musset, P. 2010. *Initial Teacher Education and Continuing Training Policies in a Comparative Perspective: Current Practices in OECD Countries and a Literature Review on Potential Effects*. OECD Education Working Papers, 48. Accessed on 6 August 2019 at http://dx.doi.org/10.1787/5kmbphh7s47h–en.

Sahlberg, P. 2016. "The Global Educational Reform Movement and its Impact on Schooling." In *The Handbook of Global Education Policy*, edited by K. Mundy, A. Green, B. Lingard, and A. Verger, 128–144. West Sussex: Wiley-Blackwell.

Swennen, A., and M. van der Klink, eds. 2009. *Becoming a Teacher Educator. Theory and Practice for Teacher Educators*. Dordrecht: Springer.

Van der Klink, M., Q. Kools, G. Avissar, S. White, and T. Sakata. 2017. "Professional Development of Teacher Educators: What Do They Do? Findings from an Explorative International Study." *Professional Development in Education* 43 (2): 163–178. doi: 10.1080/19415257.2015.1114506.

White, E., C. Dickerson, and K. Weston. 2015. "Developing an Appreciation of What It Means to Be a School-Based Teacher Educator." *European Journal of Teacher Education* 38 (4): 445–459. doi: 10.1080/02619768.2015.1077514.

2

BEING A REFLECTIVE TEACHER EDUCATOR

Professionalism or Pipe Dream?

Paul Holdsworth

Introduction

'Reflection' is widely accepted as a key competence for teachers that has been adopted in initial teacher education around the world (for example, Loughran 2002; Russell 2013; Collin, Karsenti, and Komis 2013), and the importance of teachers practising reflection is stressed in both academic literature (e.g., Cochran-Smith 2003; Zeichner 2005; Jones and Jones 2013) and policy guidance (e.g., Teaching Council of Ireland 2011; General Teaching Council Scotland 2012; Council of European Union 2014). Reflective practice is a key competence for teacher educators (e.g., Cochran-Smith 2005; ATE 2008).

The concept of reflective practice has developed in multiple directions (e.g., Schön 1983, 1987; Zeichner and Liston 1996; Pollard et al. 2005), so that it is "a term that carries diverse meaning" (Loughran 2002, 33) and "there is no agreement on what reflective practice is" (Collin, Karsenti, and Komis 2013, 109). As Beauchamp (2015, 126) notes, "The concept of reflection and [its] application . . . in teaching contexts continues to provoke criticism and raise cautions" because it is defined in many different ways, using shifting terminology from different epistemological approaches; and "[e]ven those who promote it do not completely understand the term" (2015, 123). Examples of what different authors consider to be key aspects of reflective practice include:

- Something more than just thinking about my professional practice; gathering evidence about my own impact and changing my professional practice (Davey and Ham 2011);
- Acquiring "a critical stance or attitude towards one's own practice and that of one's peers" (Johnston and Badley 1996);
- Problem-finding and problem-solving (Leitch and Day, 2000);

- Questioning the social and political context in which I work (ibid);
- Questioning my tacit professional assumptions, values, and beliefs (Zeichner and Liston (1996); and
- Confronting my professional reality with public theory (Zeichner and Liston 1996; Warwick 2015).

Several authors note a gap between the theory and its classroom implementation (e.g., Mena Marcos, Sánchez, and Tillema 2008; Postholm 2008; Atkinson 2012) and the crucial question of whether or not teachers' reflective practice has an impact on teaching or learning remains largely unanswered. Collin, Karsenti, and Komis (2013) highlight the dearth of effective empirical studies. Jaeger reviewed studies of different approaches to reflection in teaching; none "presents clear evidence of a connection between teacher reflection . . . and detailed or robust measures of teaching proficiency" (2013, 99; see also Akbari 2007). In addition, there are "many ambiguities" about how reflective thinking should be taught to student teachers (Jones and Jones 2013, 73). Davey and Ham (2011, 234) note that the literature shows evidence of "only a general consensus on what critical reflection . . . looks like, and . . . considerably less consensus on . . . the most effective methods . . . to develop or promote it". For many, reflective practice should be taught explicitly, because it is not intuitive (Williams and Grudnoff 2011; Ryan 2013); teacher educators must "explicitly facilitate the process of reflection and make transparent the metacognitive process it entails" (Nagle 2008, 86); student teachers require "carefully constructed guidance" and "multifaceted and strategically constructed interventions" to reflect effectively on their practice (Larrivee 2008, 345). Lane et al. list ways for teacher educators to promote reflective practice in pre-service teachers, such as discussions of a teaching situation, reflective interviews or essays, action research, journaling, or blogging (2014). Hatton and Smith conclude that teacher education programmes use a range of strategies to encourage student teachers to reflect, but find "little research evidence to show that this [aim] is actually being achieved" (1995, 36).

Empirical research on teacher educators' professional practice is scarce (Willemse, Lunenberg, and Korthagen 2005), and there is little evidence about whether or how they themselves deploy reflective practice, and whether or how they teach it. Teaching how to reflect requires teacher educators to deploy specific competences (Gelfuso and Dennis 2014). However, Dyment and O'Connell (2014) noted that experienced teacher educators had received no training in using reflection and, in turn, did not give such training to their students: both parties were expected to know how to reflect. Many writers (e.g., Loughran and Berry 2005; Russell 2013) advocate for teacher educators to act as models of reflective practice: how they teach their students should be congruent with the approaches they expect their students to adopt with pupils. However, teacher educators do not always 'teach as they preach' (Lunenberg and Korthagen 2003).

Teacher educators need to be aware of their own tacit theories of teaching and able to connect them overtly to public theory (Swennen, Lunenberg, and

Korthagen 2008). However, teacher educators base their teaching decisions on 'common sense' more than on public theory (Lunenberg, Korthagen, and Swennen 2007, 590), and struggle with modelling (Loughran and Berry 2005). Russell (2013) asserts that teacher educators rarely model reflective practice, fail to link reflection clearly and directly to professional learning, and rarely explain what they mean by reflection, so that student teachers complete their initial teacher education with "a muddled and negative view of what reflection is and how it might contribute to their professional learning" (2013, 87); these problems arise because teacher educators have not sufficiently explored how theories of reflective practice relate to their own teaching, so have not made the necessary "paradigmatic changes" which they expect their students to make (2013, 83).

Teachers' beliefs (their convictions, the ideas they hold to be true) play a key role in their professional behaviour (Pajares 1992) but are highly resistant to change (Block and Hazelip 1995, cited in Kane, Sandretto, and Heath 2002). Similarly, teacher educators' prior beliefs and attitudes influence the development of their identity (Izadinia 2014) and practice (Tillema and Kremer-Hayon 2005). In sum, the literature shows that the concept of reflective practice is widely promoted in teaching, but there is not consensus about its conceptualisation or about how it should be operationalised by teachers or taught by teacher educators, and there is little evidence about whether or how teacher educators themselves deploy reflective practice.

My research asked: (1) To what extent are teacher educators attached to the concept of reflective practice? (2) How do they conceptualise reflective practice? (3) How do their beliefs and conceptualisations inform their professional practice? and (4) What underlying factors influence (2) and (3)?

Methodology

The research adopted a mixed-methods approach and was in two stages. In stage 1, quantitative data were gathered about the extent to which they promote reflective practice and the frequency with which they engage in it. In stage 2, these data were illuminated by qualitative data from a sample of participants about their theories and conceptualisations of reflective practice in teacher education and their perceptions of their own engagement in reflective practice.

In stage one, 48 self-selected members of the Association for Teacher Education in Europe (ATEE) from 24 countries around the world responded to an e-mail invitation to complete an on-line questionnaire. The sample comprised almost entirely experienced teacher educators, nearly two-thirds with a doctorate. The survey sought their beliefs about reflective practice (for teachers and for teacher educators), and asked which reflective practices they had employed in the previous year, in addition to requesting background information. Respondents were asked, for example, whether they strongly agreed, agreed, disagreed, or strongly disagreed with statements like: "I think it is important that my students become reflective teacher practitioners", "I explicitly model reflective teaching practices to my students", or "It is possible to be an effective teacher without being a reflective practitioner".

Stage 2 involved nine out of the 48 online respondents. Table 2.1 summarises their profiles. The interviewees were a self-selected sample: they were the only online respondents who also made themselves available to be interviewed. All were women (here called Ada, Bea, Cora, Dot, Eva, Fay, Gail, Hope, and Jo); they came from eight education systems (six in Europe and two in North America); five had more than ten years' experience as a teacher educator; all except two had a doctorate; all work in initial teacher education in higher education (HE), except Dot,

TABLE 2.1 Profile of interviewees

Name	Profession	Field of teacher education	Country	Highest qualification	Years of experience
Ada	Primary teacher; mentor of student teachers	Initial teacher education: teaching practice (primary)	Hungary	MA	10+
Bea	Part-time teacher educator; PhD student	Initial teacher education (equity, equality)	Scotland	MA	4–9
Cora	Full-time teacher educator, university college lecturer	Initial teacher education	Norway	PhD	4–9
Dot	Full-time teacher educator; university professor	Formerly initial teacher education; currently works with practising teachers' CPD	Scotland	PhD	10+
Eva	Full-time teacher educator; university associate professor	Initial teacher education (secondary, physics)	England	PhD	4–9
Fay	Full-time teacher educator; university lecturer	Initial teacher education (EFL); teaching practice supervisor; inspector	Poland	PhD	10+
Gail	Full-time teacher educator; university lecturer	Initial teacher education	Portugal	PhD	10+
Hope	Retired teacher educator; university professor emerita	Initial teacher education (English, history)	USA	PhD	10+
Jo	Full-time teacher educator; university associate professor	Initial teacher education (primary, art)	Canada	PhD	4–9

who currently works with practising teachers, and Ada, who is a school-based mentor of trainees. The Skype interviews used a semi-structured framework, to identify the motivations behind the behaviours and beliefs that had been uncovered in stage 1. Interviewees received a pen-portrait of a 'typical' respondent to the online survey, and a list of 15 phrases, taken from the literature, describing key aspects of reflective practice. The interview questions addressed, for example, how they understand the term 'reflective practice', the factors that influence their belief in reflective practice (e.g., own experience, peer opinions, government policy, organisational culture, research evidence), how they embed reflective practice in their daily work, how they teach it, and how students would know that they are reflective practitioners.

Interviews were transcribed; texts were analysed using a constant comparative method (Thomas 2009) to identify themes or categories that summarise the contents of the data. Coding was done manually, by the author alone. Recurring themes comprised both issues that were known in advance (e.g., from the literature) and issues that arose from the interviewees. Data sharing the same code were analysed to seek associations and connections, similarities and dissimilarities. Key conclusions were cross-checked against the literature review for similarities and discrepancies. This research adhered to the BERA ethical standards.

Findings

This section describes the main findings of this research about: (1) the extent of teacher educators' attachment to reflective practice, (2) how they conceptualise it, (3) how they operationalise it, and (4) the underlying factors that influence (2) and (3).

The extent of teacher educators' attachment to reflective practice

Of those surveyed, 88% believe reflective practice is essential for teachers to be effective; only 12% think it possible to be an effective teacher without being a reflective practitioner.

All respondents (100%) want their students to be reflective practitioners (even those who do not think it essential for effective teaching) and all say they encourage their students to become reflective practitioners. Most (92%) say they model reflective practice for their students; 85% model explicitly.

Teacher educators' strong belief in the value of reflective practice for their students is matched by a strong belief in its value for themselves: almost all (94%) self-identify as reflective practitioners and believe that "all teacher educators need to engage in reflective practice". However, 20% of the sample believes it possible to be an effective teacher educator without being a reflective practitioner (but nevertheless thinks all teacher educators – and all teachers – should engage in reflective practice).

How do teacher educators conceptualise reflective practice?

I explored what reflective practice means for the interviewees by inviting them to comment on brief definitions of aspects of reflective practice, drawn from the literature.

The core of reflective practice

When these responses are analysed by frequency, few aspects emerge on which there is consensus about their importance in reflective practice. All interviewees agree on three core aspects of reflective practice: it entails "more than just thinking about one's professional practice", it involves "questioning tacit professional assumptions and beliefs" and it is based on "critical professional dialogue with colleagues". Around this narrow common core are other aspects with differing degrees of support.

Reflective practice and professionalism

A majority of interviewees agreed that reflective practice involves "adopting a critical stance towards one's professional practice and that of peers" and six saw reflective practice as helping them to "become more skilful [or knowledgeable]" and to "continue to develop as professionals". However, only a minority mentioned "examining and understanding what makes for good practice in my profession as a teacher educator'" and "confronting my professional reality with public theory" as key to reflective practice.

Meaning-making and understanding

Also attracting support from a majority of interviewees are these aspects of reflective practice that relate to understanding: "solving specific problems or dilemmas encountered at work"; "making meaning and developing understanding"; "questioning the social and political context"; "developing one's personal theories".

Changing myself through reflective practice?

Perhaps surprisingly, the aspects of reflective practice that interviewees highlighted least often were those relating to changing or developing their professional practice: "gathering evidence about my own impact", "changing my professional practice", and "making sure I don't carry out professional activities in a routine, unthinking way" were mentioned by four.

Overall, the message seems to be that this small sample of teacher educators equates reflective practice with questioning, discussing, and adopting a critical stance; and while many are interested in reflective practice to help them solve problems, examine professional practice and seek understanding, few see reflective practice as involving them in making changes in their professional behaviour. Only to a limited extent do these teacher educators share a common understanding about reflective practice and its implications for their professional lives: outside a narrow zone of consensus, they are have different understandings of what it means and what it implies for them. Indeed, several highlighted the vagueness of the term.

For Dot:

> I think you could attach all sorts of words to what we've been talking about.

For Hope:

> We were asking those reflective questions before we knew what it was called; it was part of being a professional educator. When I started thinking of it as reflective practice, it wasn't a new thing, it was a new term; when I started it was 'self-examination', but it all describes that ability to look at what you've done, look at what your students have learned, look at what your ultimate goals are, and to reflect on how well you're doing that stuff.

Bea questioned the utility of the term; she felt that many activities defined as reflective practice are in fact 'just part of the job':

> To me it's pretty much the same as constantly asking yourself why you're doing this: 'what's important here?' 'what is the goal?'; whether you call it philosophy – which asks for the aims of education – or whether you call it being reflective, to me that's the same thing.

Jo, a teacher education professor for seven years, felt unsure about her grasp of the concept:

> I was wondering if I'm really someone you want to interview because I'm certainly not really knowledgeable about [reflective practice].

For this sample of teacher educators, then, not only is the area of shared understanding about reflective practice limited, but also the boundaries between it and other concepts in the field of teacher education are not tightly drawn or not well understood.

How do teacher educators operationalise the concept of 'reflective practice'?

Reflective practice in professional life

The online survey uncovered the extent to which teacher educators deploy behaviours that the literature refers to as useful in reflective practice in education. Most often undertaken were: taking part in conferences or seminars (92% had done so in the previous year); reading research (96%); undertaking research (85%); discussing one's practice with a 'critical friend' (81%); collecting evidence about the effects of one's own practice (75%); collaborative study with other teacher educators (70%); self-study of one's own practice (68%); and observing the practice of other teacher educators (65%). Thus, respondents had undertaken a wide range of activities that contribute to reflection, though it could be argued that these are activities that would be seen as key elements of professional practice by many other academics – even those who do not identify as 'reflective'.

It can also be noted that (more demanding?) activities, such as self-study or collecting evidence about the effects of their own practice, were undertaken by fewer respondents than were activities such as reading research or attending conferences. This connects with the varied ways in which teacher educators understand the term, as outlined in the previous section.

Much less popular with teacher educators were: keeping a journal (38%) and having in-depth learning conversations with a mentor (26%), a curious finding given that these activities are often used by teacher educators with beginning teachers.

Reflective practice in teaching

How, then, do teacher educators integrate reflective practice into their teaching? The interviews uncovered a heterogeneous picture of the teaching of reflective practice and its incorporation into the curriculum of student teachers. The activities that interviewees most frequently said they use to encourage students to reflect were: "discussions" and "dialogue with students"; but these are, of course, widely used in many university disciplines and are not specific to reflective practice in teacher education. The range of other 'reflective' activities mentioned is narrower than the variety identified in the literature as promoting reflection: no interviewee mentioned using action research, case studies, or video-recording, for example. No interviewee mentioned teaching their students different techniques of reflective practice; two employ 'scaffolding' to assist students' first steps in reflection.

This raises the question of exactly how these teacher educators – who, after all, overwhelmingly support reflective practice – actually teach it. Both the online survey and the interviews show that they place great faith in 'modelling': 92% of survey respondents said they model reflective teaching practices to their students, and 85% said they do so explicitly.

Interviewees were asked, "How would your students know that you are a reflective practitioner?" Their answers range from "talking about" reflective practice (3 mentions), through implicit modelling (5) to explicit modelling (4).

For Cora:

> As often as possible [I] discuss and evaluate and reflect with the students how this relates to their way of thinking, how they feel that this session moved their thinking on, or how it could be coupled with their practicum, and so on.

For Hope:

> I believe that teacher educators should be reflective; but I also believe that if
> I'm doing that well, my students will see it. It's almost subliminal; I don't say
> "you must be reflective" but I ask them to reflect.

For Bea:

> I think they would know if they see and hear me . . . not just having answers
> all the time, but looking for answers with them and making the answers
> together. I think that's being reflective. But do they know that I'm reflective?
> I don't know.

Modelling is the main way this sample of teacher educators teaches reflective practice. However, as described earlier, their conceptualisation of reflective practice,
and their ways of integrating it into their professional lives, varies significantly. This
raises questions: What exactly is being modelled? Are the students of these teacher
educators all developing similar knowledge and competences in reflective practice?

Reflective practice in the teacher education institution

Of course, most student teachers encounter more than one teacher educator, so a
question also arises about the place of reflective practice in the teacher education
institution as a whole. More than half of respondents say they work in an institution where there is no shared understanding of what reflective practice involves for
teacher educators; however, slightly more believe that their institution has a shared
understanding of what the concept means for teachers.

The extent to which reflective practice is supported by the institution also varies
greatly. For most interviewees, their institution was neutral about reflective practice; only one works in an institution with a policy promoting reflective practice
amongst staff. Fay noted that reflective practice is done as a personal choice, by
a few staff. There is no encouragement from the institution; there is no shared
'policy' or 'philosophy'. As a result, she notes, student teachers receive mixed messages about the value of reflective practice. Three interviewees also raised the issue
of their own professional development.

Eva noted that:

> There's very little formal training for teacher educators; there's an awful lot of
> learning on the job, it's quite an apprentice model actually, with a great deal
> of expectation for you to learn through reading research and other things.

The previous three sections have shown that this sample of teacher educators –
those surveyed and those interviewed – have in common that they rely heav-
ily upon modelling as their approach to teaching reflective practice; however, it

has also been shown that the interviewees each understand and operationalise the concept in very different ways, often do not work in an institution with a shared understanding of the concept, and have not received training in it.

So why exactly does a concept that is – to say the least – ambiguous attract such overwhelming support?

What factors influence how teacher educators conceptualise and operationalise reflective practice?

Interviewees were asked directly on what evidence their belief in reflective practice was based. No interviewee said that her attachment to reflective practice was linked to public policy; indeed, several identified aspects of public policy as inimical to reflective practice.

Evidence for the benefits of reflective practice

No interviewee claimed her support for reflective practice was based on empirical evidence about its benefits for pupils, teachers, or teacher educators. Thus, even Eva, who works in a "research intensive institution", did not adduce empirical evidence to justify her strong belief in reflective practice; her motivation was her attachment to the scientific method of enquiry itself, rather than any evidence about the benefits of reflective practice.

Six interviewees identified, from their experience, benefits to their students of the students' own reflective practice. Three thought that reflective practice enabled student teachers to acquire key qualities such as better grounding of professional knowledge or better learning. Two referred to students acquiring a greater awareness of what they do and an ability to articulate their views about teaching. One said that reflective practice enabled students to gain an awareness of the complexity of the teaching act. Hope referred to combining evidence about reflective practice from several sources (e.g., philosophical, theoretical, practical, experiential, among others):

> I've worked with teachers for a long time and the ones that are reflective are better teachers. So, for me it's partly evidence; it's partly a philosophical belief that [teaching] is a reflective profession.
>
> Can I say that a reflective teacher leads to more student learning? I can philosophically make that connection, but my evidence is qualitative: it says that teachers who are reflective do a better job, and if you do a better job, then your students will, on the whole, learn more.

The benefits of teacher educators' reflective practice

The benefits to student teachers of their teacher educators' own reflective practice were seldom spontaneously mentioned by interviewees. Four interviewees could identify some benefits for themselves, as teacher educators, of their reflective practice. These related to: developing learning from experience; developing (applicable) professional knowledge; transforming their personality – becoming a better person; and thinking for oneself, enabling one to 'defend one's ground'. It is interesting to note that no interviewee had undertaken research into the effects of reflective practice.

This group of teacher educators' very strong belief in the value of reflective practice, for themselves and for school teachers, is not based upon evidence from empirical research, and none had undertaken any. For some, it is based upon their own experience, although these respondents did not point to any structured evidence-gathering about the benefits of reflective practice to which they referred anecdotally. For some, their espousal of reflective practice is based on their understanding of theory (which was found in the previous sections to be open to various interpretations), but also on their beliefs.

Teacher educators' values and beliefs drive their espousal of reflective practice

A theme that emerged from the interviews is a strong connection between interviewees' personal beliefs or values and their espousal of reflective practice. This was true for eight of the nine interviewees. This group of influences can be broken down into (a) beliefs about education, (b) core personal values, and (c) values related to sense of personal identity.

The most frequently mentioned factor influencing interviewees' belief in reflective practice, for seven out of nine interviewees, was their – very varied – educational beliefs or values. A common thread is a belief in the value of questioning: questioning one's own practice, questioning the purpose of education/teacher education.

Cora is motivated by a belief in education as dialogic, interactive and constructive:

> It's not a cognitive process that you do by yourself, it's physical, active, agentic; you have to be an agent in relation to other agents to be able to reflect on your practice and that's how I define the reflective practice.

Gail was driven by a vision of a better kind of schooling: reflective practice enables her and her students to look critically at the current situation in education.

For four interviewees, support for reflective practice was closely linked to their core personal values.

For Bea, the critical questioning stance of reflective practice matches her philosophy of life:

> Critical thinking is something that guides me, not just in teaching the students, but in life in general; it's something I grew up with: believing there's many perspectives in this world.

Both Ada and Hope shared a desire always to do the job to the best of their ability for the sake of their learners. Hope said:

> [In] nursing and education – what we do has an impact on people's lives; if you're nursing you can actually kill a person; if you're teaching you can kill a kid, intellectually; and I think that means it's more important to be reflective: to do the best you can do.

For these three interviewees, there seems to be a strong connection between their reflective practice and their sense of personal identity: they see reflective practice as helping them grow and develop not only as professionals but also as people.

Hope said:

> The most important part of critical reflection/reflective practice for me is making sure that I continue to grow and learn and develop as a professional, *and as an adult* [her emphasis]. So it's not just what I do as a professional instructor, as a faculty member, but often the answers to questions that I ask myself come down to 'who am I?': 'how do I, interact with the professional me?' 'Cos there is a difference.

What emerges is a strong connection between interviewees' espousal of reflective practice and their beliefs about education, their core personal values, and their sense of identity.

Implications and conclusions

The findings suggest the following answers to the research questions. The teacher educators in this sample are significantly attached to, and say they promote, reflective practice, both for their students and for themselves. However, their conceptualisation of the term – what they understand by it and its implications for them – is broad and loose, and they operationalise it in a very wide variety of ways, so that, in practice, it means different things to each. The factors that influence teacher educators' conceptualising and operationalising of reflective practice are related much more to their belief systems – personal and professional – than to empirical evidence about the value of reflective practice itself.

All in all, the findings present a paradoxical situation. Almost all teacher educators believe strongly in, and think that they pass on to their students, an approach to professional practice called reflective practice; they almost all claim to model it; they almost all claim to live it in their professional lives. However, they understand the concept in very different ways; for some, reflective practice seems only to mean the same as 'good professional practice'.

Perhaps unsurprisingly, then, the range of reflective behaviours most often exercised by these 'reflective' teacher educators – attending conferences, reading and doing research, discussing with colleagues – are the kind that might be considered core activities for any academic in any discipline; among these teacher educators, activities like journaling, being mentored, or self-study, which perhaps require a deeper level of personal engagement – and are often assigned to student teachers – appear less popular. These teacher educators believe it is not possible to be an effective professional without being a reflective practitioner; however, there is no consensus that reflective practice necessarily involves a structured or rigorous examination of, or change in, one's professional practice; professional activities that require a sustained self-analysis are not adopted by a large share of the sample. The link between reflective practice and developing effective professional practice therefore seems unclear in the minds of this sample.

The literature attaches much importance to modelling behaviour by teacher educators (e.g., Lunenberg and Korthagen 2003; Loughran and Berry 2005; Russell 2013), so it is interesting that these teacher educators say they model reflective practice in the way they teach; but, given the lack of consensus about what reflective practice means, we must assume that each teacher educator is modelling what s/he individually understands to be reflective practice. It therefore seems possible that students of different teacher educators may acquire different understandings of what the concept means, and how to operationalise it; this seems unlikely to promote clarity in the long term. Apart from this 'modelling', the ways that these teacher educators teach reflective practice seem to have little in common, and little to suggest that they do succeed in promoting reflection amongst students.

The interviews uncovered a heterogeneous picture of the teaching of reflective practice and its incorporation into the curriculum of student teachers, reflecting the "many ambiguities" referred to by Jones and Jones (2013, 73). No interviewee mentioned teaching her students different techniques of reflective practice, as advocated by Nagle (2008, 86) or the "carefully constructed guidance" advocated by Larrivee (2008, 345). The findings corroborate Dyment and O'Connell's (2014) observation that teacher educators received no training in reflection, and did not give such training to their students. This research therefore supports the findings of Beauchamp (2015) and Collin, Karsenti, and Komis (2013) that there is little consensus about what reflective practice is, or should look like. More generally, these testimonies also fit with the body of research showing that the professional development of teacher educators is often neglected (e.g., Snoek, Swennen, and van der Klink 2009; Caena 2012).

No interviewee claimed that her support for reflective practice was based on empirical evidence about its benefits for pupils, for teachers, or for teacher educators. This is perhaps unsurprising, given the dearth of such evidence (Collin, Karsenti, and Komis 2013, 109; Jaeger 2013). However, in a profession that many would wish to be evidence-informed, it is striking that teacher educators' very strong belief in this approach is not based upon an assessment of systematic evidence from their own, or others', research about its value or impact. In fact, teacher educators' support for, belief in, and use of reflective practice is based less on any quality of the concept itself and more on the qualities of teacher educators themselves: their beliefs, values, and identity. This supports the evidence that teacher-educators' (and teachers') beliefs influence their teaching practice and behaviour (Pajares 1992; Kane, Sandretto, and Heath 2002; Tillemaa and Kremer-Hayon 2005, 204).

Perhaps the heterogeneity in mental representations of the concept and in how it is operationalised in professional practice is connected to the fact that most teacher educators receive no training in reflective practice (and no encouragement to be reflective); they thus each translate their individual concept of reflective practice into their own practice in their own way. However, curricula and prospectuses for initial teacher education courses regularly make claims about the importance of reflective practice in their institutions, so it seems reasonable to ask why the institutions of this sample of teacher educators offer no encouragement or training in this approach to those who must teach it.

This chapter draws upon a small-scale research project on an under-researched topic. Strong points were the international sample of respondents and interviewees, and the mixed design which allowed quantitative data, gathered in stage 1, to be illuminated by qualitative data, in stage 2. Weaker points were that respondents were all members of a professional association of teacher educators who replied to a request for participants in a survey on reflective practice. This may have biased the sample towards those with a particular interest in reflective practice. The semi-structured interview approach enabled interviewees to raise topics that the interviewer had not previously identified, but meant that not every planned topic was addressed in every interview, leading to some gaps in the data set. The involvement of a second researcher to code the data could have improved the quality of the analysis of interview data.

The fact that so many teacher educators believe so strongly in the concept of reflective practice suggests that it has potential to contribute to the development of the teacher educator profession; however, there needs to be debate – informed by evidence – about the usefulness (or not) of this widely used concept. Research with a larger international sample could test whether the results of this study are replicated, and could usefully compare and contrast teacher educators' approaches to reflective practice in different educational systems and contexts, leading to a better understanding of what it means in practice for a teacher educator (and a teacher) to be a reflective practitioner. Research could also seek to identify the impact on student teachers of teacher educators' different approaches to reflective practice, enabling the profession to promote a more coherent approach to training teacher educators in reflective practice.

If 'reflective practice' is to be a useful concept in teacher education, it seems reasonable to hope that the profession will find ways to arrive at a shared understanding that could inform both the professional development of teacher educators and the curricula of initial teacher education institutions.

References

Akbari, R. 2007. "Reflections on Reflection: A Critical Appraisal of Reflective Practices in L2 Teacher Education." *System* 35: 192–207.

ATE (Association of Teacher Educators, USA). 2008. *Teacher Educator Standards.* Winter Conference Standards Clinic. New Orleans.

Atkinson, B. 2012. "Rethinking Reflection: Teachers' Critiques." *The Teacher Educator* 47: 175–194.

Beauchamp, C. 2015. "Reflection in Teacher Education: Issues Emerging from a Review of Current Literature." *Reflective Practice: International and Multidisciplinary Perspectives* 16 (1): 123–141.

Block, J., and K. Hazelip. 1995. "Teachers' Beliefs and Belief Systems." In *International Encyclopaedia of Teaching and Teacher Education,* edited by L. Anderson, 2nd ed., 25–28. New York: Pergamon Press (cited in Kane et al. 2002).

Caena, F. 2012. "Perspectives on Teacher Educator Policies in European Countries: An Overview." Paper prepared for European Commission conference *Education²: Policy Support for Teacher Educators.* Accessed August 2013 at http://ec.europa.eu/education/school-education/teacher-educator_en.htm.

Cochran-Smith, M. 2003. "Learning and Unlearning: The Education of Teacher Educators." *Teaching and Teacher Education* 19: 5–28.

Cochran-Smith, M. 2005. "Teacher Educators as Researchers: Multiple Perspectives." *Teaching and Teacher Education* 21: 219–225.

Collin S., T. Karsenti, and V. Komis. 2013. "Reflective Practice in Initial Teacher Training: Critiques and Perspectives." *Reflective Practice: International and Multidisciplinary Perspectives* 14 (1): 104–117.

Council of the European Union. 2014. "Conclusions on Effective Teacher Education." Brussels: Council of the European Union.

Davey, R., and V. Ham. 2011. "'It's all about paying attention!' . . . but to what?" In *The Professional Development of Teacher Educators,* edited by Bates et al., 232–247. London: Routledge.

Dyment, J., and T. O'Connell. 2014. "When the Ink Runs Dry: Implications for Theory and Practice When Educators Stop Keeping Reflective Journals." *Innovation in Higher Education* 39: 417–429.

Gelfuso, A., and D. Dennis. 2014. "Getting Reflection off the Page: The Challenges of Developing Support Structures for Pre-Service Teacher Reflection." *Teaching and Teacher Education* 38: 1–11.

General Teaching Council for Scotland. 2012. *Standards for Registration: Mandatory Requirements for Registration with the General Teaching Council for Scotland.* Edinburgh: GTCS.

Hatton N., and D. Smith. 1995. "Reflection in Teacher Education: Towards Definition and Implementation." *Teaching and Teacher Education* 11 (1): 33–49.

Izadinia, M. 2014. "Teacher Educators' Identity: A Review of Literature." *European Journal of Teacher Education* 37 (4): 426–441.

Jaeger, E. 2013. "Teacher Reflection: Supports, Barriers and Results." *Issues in Teacher Education* 22: 89–105.

Johnston, R., and G. Badley. 1996. "The Competent Reflective Practitioner." *Innovation and Learning in Education* 2: 4–10.

Jones, J., and K. Jones. 2013. "Teaching Reflective Practice: Implementation in the Teacher-Education Setting." *The Teacher Educator* 48 (1): 73–85.

Kane, R., S. Sandretto, and C. Heath. 2002. "Telling Half the Story: A Critical Review of Research on the Teaching Beliefs and Practices of University Academics." *Review of Educational Research* 72 (2): 177–228.

Lane, R., H. McMaster, J. Adnum, and M. Cavanagh. 2014. "Quality Reflective Practice in Teacher Education: A Journey Towards Shared Understanding." *Reflective Practice: International and Multidisciplinary Perspectives* 15 (4): 481–494.

Larrivee, B. 2008. "Development of a Tool to Assess Teachers' Level of Reflective Practice." *Reflective Practice: International and Multidisciplinary Perspectives* 9 (3): 341–360.

Leitch, R., and C. Day. 2000. "Action Research and Reflective Practice: Towards a Holistic View." *Educational Action Research* 8 (1): 179–193.

Loughran J. 2002. "Effective Reflective Practice: In Search of Meaning in Learning about Teaching." *Journal of Teacher Education* 53: 33–43.

Loughran J., and A. Berry. 2005. "Modelling by Teacher Educators." *Teaching and Teacher Education* 21: 193–203.

Lunenberg, M., and F. Korthagen. 2003. "Teacher Educators and Student-Directed Learning." *Teaching and Teacher Education* 19: 29–44.

Lunenberg, M., F. Korthagen, and A. Swennen. 2007. "The Teacher Educator As a Role Model." *Teaching and Teacher Education* 23: 586–601.

Mena Marcos, J., E. Sánchez, and H. Tillema. 2008. "Teachers Reflecting on Their Work: Articulating What Is Said About What Is Done." *Teachers and Teaching* 14 (2): 95–114.

Nagle, J. 2008. "Becoming a Reflective Practitioner in the Age of Accountability." *The Educational Forum* 73 (1): 76–86.

Pajares, M. 1992. "Teachers' Beliefs and Educational Research: Cleaning Up a Messy Construct." *Review of Educational Research* 62 (3): 307–332.

Pollard, A., J. Collins, N. Simco, S. Swaffield, J. Warin, and P. Warwick. 2005. *Reflective Teaching*. 2nd ed. London: Continuum.

Postholm, M. 2008. "Teachers Developing Practice: Reflection As Key Activity." *Teaching and Teacher Education* 24: 1717–1728.

Russell, T. 2013. "Has Reflective Practice Done More Harm Than Good in Teacher Education?" *Phronesis* 2 (1): 80–88.

Ryan, M. 2013. "The Pedagogical Balancing Act: Teaching Reflection in Higher Education." *Teaching in Higher Education* 18 (2): 144–155.

Schön, D. 1983. *The Reflective Practitioner: How Professionals Think in Action*. New York: Basic Books.

Schön, D. 1987. *Educating the Reflective Practitioner*. San Francisco: Jossey Bass.

Snoek, M., A. Swennen, and M. van der Klink. 2009. "The Teacher Educator: A Neglected Factor in the Contemporary Debate on Teacher Education." In *Advancing Quality Cultures for Teacher Education in Europe: Tensions and Opportunities*, edited by B. Hudson, B. Zgaga and P. Åstrand, 288–299. Umeå: Umeå University.

Swennen, A., M. Lunenberg, and F. Korthagen. 2008. "Preach What You Teach! Teacher Educators and Congruent Teaching." *Teachers and Teaching: Theory and Practice* 14 (5): 531–542.

Teaching Council of Ireland. 2011. "Policy on the Continuum of Teacher Education." Dublin: Teaching Council of Ireland.

Thomas, G. 2009. *How to Do Your Research Project*. London: Sage.

Tillema, H., and L. Kremer-Hayon. 2005. "Facing Dilemmas: Teacher-Educators' Ways of Constructing a Pedagogy of Teacher Education." *Teaching in Higher Education* 10 (2): 203–217.

Warwick, P. 2015. "Reflective Practice: Some Notes on the Development of the Notion of Professional Reflection." Accessed on 11 August 2019 at https://dera.ioe.ac.uk/13026/1/3573.pdf

Willemse, M., M. Lunenberg, and F. Korthagen. 2005. "Values in Education: A Challenge for Teacher Educators." *Teaching and Teacher Education* 21: 205–217.

Williams, R., and L. Grudnoff. 2011. "Making Sense of Reflection: A Comparison of Beginning and Experienced Teachers' Perceptions of Reflection for Practice." *Reflective Practice: International and Multidisciplinary Perspectives* 9: 177–184.

Zeichner, K. 2005. "Becoming a Teacher Educator: A Personal Perspective." *Teaching and Teacher Education* 21: 117–124.

Zeichner, K., and D. Liston. 1996. *Reflective Teaching: An Introduction.* Mahwah, NJ: Lawrence Erlbaum Associates.

3

UNDERSTANDING THE REFLECTIVE PROCESS THROUGH SELF-STUDY

A teacher educator's journey towards continuous professional development

Karl Attard

Introduction

An increasingly important part of engaging in professional behaviour is the ability of both teachers and teacher educators to make informed decisions emerging from reflection and analysis of professional practice (Calderhead 1989; Livingston 2012). As a result, teacher education institutions have in the past three decades increasingly attempted to support pre-service teachers' development into reflective professionals as a preparation for increasingly complex and ever-changing classroom scenarios (Toom, Husu, and Patrikainen 2015; Mena-Marcos, Garcia-Rodriguez, and Tillema 2013; Hatton and Smith 1995). Subsequently, rather than being presented with a set of skills that needed to be mastered, the focus started shifting towards how teachers learn about teaching and ultimately how teachers learn about their own and their students' learning (Calderhead 1987). Therefore, teachers' cognitive processes before, during, and after teaching assumed increasing importance in understanding teachers' professional development as part of their daily lives. Such theoretical underpinning, in parallel with my difficult experiences of trying to support pre-service teachers' development into reflective professionals, led me to ask: "How can teacher educators help pre-service teachers become reflective? What is the best way to do so?" Unfortunately there is no clear answer to these questions, as there is a void in research efforts that might answer teacher educators' questions on how best to support pre-service teachers' development of reflection (Pellicone and Raison 2009; Mena-Marcos, Sánchez, and Tillema 2011; Mena-Marcos, Garcia-Rodriguez, and Tillema 2013). This is paradoxical, considering that teacher educators have promoted themselves as proponents of reflection (Mena-Marcos, Garcia-Rodriguez, and Tillema 2013; Stapleton 2011).

Considering my role as a teacher educator trying to support pre-service teachers' reflective development, I chose to position this study within a socio-constructivist framework. My professional interaction with my students, and interactions between students themselves, were my main opportunities to promote reflective engagement, especially when considering that social interaction is the medium by which knowledge is constructed. According to Vygotsky (1978), such social interaction provides the individual with assistance from others that promotes the learning of a task that might be rather difficult to achieve alone.

This chapter therefore aims at aiding the reader to understand the reflective process undertaken by a teacher educator, and how this has an impact on the teacher educator's professional development with the aim of improved professional practice that can have a positive impact on pre-service teachers' learning.

Self-study and reflection

Over the past three decades, self-study has emerged as a prominent way of researching both teacher education practices and teaching in general through a reflective approach (Ovens and Fletcher 2014). It revolves around the notion that the practitioner can engage in reflective analysis of his/her own professional practice (Ham and Kane 2004). Although self-study through reflection has been earmarked as having potential for ongoing professional development in the workplace, Loughran (2004) also highlights how difficult it is at times to linearly describe the methodology entailed when engaging in such research practices. The fact that self-study is used as both a research process and an ongoing form of professional development emerging directly from professional practice makes it dissimilar to other, more traditional types of research methodologies. Loughran (2004) in fact describes it as a research practice oriented more by the study's focus and attention to applicability of immediate findings, rather than by its methods for conducting enquiry. It also offers ways of understanding that embrace non-linearity, the tolerance of uncertainty, and the messiness that is part and parcel of the world of teaching. In summary, self-study is the practitioner's effort to systematically learn from research that studies the practitioner's own professional actions and experiences. Such learning however, is not isolated, as it has a lot to offer to educational researchers, teacher educators, and teachers.

> Self-study as an area of research . . . is in its infancy. Its endurability as a movement is grounded in the trustworthiness and meaningfulness of the findings both for informing practice to improve . . . and also for moving the research conversation . . . forward. Like other forms of research, self-study invites the reader into the research process by asking that interpretations be checked, that themes be critically scrutinised, and that the 'so what' question be vigorously pressed. In self-studies, conclusions are hard won, elusive, are generally more tentative than not.
>
> *(Bullough and Pinnegar 2001, 20)*

Schön (1983) considers reflection as essential when it comes to learning from experience, and it is unsuprising, perhaps, that reflection is commonly used in self-study research. As a matter of fact, reflection is my main vehicle for analysing, understanding, and interpreting. Yet, reflection is hard to define. Loughran (2002) confirms that a number of diverse definitions are given in the literature and it seems that no universally accepted definition exists. I take this as no surprise since people tend to think, reflect, and analyse lived experiences in diverse ways. Put simply, reflection is systematic and intentional enquiry into one's own thoughts, actions, and experiences (Loughran 1996; Mason 2002), and is thus assumed to provide "a heightened awareness of the self, acting in the social worlds" (Elliott 2005, 153). From my experience with reflection, I contend that such *heightened awareness* is attained after a specific process. I firstly observe my practice and reflect on perceived problems, value conflicts, and newly encountered situations. Then I try to analyse the situation from varying viewpoints, giving hypothetical reasons for what happened. I subsequently consider possible alternatives as solutions to the problems. Finally I try to translate my new learning into action that is relevant for my particular context.

It is imperative to note, however, that the reflective process is not simply some form of loose experimentation. In teaching there is an ethical imperative to consider the impact of teachers' and teacher educators' actions upon their students (Husu and Tirri 2003), and reflection is helpful because it provides the opportunity of considering possibilities and consequences of pedagogical ideas and planned action (Tickle 2000). Additionally, through previous studies, I have come to the conclusion that ongoing reflection results in the questioning, challenging, and possibly the alteration of personal practical theories which form the foundations of teacher educators' professional beliefs, assumptions, and ultimately practice (Attard 2014, 2016). Such challenging of personal practical theories allows for another important step in the ongoing professional development of a teacher educator; that of using other sources like relevant research literature and engaging in collaborative reflection, to test previously held and/or newly formed professional beliefs and held practical theories. Any slight shift in such theories and beliefs should ultimately have an impact on professional practice, as the foundations upon which such practice is based have shifted, and therefore professional practice itself is expected to reflect such a shift.

It is important to highlight that throughout my engagement with self-study, shifts in understanding as well as alteration to professional assumptions and to professional practice also had an impact on the research process itself. Analysis of practice led to increased awareness and change to professional practice, and these subsequently impinged on the direction of the study. My practice today depends on my previous learning, and what literature I search for depends on the identification of problematic aspects that need to be delved into. What I analyse also depends on my professional practice and the feedback I get from my students. After all, if the views, opinions, understandings, and professional practice of a teacher educator do not change while engaging in self-study, then the impact of the entire process is null. This is why self-study is both a research process as well as a strong professional development opportunity in its own right. Hence, self-study as a research methodology should not be regarded as a linear and perfectly pre-planned and organised research methodology. The teacher educator's learning from engagement in self-study necessitate the shaping and re-shaping of the steps to be taken.

Methodology

This study is a longitudinal self-study spanning 11 years. It started in 2007 when, as part of the Faculty of Education at the University of Malta, I was given responsibility to help pre-service teachers develop reflection; and it is ongoing up to this present day. The impetus to engage in reflective self-study originated from the fact that I felt lost and confused, not knowing how to help pre-service teachers engage in analysis of professional practice through reflection. My initial attempts to support pre-service teachers' development regarding reflection on professional practice were failing miserably. The literature available mostly presented reflection to pre-service teachers as a set of steps to follow (Pellicone and Raison 2009; Mena-Marcos, Sánchez, and Tillema 2011; Mena-Marcos, Garcia-Rodriguez, and Tillema 2013). This was also problematic as reflection became a technical endeavour where a set of questions simply needed to be answered. This was not a good way of treating prospective teachers as active learners, as Putnam and Borko (1997) had suggested long ago. When analysing pre-service teachers' self-evaluations of professional practice, I quickly realised that their writing mainly contained descriptive elements rather than attempts at analysis of practice through reflection. This was surely not effective in promoting analysis of knowledge, beliefs and practice. My experiences with reflection as a teacher in the past were very different. I thus came to the realisation that I knew how to reflect but I had no idea how to promote it and support its use with pre-service teachers. The students' self-evaluations served as data early in the self-study process. This helped me, as a teacher educator to highlight the problem and focus my professional development on trying to improve the impact my practice was having on student learning.

Data were systematically gathered throughout the 11-year period with the use of a reflective journal. This journal included systematic descriptions and observations of practice (with an entry for every tutorial focusing on reflection), reflection on my professional practice, analysis of my students' reflective writing, reflection on conversations with colleagues and students, identification of professional aspects that I needed to better understand, the incorporation of various viewpoints coming from professional sources, and decisions about future directions. For this study, a total of 556 entries were assessed using thematic analysis. Initially, I read the entire dataset to familiarise myself with the data. Considering that in self-study, data represent the researcher's own thoughts, reflections and experiences, this process helped me in re-visiting my original experiences and reflections of the past; and noticing in the process changes to my own views, understandings, and professional assumptions. This stage was followed by coding, wherein lengthy extracts were coded so that data directly relevant to this study could be easily identified at a later stage. Once the coding phase was over, I re-read the entire dataset looking for themes with the help of the codes originating from the previous phase. Codes were here clustered to form the themes that are relevant for this particular chapter. The final stage consisted of making links between themes by re-visiting the emergent themes and looking for codes within the specific themes that had an impact on other themes. This final stage was inevitable due to the messiness mentioned earlier and due to the fact that all of my reflections were ultimately linked and not separated into neatly packed boxes. Four major themes emerged:

1   Understanding the need for reflection;
2   The importance of questioning and conversing;
3   Relevance of learning creates the need for learning;
4   A continuous quest to engage in informed practice.

It is important to read this chapter as a teacher educator's learning journey. Therefore, outcomes related to learning how to support pre-service teachers' reflective thinking should be analysed as the outcome of a process of reflection by the teacher educator to improve his/her professional practice. Such outcomes are included in this chapter in order to highlight such ongoing learning by the teacher educator. The continuous analysis of students' work and feedback should not be overlooked in this self-study. These were systematically captured and analysed in the aforementioned reflective journal, and thus form part of the 556 entries analysed for this research.

Findings and discussion

Understanding the need for reflection

One lesson I have learnt over the years is that engagement with systematic reflection is hardest in the initial stages. At the start of such a journey, the teacher educator is not well versed in analysis of practice through reflection. The problem is complicated when the aim is to engage in systematic reflection as a research process, since the practitioner might also find her- or himself wondering what she/he is going to reflect about. If this happens in the early stages of a journey of ongoing professional development through reflection on professional practice, the chances of teacher educators, as well as teachers, enduring such a process is limited, simply because they do not experience the need to reflect. Therefore, reflection should not be imposed on oneself or others, as this would hinder its effectiveness and ultimately the relevance of learning that emerges from the process. This I learned when the great majority of pre-service teachers made repetitive arguments that engaging in self-reflection is just another useless and time-consuming task. The analysis of one's own practice and development was a compulsory task during practicum and field placements. Such arguments hit me like a stone. It was a critical incident that made me reconsider my previous learning emerging from my own professional experiences. I was a young teacher educator who had experienced first-hand how powerful reflection can be with regard to one's own professional growth and development. I was continuously asking myself how these pre-service teachers were blind to the benefits of reflection on professional practice.

> What am I to do? I feel lost and confused. How can something which is so obvious to me and in which I firmly believe, be so difficult for my students to appreciate and understand? But if the great majority of my students are not understanding the role and benefits of reflection, there must be a missing link. Maybe analysing their reflective writing might give me a hint into why this is happening.
>
> *(29 March 2007)*

Upon analysing their written reflections, I realised that pre-service teachers did not understand the benefits of reflection because they were not really engaging in reflection. Because they saw it just as a useless component of their practicum, they put little effort into it. It was simply something that had to be done. The problem was that they merely described their practice without reflecting upon it; and one cannot see the benefit of something if that something is inexistent.

> No wonder they do not appreciate reflection–on–action as an important tool for their professional development and ultimately improvement to professional practice. They are simply not engaging in reflection; and they are therefore not experiencing reflection. Their reflective writing is simply descriptive and they just stop short at analysing their practice. Maybe I, and tertiary institutions in general, have a blame here. It is assumed that people can be reflective. I am naturally reflective and analytical, but for some it is a learned behaviour. How did I expect prospective teachers to reflect without modelling such reflection and having reflective conversations? How do I expect them to reflect if they do not feel the need to reflect?
>
> *(19 April 2007)*

I therefore decided that my first major task was to create a link between their reflective writing, their own professional development, and future practice. I wanted to create, or rather highlight, that *need* for reflection. I wanted to model reflection by analysing together problematic situations pre-service teachers themselves identified. My plan was that through such modelling of reflective conversation, they could understand how analysis of professional practice through reflection could have an immediate impact on their professional development and professional practice. Yet, this was more difficult than anticipated because most pre-service teachers in 2007 held a view that professional development of teachers happens through a transmission model, in which teachers are taught and told what needs to be done, supporting a technocratic, skill-based view of teaching (Kennedy 2005). This became mostly evident during the first few group meetings, where pre-service teachers asked me questions related to problematic aspects of practice, as they perceived me to be the expert whose role was to give them answers and teach them the skills of teaching. They were surprised when I said that they were in a better position than me to answer such questions. Ultimately, however, such group meetings served as a setting where reflective conversation was being modelled in a collaborative manner. Slowly but surely, pre-service teachers started seeing the need and the benefits for reflection.

> In these past eight years I have come a long way in understanding how reflection can be taught. Well, in reality reflection is not taught. My role is more of a facilitator, where I help prospective teachers experience reflection by creating the conditions that help them reflect; such as creating a need why professional practice should be analysed; asking challenging questions; and working in an environment where they can feel at ease with experimenting new ideas. Yesterday was the first time in eight years where I shared my own reflections with students regarding my constant endeavour to improve the facilitation of reflection by my students. They were initially surprised that someone who is helping them reflect-on-action, actually reflects on his own professional practice. Of most importance, however, is that nearing the end of their initial teacher education, I rarely ask challenging questions to help prospective teachers reflect. They are capable of asking such questions themselves, and this is happening with different groups over the past few years.
>
> *(21 April 2015)*

My learned ability as a teacher educator to model questioning that promotes reflective thought became a powerful educational instrument. It led to pre-service teachers increasingly engaging in self-questioning, and subsequently analysis of practice. In short, I managed to explicitly model a desirable behaviour while trying to facilitate its transition into prospective teachers' own practice (Lunenberg, Korthagen, and Swennen 2007).

The importance of questioning and conversing

Over the years, I have used two ways of promoting the need to engage in reflection. The first one is simply writing what I observe during practice. This helps me focus my thinking and highlight aspects of practice that might need attention. Of most importance is that through such a process I engage in self-questioning, and it is this that really promotes my analysis of practice, as it helps me to enter into a conversation with myself. As I argued elsewhere:

> The unpredictable course of thinking while writing is very similar to when two or more people converse. During informal conversation, one thing leads to another, and nobody can precisely predetermine the outcome of such

conversations. Since narrative writing can promote an internal reflective dialogue – a conversation with oneself – the same unpredictability found in informal conversation is present in reflective narrative writing.

(Attard 2012b, 166)

The second way that promotes the need to engage in reflection is conversation with other teacher educators about professional practice. I have noticed that although the initial stages of such conversations are rather superficial and usually simply describe a situation, the level of analysis increases as the conversation proceeds. However, it seems that this depends on questions asked by the people involved. Learning through self-study that these two simple methods have promoted my reflective analysis throughout the years, I chose to use such methods to promote the need for reflection with my students. I started modelling reflection using these two methods; promoting reflection both collaboratively and individually. What is common in these two methods mentioned here, is that questioning promotes further conversation and reflection. After all, a question invites an answer. When a teacher educator finds it difficult to articulate an answer, or realises that s/he has no clear answer to a question, then s/he starts to think, mulls things over, formulates hypotheses, and reflects about possibilities and different scenarios. This is what happens to me. Maybe, therefore, prior to engaging in reflection, teacher educators need to learn how to challenge their understandings through questioning and be open-minded when entering professional conversations. This, over the years, has become my most compelling form of professional development, and challenging my prior learning through challenging questions has become my most treasured tool. In Mills' (1959, 201) words:

I do not know the full social conditions of the best intellectual workmanship, but certainly surrounding oneself by a circle of people who will listen and talk – and at times they have to be imaginary characters – is one of them.

This intellectual conversation focussing on professional practice is necessary for reflection to take place; be it with oneself and/or with colleagues. The reason is that questioning and conversing help us in putting under the spotlight our tacit understandings and professional assumptions. This is a necessary precursor to examining them and modifying them if necessary. Upon realising the importance of questioning tacit understandings, I started to increasingly focus my observation of practice on this aspect. For example:

[Student] is finding it so hard to examine and challenge his professional beliefs and assumptions. These are taken for granted and held strongly. For example . . . what [he] is experiencing during lessons does not fit neatly into his pre-existing frame of what should be regarded as a successful lesson. Rather than question his beliefs, he brushes off the problem as coming from the students and he can do little about it. . . . He needs to question such taken-for-granted assumptions.

(6 March 2012)

Almost two months later:

[This student] is realising that his taken-for-granted assumptions are flawed and need to be reconsidered. At this point I asked all those present to comment on what he was saying and everyone gave his/her view upon the issue.

(3 May 2012)

As can be seen in these extracts, when professional beliefs and assumptions are taken for granted and unquestioned, they tend to influence how we view our surroundings, experiences, and analysis. However, when a person realises that his or her professional views might be somewhat flawed, then s/he suddenly becomes more prone to analysing them, and this is why conversation becomes even more important at this stage, since conversation can provide new insights to the person. This is where socio-constructivism comes in strongest, for it is here that practitioners can analyse situations together and create knowledge together. It is unsurprising, therefore, that once students realise that their professional beliefs and assumptions are not congruent to their professional experiences, as a teacher educator, I immediately invite others to talk about that particular aspect of professional practice.

The ability and openness to question and challenge one's own professional assumptions is crucial because these, together with personal practical theories, shape the way we interpret professional experience, and therefore have an impact on future learning (Nissilä 2005; Orland-Barak 2006). Needless to say, the questioning and challenging of one's own personal practical theories through reflection is a longitudinal process. Similarly, the construction of learning and the formation of professional insights take time and effort, as do their progressive alteration. Sometimes, the practitioner has no answers to the questions he poses, and has no option but to postpone construction of knowledge until further observations are made (Conle 2000). The practitioner enters a *suspended state* of *not knowing*. Yet, it is the tolerance of being in a suspended state that promotes further enquiry, observation, and analysis. In fact, practitioners who can tolerate uncertainty are better at analysing practice and learning from it (Attard 2008). Here, the importance of experience and of reflection upon experience as described by Schön (1983) take on added meaning as professionals start observing their own practice with a purpose; the purpose being targeted learning that is specific and relevant for the learner.

Relevance of learning creates the need for learning

As a teacher educator I often make the argument that teachers need to make learning relevant to their students' needs. I firmly believe that such a statement also holds for teachers' learning; that is, teacher educators need to make learning relevant to pre-service teachers' needs (Hochberg and Desimone 2010). Once learning is perceived as relevant, the need for that learning is made evident. This was evident in a previous study I conducted with in-service teachers (Attard 2012a) and confirmed through analysis of pre-service teachers' reflective development throughout this past decade. Although reluctant at first to engage in reflection on practice, by the end of their journey, the majority understand the benefits of ongoing professional development through reflection, and actually use it as a necessary tool for professional development, rather than as a compulsory task that needs to be done. In fact, while reflecting on a particular tutorial I wrote:

> [Student] argued that reflection-in-action should be supplemented with reflection-on-action through self-questioning. He argued that through his self-evaluations he is in a better position to learn from experience, as well as make informed decisions for the future – and this includes lesson planning. He argued that through continuous improvement with the help of reflection-on-action, his reflection-in-action can be targeted at other aspects of his teaching that were not delved into beforehand. He argued that without reflection-on-action, learning is limited and the focus of reflection-in-action might remain on one or a few aspects of teaching.
>
> *(25 April 2013)*

Two days later, another student shared the following quote obtained from relevant literature with the other pre-service teachers, showing that professional conversations (with others and oneself) went on beyond the physical meeting place. This shared quote read:

> Reflection-in-action is always going to be limited or pre-empted by an individual's previous experiences where unprocessed or confused emotions predominate. Reflection-on-action is, therefore, a prerequisite for reflection-in-action to be manifested effectively.
>
> *(Leitch and Day 2000, 187)*

In this case, it was my students who were connecting desirable behaviour with theory, and this, according to Lunenberg, Korthagen, and Swennen (2007) and Swennen, Lunenberg, and Korthagen (2008), is a key issue in teacher education. Through socio-constructivism, the journal entry also positioned me as a learner. It helped me realise my own learning process when engaging in reflection. While in action, it is humanly impossible for me as a teacher educator to be alert to every minute detail of practice, considering that an infinite amount of variables shape our professional practice. It is after the act of teaching ends that writing in a journal helps my thinking become more focussed while helping me analyse various aspects of my practice. The heightened awareness that can be achieved through reflection-on-action can then be effective during the act of teaching itself, where the professional can use prior learning while also paying increased attention to aspects of practice that might have gone unnoticed in earlier stages.

However, the question as to what learning is relevant to pre-service teachers' needs at a specific moment in time still has to be answered. The easiest way of planning lectures and tutorials with our students is to have an agenda, where a pre-planned list of topics need to be discussed. Yet, while reflecting upon my past experiences with professional development opportunities, I quickly realised that such opportunities need to be transformative rather than transmission models. After all, my aim as a teacher educator is to help pre-service teachers learn how to analyse their own practice, which should subsequently lead them to taking informed decisions about their own professional practice. I try to stay at arm's length from giving them ready-made solutions to practice. Therefore, after the first few weeks of engaging in this self-study, I realised that if learning is to be relevant for my students, it has to stem from their own practice. I therefore opted to do away with a pre-set agenda, and asked my students to identify aspects of practice they wanted to discuss during our meetings. This had a major impact upon their learning, the relevance of that learning, and their realisation that continuous professional development is a need. I later used this model of having no pre-set agenda with in-service teachers too, and a participant argued:

> Having the freedom to reflect upon and discuss topics we deem as relevant has indeed made this a positive experience, as my enthusiasm to dive into the world of professional learning has increased.
>
> *(Attard 2012a, 208)*

Therefore, relevance of learning is both a need as well as a motivation for further engagement with professional development opportunities. As a teacher educator, I simply needed to have more patience with teachers' learning, stay away from giving them pre-fabricated solutions, and most importantly, give them a voice in how they wanted to focus their learning.

A continuous quest to engage in informed practice

What denotes professional practice are the informed choices of the professional (Helterbran 2008). It is hence of utmost importance that teacher educators, as well as teachers, avoid developing routines without an attempt to analyse how such routine practice can affect student learning and future practice. Teacher educators in their induction phase, as well as pre-service teachers and newly qualified teachers, tend to focus on survival in their agenda (Brouwer and Korthagen 2005), and a common survival strategy is to simply copy what seems to work for others without much attention to how such practice affects the teaching and learning process. It is unsurprising perhaps that during our tutorials, pre-service teachers were looking for quick-fix solutions when faced by problems in practice. They acted as technicians rather than professionals as their main aim was surviving the present.

As I gained more experience and progressively realised that quick-fix solutions do not aid pre-service teachers' continuous professional development, I tried to keep away from offering such solutions. Instead I opted to challenge pre-service teachers by re-directing questions at them. The aim behind the use of such questions was to model the type of questions that promote analysis of practice as well as practical theories. In my initial years as a teacher educator, I felt obliged to act as the expert and offer solutions to perceived problems. This, however, had a negative impact on pre-service teachers' ability to analyse practice. Now I have come to realise that my expertise is not about every possible teaching situation but on how to analyse professional practice. This shift in my practical theory has had a huge impact upon how pre-service teachers view their role and their professional development. My aim is to help them realise that their decisions and actions have to be informed.

If teacher educators and teachers fail to analyse their own practice, then the aforementioned survival strategies will in time help to create a comfort zone comprising routines where analysis of practice is at best limited. Such professionals can still learn from unanalysed practice, but such learning leads to habits gained from such unquestioned practice (Schön 1983; Mason 2002). This is why it is fundamental for teacher educators and teachers to analyse their practice as early as possible in their career. Needless to say, when discussing teacher learning with my students I make the claim that the creation of habitual practice is not an evil in itself. In the immediacy of the class, teachers cannot think about every possible aspect that crops up in practice. "What is harmful to professional practice is that if such habitual routines and professional beliefs are never analysed and modified where necessary, our practice never changes, whether or not these practices are achieving the results they are set to achieve" (Attard 2007, 159). This also holds for teacher educators, and my continuous engagement with reflective self-study resulted in the ongoing questioning of what I had previously taken for granted: the analysis of student learning; understanding what aspects of my professional practice needed to be altered in order to positively affect student learning; and most importantly, having reasons backing every decision I take. Ongoing reflection has therefore made me "an informed decision-maker and afforded me better control and understanding of my actions and the context in which I operate" (Attard 2007, 159).

Conclusion: reflection, like learning, should be a dynamic process

"Researchers on teacher thinking say: be very thoughtful, reflective, self-conscious, and intentional all of the time. This is the secret of good teaching" (Clark 1995, 20). Through my experience I found this advice valid both for me as a teacher educator and for my students in their role as pre-service teachers. Yet, learning acquired through the reflective process should not be seen as linear. It needs to be revisited, because what we learn today might be better than that of yesterday but still incomplete or flawed for future practice. Once I realised this, I sometimes found myself reflecting again on my past reflections and analysing past data, for the scope of this study has helped me in this respect. Mostly, however, such re-analysis happened when insights and new understandings were made problematic due to further observation and analysis of professional practice not fitting nicely into my professional beliefs. Chetcuti (2002, 154) sees this as keeping an open mind, describing it as:

> [a]n active desire to listen to more sides than one, to give full attention to alternate possibilities, and to recognise the possibility of error even in the beliefs that are dearest to us. Being a reflective teacher means that you keep an open mind about the content, methods and procedures used in your class-room. You constantly re-evaluate your worth in relation to the students currently enrolled and to the circumstances. You not only ask why things are the way they are, but also how they can be made better.

This is what has made reflection on teacher education practices an ongoing process in my case. It is a never-ending journey where the main aim is my own professional development, which will ultimately have an impact upon my students' learning and development. Therefore, this study included 11 years of data, not because it took me this long to understand how reflection can be used by a teacher educator as a professional development tool, but because my own professional development as a teacher educator, through systematic reflection, is still ongoing. Through my engagement in reflective self-study as a research methodology and as a form of professional development, I have learned about my teacher education practices and how these can be improved. I learned that analysis of practice usually triggers in me a need to better understand various aspects. I learned to interrogate these problematic aspects of practice through challenging questions. As a result, I usually focus my observations on these aspects, while in my reflective journal, I delve into other issues that capture my professional attention. I have also come to appreciate alternative viewpoints. Exposing myself to the viewpoints of other teacher educators and students through professional conversation has indeed aided my professional growth, and subsequently my professional practice. Such exposure to alternative viewpoints is also buoyed by the reading of relevant academic literature. The information available in educational research is analysed and integrated into my existing knowledge. However, the most important aspect is when such reading and/or conversations either put my prior understandings under the spotlight or offer an alternative viewpoint through which I can analyse my teacher education practices. It is important to note that such learning is immediately relevant because I, the learner, choose the literature as well as the topic of conversation.

All this happened in parallel to support the development of reflective analysis of pre-service teachers. I thus implemented the aforementioned learning about my reflective process as a teacher educator with my own students, where I could re-assess my understanding through further observation of my own professional practice. This, I found, was how I could immediately use what I learned from this process with my students to enhance the support provided. This is why my improved understanding of reflection as a form of professional development for the teacher educator was so intertwined with my aim to help pre-service teachers develop into reflective professionals.

It is important to highlight that the focus of this chapter is on understanding various features that tend to promote reflection as a learned behaviour, and not specifically on particular outcomes. Hence, various aspects that aim to promote a deeper understanding of the process were discussed. Such aspects include reflection as a corrective measure to over-learning of habitual practice; reflection as promoting learning that has immediate relevance to the practitioner; the importance of questioning and conversation in reflection; and the dynamicity of learning that emerges from systematic reflection.

Findings show that neither teacher educators nor pre-service teachers can be expected to engage in reflection solely by being taught about reflection. First of all, they need to experience it firsthand, and this is how I learned about the process and benefits of reflection in my role as teacher educator. Practitioners need to move from practice to theory to practice. They also need to be convinced of reflection's worth, and such conviction should improve once they start to experience its positive results on their own professional development as well as on improved professional practice. In addition, it would be helpful to guide teacher educators and teachers who are not proficient in the use of reflection. This can be done through modelling reflection, as well as observing reflective thought through verbal or written conversation, as these emerged in this study as powerful guides towards promoting and supporting reflection. Most important, these professionals must feel the need to engage in self-study and reflection if such behaviour is to become part of what they understand as being a professional educator.

References

Attard, K. 2007. "Habitual Practice vs. the Struggle for Change: Can Informal Teacher Learning Promote Ongoing Change to Professional Practice?" *International Studies in Sociology of Education* 17 (1/2): 147–162.

Attard, K. 2008. "Uncertainty for the Reflective Practitioner: A Blessing in Disguise." *Reflective Practice* 9 (3): 307–317.

Attard, K. 2012a. "Public Reflection within Learning Communities: An Incessant Type of Professional Development." *European Journal of Teacher Education* 35 (2): 199–211.

Attard, K. 2012b. "The Role of Narrative Writing in Improving Professional Practice." *Educational Action Research* 20 (1): 161–175.

Attard, K. 2014. "Self-Study as Professional Development: Some Reflections from Experience." In *Self-Study in Physical Education Teacher Education: Exploring the Interplay of Practice and Scholarship*, edited by T. Fletcher and A. Ovens, 29–43. New York: Springer.

Attard, K. 2016. "Teachers Perceived as Professionals or Technicians: A Longstanding Contemplation that Impacts the Type of Professional Development Offered and/or Sought." In *Professional Development: Recent Advanced and Future Directions*, edited by T. Norton, 103–119. New York: Nova Science.

Brouwer, N., and F. Korthagen. 2005. "Can Teacher Education Make a Difference?" *American Educational Research Journal* 42 (1): 153–224.

Bullough, R., and S. Pinnegar. 2001. "Guidelines for Quality in Autobiographical Forms of Self-Study Research." *Educational Researcher* 30 (3): 13–21.

Calderhead, J. 1987. *Exploring Teachers' Thinking*. London: Cassell Education.

Calderhead, J. 1989. "Reflective Teaching and Teacher Education." *Teaching and Teacher Education* 5 (1): 43–51.

Chetcuti, D. 2002. "Becoming a Reflective Practitioner." In *Inside Secondary Schools: A Maltese Reader*, edited by C. Bezzina, A. Camilleri Grima, D. Purchase and R. Sultana, 154–165. Malta: Indigobooks.

Clark, C. 1995. *Thoughtful Teaching*. London: Cassell.

Conle, C. 2000. "Narrative Inquiry: Research Tool and Medium for Professional Development." *European Journal of Teacher Education* 23 (1): 49–63.

Elliott, J. 2005. *Using Narrative in Social Research: Qualitative and Quantitative Approaches*. London: Sage Publications.

Ham, V., and R. Kane. 2004. "Finding a Way through the Swamp: A Case for Self-Study as Research." In *International Handbook of Self-Study of Teaching and Teacher Education Practices*, edited by J. Loughran, M. Hamilton, V. LaBoskey and T. Russell, 103–150. Dordrecht: Kluwer.

Hatton, N., and D. Smith. 1995. "Reflection in Teacher Education: Towards Definition and Implementation." *Teaching and Teacher Education* 11 (1): 33–49.

Helterbran, V. 2008. "Professionalism: Teachers Taking the Reins." *The Clearing House: A Journal of Educational Strategies, Issues and Ideas* 81 (3): 123–127.

Hochberg, E., and L. Desimone. 2010. "Professional Development in the Accountability Context: Building Capacity to Achieve Standards." *Educational Psychologist* 45 (2): 89–106.

Husu, J., and K. Tirri. 2003. "A Case Study Approach to Study One Teacher's Moral Reflection." *Teaching and Teacher Education* 19: 345–357.

Kennedy, A. 2005. "Models of Continuing Professional Development: A Framework for Analysis." *Journal of In-service Education* 31 (2): 235–250.

Leitch, R., and C. Day. 2000. "Action Research and Reflective Practice: Towards a Holistic View." *Educational Action Research* 8 (1): 179–193.

Livingston, K. 2012. "Teachers Engaging in Peer-Mentoring to Improve Pupil Learning." In *Create Leaning for All – What Matters?* edited by U. Lindqvist and S. Pettersson, 13–30. CIDREE yearbook.

Loughran, J. 1996. *Developing Reflective Practice: Learning about Teaching and Learning through Modelling*. London: Falmer Press.

Loughran, J. 2002. "Effective Reflective Practice: In Search of Meaning in Learning about Teaching." *Journal of Teacher Education* 53 (1): 33–43.

Loughran, J. 2004. "A History and Context of Self-Study of Teaching and Teacher Education Practices." In *International Handbook of Self-Study of Teaching and Teacher Education Practices*, edited by J. Loughran, M. Hamilton, V. LaBoskey and T. Russell, 7–39. Dordrecht: Kluwer.

Lunenberg, M., F. Korthagen, and A. Swennen. 2007. "The Teacher Educator As a Role Model." *Teaching and Teacher Education* 23: 586–601.

Mason, J. 2002. *Researching Your Own Practice: The Discipline of Noticing*. London: RoutledgeFalmer.

Mena-Marcos, J., M. Garcia-Rodriguez, and H. Tillema. 2013. "Student Teacher Reflective Writing: What Does It Reveal?" *European Journal of Teacher Education* 36 (2): 147–163.

Mena-Marcos, J., E. Sánchez, and H. Tillema. 2011. "Promoting Teacher Reflection: What Is Said to Be Done." *Journal of Education for Teaching* 37 (1): 21–36.

Mills, C. 1959. *The Sociological Imagination*. New York: Oxford University Press.

Nissilä, S. 2005. "Individual and Collective Reflection: How to Meet the Needs of Development in Teaching." *European Journal of Teacher Education* 28 (2): 209–219.

Orland-Barak, L. 2006. "Convergent, Divergent and Parallel Dialogues: Knowledge Construction in Professional Conversations." *Teachers and Teaching: Theory and Practice* 12 (1): 13–31.

Ovens, A., and T. Fletcher. 2014. "Doing Self-Study: The Art of Turning Inquiry on Yourself." In *Self-Study in Physical Education Teacher Education*, edited by A. Ovens and T. Fletcher, 3–14. London: Springer.

Pellicone, L., and G. Raison. 2009. "Promoting the Scholarship of Teaching through Reflective E-Portfolios in Teacher Education." *Journal of Education for Teaching* 35 (3): 271–281.

Putnam, R., and H. Borko. 1997. "Teacher Learning: Implications of New Views of Cognition." In *International Hanbook of Teachers and Teaching*, edited by B. Biddle, T. Good, and I. Goodson. Dordrecht: Kluwer.

Schön, D. 1983. *The Reflective Practitioner: How Professionals Think in Action.* London: Temple Smith.

Stapleton, P. 2011. "A Survey of Attitudes Towards Critical Thinking among Hong Kong Secondary School Teachers: Implications for Policy Change." *Thinking, Skills and Creativity* 6 (1): 14–23.

Swennen, A., M. Lunenberg, and F. Korthagen. 2008. "Preach What You Teach! Teacher Educators and Congruent Teaching." *Teachers and Teaching* 14 (5–6): 531–542.

Tickle, L. 2000. *Teacher Induction: The Way Ahead.* Buckingham: Open University Press.

Toom, A., J. Husu, and S. Patrikainen. 2015. "Student Teachers' Patterns of Reflection in the Context of Teaching Practice." *European Journal of Teacher Education* 38 (3): 320–340.

Vygotsky, L. 1978. "Interaction between Learning and Development." *Readings on the Development of Children* 23 (3): 34–41.

4

DEVELOPING AS TEACHER EDUCATORS

Lessons learned from student voices during practice and research

Tom Russell and Maria Assunção Flores

Introduction

Teacher educators' work, identity, and professional development opportunities have attracted a number of researchers in recent years. However, the questions about who they are, what they do, and how they understand their roles seem to have different answers in the existing research literature (e.g., Izadinia 2014; Livingston 2014; Czerniawski, Guberman, and MacPhail 2017; Meeus, Cools, and Placklé 2018; Bouckaert and Kools 2018; White 2019). In general, they are described as teachers of teachers who are engaged in the professional learning of teachers-to-be (Murray, Swennen, and Shagrir 2009). In a recent review of research articles, Ping, Schellings, and Beijaard (2018) found that while research on teacher educators' professional learning appears to be a growing field of interest, it is fragmented in focus. The same authors also concluded that 1) there is no clear knowledge base that is essential for teacher educators' work, 2) teacher educators undertake different activities from which to learn, and 3) teacher educators generally experience the need to learn to do their work as teacher educators. In addition, teacher educators have been identified as a unique group of teachers because their instructional practices are significantly different from those of other higher education faculty in terms of the use of various types of traditional and constructivist strategies (Goubeaud and Yan 2004).

Despite the lack of consistency in existing literature regarding their identities and professional learning and development opportunities, teacher educators are seen as "crucial players for maintaining – and improving – the high quality of the teaching workforce" (European Commission 2013, 4). As such, teacher educators are seen as agents of transformative "local reforms" that respond to educational and social demands (Moreira and Vieira 2012). There is, therefore, a need to learn more about how they learn, how they teach how to teach, and how they look at their practice. In this context, self-studies of teacher education have highlighted their key role in understanding and challenging teacher education programmes, processes, and practices (e.g., Kitchen 2005; Schulte 2005; Loughran 2005, 2009;).

In this chapter we focus on data from self-studies of our teacher education practices conducted in 2018 and 2019. Our aim was to investigate our practices as teacher educators through the eyes of our student teachers in order to understand and improve teacher education from within.

Studying teacher educators' practices

Self-study of teacher education practices is not an end in itself, as it entails consideration of the long-range goal of improving teacher education and schooling (Russell and Loughran 2005). Self-study becomes a key element in developing a pedagogy of teacher education (Loughran 2005). The self-studies reported in this chapter were conducted collaboratively in two countries: Portugal and Canada. Our focus is on the value of listening to student teachers and how we interpreted and responded to what we heard. Overall, listening and responding yielded positive responses from student teachers. Our goal in this chapter is to illustrate several ways of listening to student teachers and the positive effects of that listening on the teacher educators and their student teachers.

The self-studies

Context

The self-study in Canada was conducted in the context of a Bachelor of Education degree that leads to certification by the Ontario College of Teachers. As described in Table 4.1, the course prepares individuals to teach physics and science in the secondary school. Situated in Terms 2 and 3 of a four-term program, the course has a duration of 72 hours (two hours a week for 18 weeks) interspersed with two practicum placements of six and four weeks. The 14 student teachers were assessed on the basis of three written assignments per term. Teaching methods included student-led presentations to provide early practice, discussion of test items focussing on conceptual physics, predict–observe–explain routines, review of physics education research, end-of-class metacognitive discussions, and completion of a small exit ticket at the end of every class. Frequent email messages were used to share additional reading materials.

The self-study in Portugal was conducted within the context of a master's degree in teaching[1] that is a mandatory requirement for all entrants into teaching (from pre-school to secondary school). The main characteristics of the Curriculum and Assessment course are presented in Table 4.1. It is a mandatory course in Year 1, Semester 1, for all master's degree student teachers with a duration of 45 hours (three hours per week). Twenty student teachers preparing to teach History, Mathematics, and Informatics were enrolled in the course, which focuses on knowledge

TABLE 4.1 Comparison of research contexts

	Canada	Portugal
Programme	Bachelor of Education (two-year degree, after four-year B.Sc. degree)	Master of Teaching (two-year degree)
Course title	Physics Teaching in Theory and Practice	Curriculum and Assessment
Nature of course or module	Compulsory for physics teachers	Foundational course (compulsory)
Duration	Two semesters (72 hours)	One semester (45 hours)
Main goals	To prepare for teaching of science/physics through in-class activities and discussion; model good teaching practices	To develop knowledge and competencies related to curriculum design and assessment of pupils' learning
Number of student teachers	14	20

and competencies in curriculum design and assessment of learning – two essentials in the construction of teachers' professional knowledge. The assessment methods used for assessing student teachers' work were chosen by them, in this case writing an individual portfolio throughout the course and taking a final written test. Various teaching methods were used, including written narratives (e.g., "my most remarkable teacher"); debates in the classroom (e.g., "Do teachers have professional autonomy? Why or why not?"); formative vs. summative assessment; national exams vs. other assessment methods; voices from pupils about their teachers' teaching; discussions; and practical work. Frequent email messages were used to provide student teachers with feedback on their portfolios. Student teachers were also asked to read and provide feedback to their peers about given entries in their portfolios (e.g., "a critical incident related to assessment" and "my most remarkable teacher").

Our rationale as teacher educators

Each author of this chapter has more than 25 years' experience as a teacher educator, and we have made significant efforts to identify and understand the reasons why we teach as we do. The following five statements indicate some of the fundamental rationales for our work as teacher educators.

Reflective practice can and should be taught (Russell 2005):

> Fostering reflective practice begins with a personal teaching-learning relationship based on mutual trust, . . . requires listening to each unique individual, . . . must include attention to what each person . . . learned in the apprenticeship of observation [as a student], . . . involves fostering

> metacognition, . . . demands explicit modelling of one's own reflective prac-
> tice, . . . focuses on learning from experience, [and] . . . must permeate every
> pedagogical move one makes.
>
> *(Russell 2014, 58–60)*

Learning to teach is a personal and reflective process; it is important to develop
pedagogies conducive to learning how to become a teacher by giving voice and
space to student teachers to challenge and change their beliefs and experiences:

> The focus on the student rather than on the curriculum, the interaction
> among student teachers, the inquiry-based work, the modeling of teacher
> educators' practice . . ., the pedagogical voice, and productive learning in
> teacher education . . . were key principles in designing the course.
>
> *(Flores 2014, 375)*

Initial teacher education is a key context for teacher identity formation, and enquiry-
based activity and reflection are key elements in learning to teach (Flores 2014).
Modeling productive learning and putting meaning into reflection through teacher
educators' own practice may contribute to developing professional identity and
enhance professional learning in a more explicit way (Russell and Martin 2014).

One of the key dimensions of initial teacher education is to provide student
teachers with opportunities to reflect on their journey to become teachers, including reflection about the visible and invisible elements of the pedagogical experience (Loughran 2009).

> Learning to teach entails a constellation of complex factors. It is a process
> that goes beyond the mere application of a set of acquired techniques and
> skills. Not only does it imply the mastery of practical and more technical
> issues, but it also encompasses the construction of knowledge and meaning
> in an ongoing and challenging dialogue with the practice.
>
> *(Flores 2001, 146)*

Methods

Research questions

We set out to collect data relevant to the following questions:

- How do student teachers see our courses in the context of their overall
  programme?
- How are our courses helping student teachers to develop their views of teaching and learning?
- How do tickets-out-of-class help both teacher and student teachers improve
  students' learning?

Participants

All participants had completed an undergraduate degree and were enrolled in a two-year teacher education programme. Class sizes of 14 and 20, respectively, were relatively small, but we believe most of our practices can be adapted successfully to larger class sizes.

Methods and procedures

The research reported in this chapter employed methods familiar in self-study of teacher education practices research. LaBoskey (2004) set out five essential characteristics, reporting that self-study research is self-initiated and focussed; aimed at improvement; interactive; uses multiple, primarily qualitative methods; and validated based on examples of normal practice. This research is focussed on improving our practices as teacher educators, supported by interaction between the two researchers, using qualitative methods to analyse data from our own student teachers as we were teaching them.

A variety of methods were used to collect data: tickets-out-of-class; questions about their views of the course in relation to other courses in the same programme; written narratives; feedback from a critical friend (classroom observation); discussion about what they have learned in a given lesson; and final reflection about their learning during the course and their views and experiences in becoming a teacher. Data were collected throughout each course/semester.

Ethical considerations

All student teachers were invited to participate in the self-studies in the two courses and all agreed and signed a voluntary, informed-consent form. Student teachers were also asked to give permission for the quotation of any of their written statements. Their questions about the research were always answered promptly and an overview of findings was reported at the end of each course.

Data: student teacher responses

In this section we present data that illustrate how student teachers looked at their experiences of learning in our two courses and how listening to their comments about our teaching led to reframing of our assumptions and changes to our practices. In this section we analyse student teachers' depictions of the courses in regard to other courses or modules in the same programme, the content and value of the tickets-out-of-class and the ways in which they influenced our teaching and how we think about our teaching. Data are presented under the following headings:

- Student teachers' views of their course in relation to other classes in their programme
- Encouraging different ways of thinking about teaching and learning to teach

- Using tickets-out-of-class
- The value of tickets-out-of-class
- Student teachers' views about a teacher educator undertaking a self-study of practices.

Student teachers' views of their course in relation to other classes in their programme

Student teachers in Canada spontaneously engaged in a discussion of unique features of their class when their professor was absent for one week to participate in research in Chile. All course meetings were video-recorded and the following points about the course were identified from the discussion on that day's recording.

- Other students ask why we are going to class if our teacher isn't there;
- We are all here for a reason, engaged in becoming the best possible physics teacher;
- We are invested in our own learning;
- Our motivation is intrinsic; we are not worried about marks or being criticised;
- This is the only place we can discuss issues freely;
- In other classes we can't express our opinions freely;
- Here the course content is not laid out as gospel;
- He sits with us and attends to what we want to get out of this class; he doesn't see himself as the sage;
- Attendance isn't forced; he wants us to be responsible for ourselves;
- I never feel that he will look down on me;
- His excitement for teaching this class comes through.

Student teachers in Portugal offered these written comments about how their course compared to other courses in the programme:

- This class is much more dynamic than the other ones. You learn a lot about various topics but in an interesting manner. Reflection and discussion are important in this class and this is great for the students to learn better.
- In this class the students may, for instance, make suggestions about how to be assessed in terms of methods and criteria. The relationship between the teacher and the students is great and we are kind of practising that for our future profession.
- This is a more dynamic class. There is a lot of interaction between students and the teacher. She is always willing to help us. I really enjoy the ways in which the lessons are conducted – it is not only about transmitting knowledge, there are good fun moments, for instance the debates. We learn in different ways.
- This module is more practical, less traditional, and it is based on discussion and debates of concepts. I also appreciate the ethics of it as the module occurs within the framework of "no opinion should be disregarded". I like that.

- In this module students' voice matters, which is not the case in other modules. Classes are dynamic and there is a lot of participation on the part of students. This module is dynamic and fundamental to my professional practice. Writing up a reflective portfolio and the debates make the module more practical and very different from other modules.
- This module allows a more practical kind of work in the classroom. There is interaction between the teacher and the students; classes have both a theoretical and a practical side. Both are key to learn the content. The availability of the teacher is a key dimension for students to learn and her feedback is always constructive.
- This module is different from others as it includes debates among students with the support of the teacher and also because of the method of assessment, namely the portfolio.

Encouraging different ways of thinking about teaching and learning to teach

Student teachers in Canada offered these responses when asked what they hope to do differently in their own classroom as a result of taking the course:

- This class has fundamentally changed my philosophy of teaching. I hope to implement an active learning approach and put more emphasis on craft knowledge in my classes, and aim to continuously study and improve my teaching.
- I hope to challenge students to make mistakes and be thinking about concepts rather than the 'right answer'.
- I think this course has fundamentally changed how I view teaching, so much of what I do 'differently' comes directly from conversations in this course. Specifically, focussing on conceptual physics is something I don't want to stop when I get my own classroom.
- I hope to try to create an environment similar to the one within this course. This course has helped me to see the importance of creating a classroom environment where people feel comfortable having discussions and expressing their opinions. I also hope to focus less on the 'math' of physics and more on conceptual understanding.
- I think an easier question would be what I plan to do the same. This class has allowed me to have open conversations with my peers to grow my own pedagogical practices. In reality I would like to encourage these conversations in my own classroom.

Student teachers in Portugal stated that their course encouraged a different way of thinking about teaching and learning to teach, as the following statements illustrate:

- This module includes a variety of concepts and topics for us to reflect [on] on a daily basis. It makes me think about various methods and what it means to be a teacher. It is really useful at a personal, social, and professional level.

- We learn various methods such as how to assess, we practice them, and we discuss the most recurring problems in teaching, and this is important for our future professional lives. We are able to understand what we think and how to teach.
- This module is giving me the possibility of learning a lot about teaching and about being a teacher. It makes it possible to learn how to teach, what you should not do as a teacher as there are many teachers who do not know what being a good teacher is.
- The module makes clear the role of the teacher and invites us to think about our professional practice as future teachers and about the ways in which students learn.
- This module makes us realise the need to adapt teaching and to use a variety of techniques that we learn from experience in the classroom.
- It is a module that makes it possible to discuss real cases, key questions, and it is always possible to debate questions emerging in the class. I have never thought so seriously about the role of assessment and in the ways in which it may influence the students' trajectories. I have changed a lot my thinking.
- It teaches us different methods of teaching by experiencing them in practice and it makes us reflect on the teaching and learning experiences we had as students in order to inform our practice.

The use of tickets-out-of-class

In both Canada and Portugal, tickets-out-of-class were used to elicit information from the student teachers at the end of each lesson. Student teachers were invited to anonymously comment on each lesson. The tickets focussed on questions that student teachers would like to have answered, on comments about the class activities, on reflections about students' learning process, on the content and topics covered, and on the questioning of beliefs.

The following comments by student teachers in Portugal are indicative of the kinds of comments a teacher educator may receive when asking for comments about students' learning:

- Today's class made me think about how many theories and methods of assessment exist. It also made me reflect on the more adequate assessment tools to assess students' learning.
- The class was important and made me think about the usefulness of assessment. Assessing is more than giving grades. As a teacher I need to be aware of that.
- I enjoyed today's class. But I am a bit afraid of doing a portfolio as I have never done it before.
- I really enjoyed the debate. It made me go back to the topics learned in class before. It was good fun trying to persuade the other group that formative

assessment is more useful within the context of basic education. It is an interesting way of learning.

* I enjoyed the interaction of both groups. I like classes like this one. They help us in being better professionals.
* I really enjoyed doing activity 2 of the portfolio [a critical incident about assessment].
* I really enjoyed this class as it is clearer to me what assessment criteria are. I cannot wait to learn more about it.
* I have been thinking about my trajectory as a student. This class is interesting and it will influence my learning and my professional life.
* I feel that sometimes the participation or comments from my colleagues were a bit confusing and not relevant. But I guess the comments were [of] value because they were leading to discussion. At the end there was clarification.
* I feel more comfortable now in discussing assessment in class.
* This class was extremely interesting as I started to make sense of assessment. I am anxious regarding the next classes about assessment. Assessment is a central topic for me as a future teacher.
* After this class I felt more curious about the Finnish system.
* I had no idea whatsoever that assessment would be so complex. For me it was about tests and grades. This class has been important for my future professional life as a teacher. Usually at the end of the class I identify issues that I am going to use in my classes.

The usefulness of tickets-out-of-class in the eyes of the students

Student teachers in Portugal were asked specifically about the value of writing a ticket at the end of every class:

* I like them because they enable me to think about what I learned and make it possible to clarify any doubts I might have as the questions or comments are discussed in the following class. It also enhances the interaction between teacher and students as we can make suggestions and comments on the class.
* They are really important [because they allow] the students to ask questions if they don't feel comfortable doing them in the class.
* I like them a lot as they foster the interaction between the teacher and the students. We can clarify some doubts. It is great to get to class and to see how our questions are answered.
* They are a good way of clarifying some doubts and interacting with the teacher. It helps to develop a better communication and to make the lessons more interesting.
* They are helpful as they allow us to make questions to clarify any doubts and make us look back on what we have learned. They help us [in] remembering

concepts and we can make comments or suggestions about what we are doing in class.

- Yes, they are useful as they allow the questioning of what we learn in class and sometimes we discuss the questions in class and it enables the revision of what we have learned.
- They are useful in the sense that they clarify what we have learned and even allow us to make a kind of summary at the beginning of the following lesson. Students might not have the same abilities in terms of expressing themselves verbally and the tickets-out-of-class enable them to expose doubts without any fear of exposing themselves.
- They are very useful as they help to clarify ideas that sometimes are not so clear. They also promote discussion and sharing of ideas in the following class. They are useful as students have a voice and they enable the teacher to know what students think about the lesson.
- They are very useful as they enable reviewing what we have learned.

Student teachers' views about a teacher educator undertaking a self-study of practices

The Canadian student teachers were told on their first day of class in September that their professor intended to study his teaching practices in his final year before retirement. Each student signed a consent form to be a participant. Several months later, in April, they were asked if they remembered how they reacted to that idea and how it affected their view of the course. Other teacher educators may be encouraged to undertake a self-study of their own practices by the comments that follow:

- I was very impressed by the dedication to continuous improvement. It has made me appreciate the importance of constantly assessing my practice of teaching with the goal of improving.
- I thought it was a great idea! There aren't many educators who are willing to look at their own instruction. I was excited for the year ahead to see what was discovered.
- I remember being blown away by this idea. Most people in this position would simply finish their final year identical to the past few. The idea of still trying to study yourself and learn and experiment with new concepts even in your final year earned a lot of respect.
- I thought it was incredible that even in his last year he was still studying his own teaching. I haven't thought much about it over the past eight months because I don't want it to influence my actions in this class. I am very interested to see what you discover though!
- My reaction was to be extremely impressed. He is one of the only profs that practices everything he preaches and as a result I have deeply respected both him and this course from day one.

- A mix of confusion and inspiration! Inspiring that you were willing and enthusiastic to continue studying your practice even beyond retirement. It set the tone for the year as well, demonstrating the importance of recording our own attitudes and practice.
- My reaction was that I was surprised that a teacher educator would continue to study his teaching. It has helped me look at this course as only the beginning of my development as a teacher. Your continuing to study your own practice has helped me to see this course as a starting point to continuously develop my own teaching.
- It made me feel as though he was actually invested in the education of teacher candidates. It gave me immediate respect and appreciation for him and made me very excited to learn from him.
- I think it was the moment I learned his attitude towards education and his students, so I felt very grateful and it made me more serious about being in this program.
- I remember admiring the way that you were still learning and reflecting on your teaching practice even in your last year of teaching.
- I thought it was interesting that you would tell us about your studies. It was also the way you presented it. I believe you told us that you wanted to try some new things. I enjoyed hearing that and it made me really buy into the activities you proposed.
- It hasn't really. Isn't the best experiment where the participants aren't consciously aware of it so they are not to bias the results? I didn't have much of a reaction while I signed it.

Conclusions

The concepts of pedagogical voice and productive learning have important implications for teacher educators who are willing to look into their practices in order to improve teacher education from within. Listening in various ways to student teachers' experiences of our courses has given them a sense of voice in the classroom while also giving us insights into the quality of their professional learning. We have both used tickets-out-of-class successfully and we have both responded to our student teachers' comments by addressing any concerns and by adapting our teaching where their suggestions are consistent with our goals and principles.

The pedagogy of teacher education is a major concern for those learning to teach: how student teachers are taught matters, for they are always thinking about how they themselves will teach. We both believe strongly in the importance of *making our pedagogy transparent* by explaining our rationales and by explaining how and why we are making changes in response to their comments. We also find it important to clarify their comments and to invite others to indicate, during discussion, whether or not they are in agreement. We began research into our own practices as teacher educators cautiously; we are now enthusiastic about its value to us and to our students. We hope that this chapter encourages others to do the same.

Note

1 As a result of the implementation of the Bologna process, the former four- to five-year undergraduate teaching degrees were replaced by a consecutive model: a three-year undergraduate degree in a given subject followed by a two-year professional master's degree in teaching, 90–120 credits.

References

Bouckaert, M., and Q. Kools. 2018. "Teacher Educators as Curriculum Developers: Exploration of a Professional Role." *European Journal of Teacher Education* 41 (1): 32–49.

Czerniawski, G., A. Guberman, and A. MacPhail. 2017. "The Professional Development Needs of Higher Education-based Teacher Educators: An International Comparative Needs Analysis." *European Journal of Teacher Education* 40 (1): 127–140.

European Commission. 2013. *Supporting Teacher Educators for Better Learning Outcomes.* Brussels: Author. Accessed on 11 August 2019 at http://ec.europa.eu/assets/eac/education/policy/school/doc/support-teachereducators_en.pdf

Flores, M.A. 2001. "Person and Context in Becoming a New Teacher." *Journal of Education for Teaching* 27 (2): 135–148.

Flores, M.A. 2014. "Developing Teacher Identity in Pre-Service Education: Experiences and Practices from Portugal." In *International Teacher Education: Promising Pedagogies (Part A),* edited by L. Orland-Barak, and C. Craig, 353–379. Bingley, UK: Emerald.

Goubeaud, K., and W. Yan. 2004. "Teacher Educators' Teaching Methods, Assessments, and Grading: A Comparison of Higher Education Faculty's Instructional Practices." *The Teacher Educator* 40 (1): 1–16.

Izadinia, M. 2014. "Teacher Educators' Identity: A Review of Literature." *European Journal of Teacher Education* 37 (4): 426–441.

Kitchen, J. 2005. "Looking Backwards, Moving Forward: Understanding My Narrative as a Teacher Educator." *Studying Teacher Education,* 1 (1): 17–30.

LaBoskey, V. 2004. "The Methodology of Self-Study and its Theoretical Underpinnings." In *International Handbook of Self-Study of Teacher Education Practices,* edited by J. Loughran, M. Hamilton, V. LaBoskey, and T. Russell, 817–869. Dordrecht: Kluwer.

Livingston, K. 2014. "Teacher Educators: Hidden Professionals?" *European Journal of Education* 49 (2): 218–232.

Loughran, J. 2005. "Researching Teaching about Teaching: Self-Study of Teacher Education Practices." *Studying Teacher Education* 1 (1): 5–16.

Loughran, J. 2009. "A construção do conhecimento e o aprender a ensinar sobre o ensino". In *Aprendizagem e Desenvolvimento Profissional de Professores: Contextos e Perspectivas* [Learning and Professional Development of Teachers: Contexts and Perspectives], edited by M.A. Flores and A. Veiga Simão, 17–37. Mangualde: Edições Pedago.

Meeus, W., W. Cools, and I. Placklé. 2018. "Teacher Educators Developing Professional Roles: Frictions between Current and Optimal Practices." *European Journal of Teacher Education* 41 (1): 15–31.

Moreira, M., and F. Vieira. 2012. "Preservice Teacher Education in Portugal: The Transformative Power of Local Reform." In *Globalism and Power: Iberian Education and Curriculum Policies,* edited by J. Paraskeva and J. Torres, 94–105. New York: Peter Lang.

Murray, J., A. Swennen, and L. Shagrir. 2009. "Understanding Teacher Educators' Work and Identities." In *Becoming a Teacher Educator: Theory and Practice for Teacher Educators,* edited by A. Swennen, and M. van der Klink, 29–44. Dordrecht: Springer.

Ping, C., G. Schellings, and D. Beijaard. 2018. "Teacher Educators' Professional Learning: A Literature Review." *Teaching and Teacher Education* 75: 93–104.

Russell, T. 2005. "Can Reflective Practice Be Taught?" *Reflective Practice* 6 (2): 199–204.

Russell, T. 2014. "One Teacher Educator's Career-Long Development of a Pedagogy of Reflection." In *International Teacher Education: Promising Pedagogies (Part A)*, edited by L. Orland-Barak and C. Craig, 55–72. Bingley, UK: Emerald.

Russell, T., and J. Loughran. 2005. "Self-Study As a Context for Productive Learning." *Studying Teacher Education* 1 (2): 103–106.

Russell, T., and A. Martin. 2014. "A importância da voz pedagógica e da aprendizagem produtiva nos programas de formação inicial de professores." In *Formação e desenvolvimento profissional de professores: contributos internacionais.* [Teacher Education and Professional Development: International Contributions], edited by M.A. Flores, 17–40. Coimbra: Almedina.

Schulte, A. 2005. "Assuming My Transformation: Transforming My Assumptions." *Studying Teacher Education* 1 (1): 31–42.

White, S. 2019. "Teacher Educators for New Times? Redefining an Important Occupational Group." *Journal of Education for Teaching* 45 (2): 200–213.

5

TEACHER EDUCATOR COLLABORATION AND A PEDAGOGY OF TEACHER EDUCATION

Practice architectures, professional learning, praxis, and production

David Powell

Introduction

This chapter seeks to make visible what happens when teacher educators collaborate. Based on one of the research questions from the doctoral study of the author, a university-based teacher educator, the chapter explores some of what happened when he collaborated with six teacher educators from a further-education college in England. These English colleges provide academic and vocational education and training to 16- to 19-year-olds and adults, including initial teacher education programmes, and are more or less similar to community colleges in the United States, Fachoberschule in Germany, Vocational Upper Secondary (MBO) institutions in the Netherlands, and Technical and Further Education (TAFE) institutions in Australia. Adopting a practical action research approach, the study sought to answer the question of what happens when teacher educators work together to explore modelling and develop their own pedagogy of teacher education.

Loughran (2014, 275) asserts that teacher educator collaboration is valuable:

> Collaborative inquiry into the shared teaching and learning experiences of teacher education practices can begin to bring to the surface the sophisticated thinking, decision making, and pedagogical reasoning that underpins pedagogical expertise so that it might not only be recognized but also be purposefully developed.

However, Korthagen (2001) observes it is also rare for a team of teacher educators to work together to explore a pedagogy of teacher education. Therefore, by documenting and analysing this collaboration, this chapter makes three contributions to teacher education. First, it examines how collaborative enquiry can promote praxis, production, and professional learning. Second, it argues that collaborative enquiry is shaped by the practice of researching, the co-labourers involved, and the site of the study. Third, it illuminates the 'practice landscape' (Kemmis et al. 2014, 4) and what shapes the practice of an under-researched group of teacher educators: further education-based teacher educators. To do this, the chapter is structured around six headings: the context for the research; the conceptual framework; the research approach; discussion of the findings; concluding thoughts and reflections; and invitations for future research into teacher educator collaboration.

The context for the research

Teacher education and what teacher educators do varies considerably between and even within countries (Kelchtermans, Smith, and Vanderlinde 2018). Most often, teacher education is associated with pre-service initial teacher education for schools, normally primary or secondary, and these programmes have been traditionally taught by university-based teacher educators. This is changing with the emergence of school-based teacher educators, who are involved in support-ing the new models of school-based teacher education in England and Europe (White, Dickerson, and Weston 2015). However, in England, there is another group of teacher educators who are involved in preparing student teachers to work in another sector: further-education-based teacher educators. Like school-based teacher educators, these teacher educators are second-order practitioners delivering initial teacher education in a first-order setting (Murray and Male 2005), normally a further-education college, to student teachers who are usually part-time and in-service. Like other teacher educators in England, they are or have been teach-ers and some, though not all, are involved in delivering university-validated initial teacher education programmes. However, the working context of these teacher educators is significantly different from those working in university-based teacher education (Simmons and Thompson 2007). For instance, their teaching load is significantly higher – for example, the co-labourers in this study were teaching more than 830 hours per year, compared with 550 for those in English universities (Powell 2016). They have been described as "invisible" by Thurston (2010, 47) and their lives as "secret" (Noel 2006) because they are "under-represented [in the literature] and under-researched" (Eliahoo 2014, 180). Significantly, the "practice conditions" (Pennanen et al. 2017, 202) of their place of work and the impact of this on their practice has not been studied.

Conceptual framework

This study employed three conceptual and analytic lenses: collaboration, practice architectures (Kemmis et al. 2014), and a pedagogy of teacher education.

Collaboration

"Collaboration is an action noun, describing the act of working with one or more other people on a joint project. It can be conceptualised as 'united labour' and might result in something which has been created or enabled by the participants' combined effort" (Lofthouse and Thomas 2017, 43). Its foundations are "respect, caring, connection and purpose", though some collaborations may be disrupted because of issues of power (Ball and Rundquist 1993, 39). It can be messy (Powell 2017) and beset with tensions as co-labourers negotiate their different priorities and "competing concerns" (Berry 2008, 32), all of which are shaped by the practice architectures (Kemmis et al. 2014).

Livingston (2014, 219) has called for greater collaboration amongst teacher educators around the integration of practice and research "to promote innovation and improvement in learning and teaching". Teachers generally report that they "would like to collaborate more" (Swennen 2015, 598) with colleagues and there is evidence that when this occurs it can support mutual professional learning for those involved (Lofthouse and Thomas 2017). However, Livingston (2014, 219) notes that collaboration is not straight-forward and necessitates "shifts in systems, cultures and practice" (ibid). Significantly, Eliahoo (2017, 183) observed that the "practice conditions" in further-education colleges, such as "shortage of time . . . [and] lack of support for research and scholarship", have mitigated against collaboration amongst further-education-based teacher educators.

Practice architectures

The theory of practice architectures adopts a "site ontological perspective on practice", which asserts that "practices unfold in sites", sites shape practices, and practices shape sites (Kemmis and Edwards-Groves 2018, 124). The practices of a site consist of three elements: "sayings, doings and relatings" (Kemmis et al. 2014, 31): that is, what we say and think (the cognitive), what we do (the psychomotor), and how we relate to others (the affective), and these "hang together" (Kemmis et al. 2014, 4) in a project – for instance, teacher educator collaboration. These practices are interconnected, through intersubjective spaces, to the practice architectures of the site. The practice architectures consist of three arrangements:

1   Cultural-discursive arrangements are "the resources" (Mahon et al. 2017, 9) that shape the "sayings" of a practice at a site – for example, the ideas of a teacher education programme and its teacher educators or a government's ideas and policies about initial teacher education.
2   Material-economic arrangements are 'the resources' that shape the 'doings' of a site – for example, the classrooms used by the teacher educators, including their layout and the availability of technology such as interactive whiteboards.

3   Social-political arrangements are the 'arrangements and resources' that shape the 'relatings' of the site – for example, the relationships between the teacher educators in a team, between the teacher educators and their student teachers, and between the teacher educators and their managers.

These arrangements are present at or imported into any educational site. They shape a project and its practices, for example, teacher educator collaboration and the associated 'actions' of the participants (Kemmis et al. 2014, 29). They 'hang together' and are themselves shaped by the practice tradition, in this case of teacher education, and the practice landscape of the site, in this case a further-education college (Kemmis et al. 2014). The interrelationship between the "sayings, doings, and relatings" and the practice architectures is called "practice-arrangement bundles" (Kemmis et al. 2014, 14). The theory is visually represented in Figure 5.1.

A pedagogy of teacher education

A pedagogy of teacher education has been described as "the pedagogy unique to pre-service teacher education" (Loughran 1997, 4). It is a teacher educator–led, "practice-centred discourse" (Heaton and Lampert 1993, 46) based on the practical problems of teaching and learning to teach. Harnessing the cognitive and affective (and practical) dimensions of student teachers' learning, it draws on their experiences of being taught and teaching to build an enquiry-led conversation about "the design of practice" (ibid, 55) and the activities and resources of the classroom. Nichol (1997, 97) asserts that one of the purposes of a pedagogy of teacher education is to disrupt student teachers' prior assumptions of how to teach, with the aim that student teachers are then able to develop their own "personal pedagogies" (Hoban 1997, 135).

Its effectiveness is a product of the interrelationship of four factors:

1   A teacher educator's ability to establish a classroom climate that fosters collaborative enquiry with student teachers (Heaton and Lampert 1993);
2   A teacher educator's "co-ordination of knowledge" (Heaton and Lampert 1993, 58), that is, his/her ability to demonstrate skilled practices and professional values, employing metacognitive and affective skills to conceptualise and articulate what is modelled (Lunenberg, Dengerink, and Korthagen 2014), then utilising listening skills and reflective skills to "decide on the spot what to say and do next" (Heaton and Lampert 1993, 48);
3   The student teachers' noticing skills (Mason 2002) and willingness and capacity to engage in a dialogue with their teacher educator and their peers about the issues raised for discussion (Heaton and Lampert 1993);
4   The student teachers' learning and subsequent personal pedagogy is dependent on their ability to utilise the "student as teacher and learner" lens (Taylor 2008, 78) and draw on "the three levels of professional learning (gestalt, schema, and theory level)" when reflecting on their experiences of teaching and being taught and the subsequent discussions about them with others (Korthagen 2001, 273).

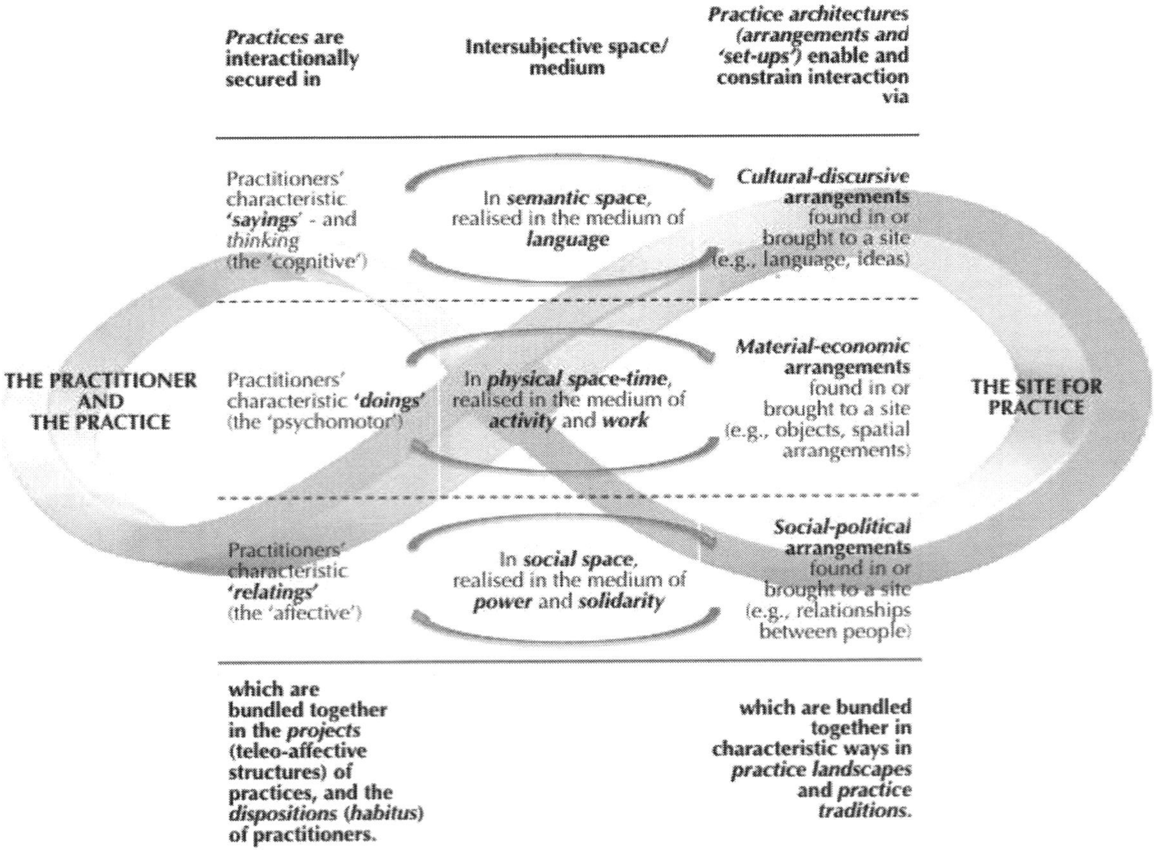

Practices are interactionally secured in

Intersubjective space/ medium

Practice architectures *(arrangements and 'set-ups') enable and constrain interaction via*

THE SITE FOR PRACTICE

Cultural-discursive arrangements found in or brought to a site (e.g. language, ideas)

Material-economic arrangements found in or brought to a site (e.g., objects, spatial arrangements)

Social-political arrangements found in or brought to a site (e.g., relationships between people)

which are bundled together in characteristic *ways in practice landscapes and practice traditions.*

In *semantic space*, realised in the medium of *language*

In *physical space-time*, realised in the medium of *activity* and *work*

In *social space*, realised in the medium of *power* and *solidarity*

Practitioners' characteristic *'sayings'* - and *thinking* (the 'cognitive')

Practitioners' characteristic *'doings'* (the psychomotor')

Practitioners characteristic *'relatings'* (the 'affective')

THE PRACTITIONER AND THE PRACTICE

which are bundled together in the *projects* (teleo-affective structures) of practices, and the *dispositions (habitus)* of practitioners.

FIGURE 5.1 The theory of practice architectures (Kemmis et al. 2014, 38)

Kemmis et al. (2014, 31) would argue that a pedagogy of teacher education is a practice of the project of initial teacher education. As such, it consists of what the teacher educator says and does, and her/his "relatings" with the student teachers, and that it is interdependent with their student teachers practice of learning to teach and their 'actions'. These practices are themselves 'pre-shaped and prefigured (but not pre-determined) [by] the intersubjective spaces' (ibid, 5) of the site.

Boyd (2014, 70) has added the idea of "a layered pedagogy of teacher education" to this field of work. Boyd's argument is that explicit modelling should be part of a layered pedagogy of teacher education that moves beyond the teacher educator modelling a value and/or behaviour to their student teacher by inviting the student teacher to adopt the modelling into their own teaching and be a role model for their students. Figure 5.2 presents Boyd's model.

The teacher educator explicitly models a teaching value and/or behaviour for their student teachers

Student teachers adopt value and/or behaviour into their practice as a teacher and role models the value and/or behaviour for their own students

Student teachers adopt value and/or behaviour into their practice as they seek to become a professional in their chosen field

---

FIGURE 5.2   Boyd's layered pedagogy of teacher education

(Adapted from Boyd 2014, 70).

This approach is underpinned by a view that student teachers' knowledge of teaching and how to teach is a result of student teachers developing their own mental map of it. In the same way, teacher educators develop their knowledge of a pedagogy of teacher education as a result of undertaking two activities: reflecting on their own practice, and researching their own practice (Tillema and Kremer-Hayon 2005).

Research approach

Previous research on developing and enacting a pedagogy of teacher education has been a product of collaborative self-study, where one teacher educator researches his/her own practice with the support and critical friendship of another teacher educator. However, this study adopted a form of practical action research called second-person practice; it is research undertaken "with" colleagues, not research "on" them (Chandler and Torbert 2003, 143). There were two reasons for selecting it. First, modelling is "complex and difficult to do and particularly difficult to develop alone" (Loughran and Berry 2005, 194). Second, when recruiting participants for my study, three teacher educators from the same college volunteered for the study and I saw this as an opportunity to respond to Korthagen's (2001) observation that teacher educators rarely collaborated. Therefore, I invited other members of the teacher education team at the college to join the study; six of the team agreed to participate. Table 5.1 provides basic data of the teacher educators in the study.

TABLE 5.1 Teacher educators in the study

Pseudonym	Subject specialty	Year they became a teacher educator
Jana (Manager)	English	2004
Tom	English	2010
Alison	English	2012
Aisha	English	2013
Benjamin	English	2007
Christine	English	2010

Before the study began, I followed McNiff's (2014) advice and invited participants of my workshop at the 2012 Collaborative Action Research Network conference to validate my chosen data collection instruments. The data collection instruments used in the study were:

1 'Teacher talk' (Hardy 2010, 131), a series of six "deliberately developed conversations" with the team of teacher educators to discuss the design of the study, their work, and their use of modelling in their practice;
2 Semi-structured interviews with five of the teacher educators (Christine said she did not want to be interviewed);
3 Filmed teacher educator's classes. Four of the teacher educators agreed to be filmed: Jana, Tom, Alison, and Aisha;
4 Stimulated recall interviews with the four teacher educators whose classes I had filmed;
5 Focus groups with the student teachers after the filmed class;
6 My "own personal experience as data" (Pennanen et al. 2017, 211).

Operationalising the action research cycle, data collection, and analysis

Traditionally, action researchers have been expected to follow Lewin's cycle of steps. However, my experience was that, whilst I intended to follow the cycle of steps, what actually happened was my "initial plans quickly [became] obsolete" (Kemmis, McTaggart, and Nixon 2014, 18) as I encountered "the human and contextual messiness" (Mockler 2017, xx) of the site and the study. Here I am using messiness to reflect the "complexity, unpredictability, difficulties, and dilemmas" of collaborative research (Adamson and Walker 2011, 29). I learned that when using practical action research I had to be "more fluid, open, and responsive" (Kemmis, McTaggart, and Nixon 2014, 18) to the participants and the study. For example, having filmed Jana, Tom, and Alison in the first cycle of the study, I was not able to go back and film them again in the second cycle because timetabling and enrolments meant that they were not teaching on the programme that year. This required us to improvise. For the second cycle, Aisha, a newly appointed teacher educator, agreed to be filmed in a class she would co-teach with Jana, who would de-brief the session in the spirit of Loughran and Berry (2005). The third cycle responded to some of the findings in the second cycle by designing and piloting a prototype Viewing Frame for teacher educators to use with their student teachers. Based on my experience, I concur with Kemmis, McTaggart, and Nixon (2014, 8) that "faithfully" following the cycle's steps should not be one of the criteria of success for practical action research. Instead we should judge its success on the extent to which its co-labourers demonstrate a "strong and authentic sense of development and evolution in their *practices*, their *understandings* of their practices, and the *situations* in which they practice" (emphasis in original; ibid, 18–19). It is against this criterion I want you to judge this study.

The interviews, 'teacher talk', focus groups, stimulated recall interviews, and filmed classes were all recorded and transcribed for analysis purposes. Thematic analysis (Braun and Clarke 2006) was combined with the study's three conceptual lenses to analyse the data and initial findings were shared with the team, and at meetings and conferences with groups of further-education and higher-education-based teacher educators for the purpose of validation (McNiff 2014).

Discussion of the findings

The analysis sought to identify the 'happenings' (Mahon et al. 2017) of this collaboration. They are presented as what happens when teacher educators collaborate, and what shapes what happens. Teacher educators' voices are used to illustrate these 'happenings' and each happening is located within existing literature on the roles of teacher educators, professional learning, collaborative research, and practice architectures.

What happens when teacher educators collaborate?

Lunenberg, Korthagen, and Swennen (2007) highlight research undertaken by Menges (1994) that suggests that teacher education collaboration offers professional learning opportunities. For example, time to reflect on and discuss a teaching session with another teacher can be a professional learning opportunity (Lahiff 2015). The four teacher educators whose classes I filmed acknowledged the value of using stimulated recall interviews to review the class with me and explain their use of modelling within it. Michael reflected: "It was useful to take that time out to go through that meta-commentary, and it was like going through guided reflective practice, which kind of allowed me to see things sometimes a bit differently and to question myself further". Alison reflected:

> I think watching the video and doing the commentary on the playback of my class was a really powerful tool for reflection actually. It also highlighted for me to remember to keep flagging that up to the students to think about the process as well as the product: to think about the way they were doing things and why in their classrooms.

Michael's and Alison's voices suggest the stimulated recall interview was a professional learning activity that allowed them to 'see into' their own practice and change it, too.

These teacher educators were also thinking more about modelling. Jana reflected that they were more aware of modelling, how it is used within the team, and strategies they can use, "so being part of the research has given me an insight into other teacher educators' practices". Michael echoed this:

> I learnt a lot from working with Ben and I became aware of certain values and things that Ben embodies as a teacher trainer and the way that they model that and I started to think about it more. Perhaps I would have done that anyway but the very fact that we were talking about modelling and that our focus was on that made me then think about what the people that I work with are doing and what I can learn from that.

It would seem that as a result of the "conversations" (Ball and Rundquist 1993, 38) and "teacher talk" (Hardy 2010), modelling has become part of the 'sayings, doings and relatings' of the team; the process of researching, discussing, and explaining their practice has turned on a modelling lens for them. These 'happenings' add to existing research, such as Menges, on teacher educators' collaborative research as professional learning and a way of supporting their work and role as 'teachers of teachers' (Lunenberg, Dengerink, and Korthagen 2014).

Another of the identities (Swennen, Jones, and Volman 2010) and roles for university-based teacher educators is being a researcher (Lunenberg, Dengerink, and Korthagen 2014). Whilst being active in research is seen as less important for further-education-based teacher educators, the 'sayings, doings, and relatings' of some of the teacher educators in this study echo BERA's (2014, 18) claims that being involved in research "can have a deep influence" on participants' conceptualisation of research and their enthusiasm for it, and result in them undertaking their own research. Being involved in the study made the participants feel they had become part of "a research community", and that they have had modelled to them how they might undertake their own research. For example, Alison observed that "you were modelling the importance of research and also of emancipatory relationships with colleagues. I felt empowered by being involved in your research". It has acted as a stimulus for Michael's own research ambitions: "being involved with you has been a motivator in terms of me thinking about my own research". Towards the end of the study, he would realise this ambition when his first journal article was published. And it would inspire Aisha to enrol in a full-time PhD course.

We modelled practitioner research to their student teachers, too. Jana pointed out that our collaboration had unintentionally modelled for their student teachers Stenhouse's notion of teachers as researchers: "it also was interesting for the students to see that we were consciously looking at our practice [by] engaging in action research ourselves. They were interested to see this being modelled to them". This example of Boyd's (2014) layered pedagogy of teacher education was an unexpected outcome for the study.

Hardy (2010, 131) asserts that "teacher talk" is "praxis" when it focuses on "committed, collaborative inquiry". An example of this occurred in the second cycle when Aisha and Jana worked with myself to jointly plan a peer teaching session based on Loughran and Berry's peer teaching (2005). Jana reflected: "in a meeting a couple of years ago we talked about modelling and then people were interested in it and everything but it is the actual doing of it that hasn't happened". At a later meeting they added:

> [T]he leitmotif that keeps reappearing is that the research has contributed to a more expansive rather than a restrictive working environment, so what we found is that it has contributed to cross-college working in terms of our COPPs – communities of professional practice – and it's developed into team teaching within our team and more widely across the college.

An instance of praxis and production (Lofthouse and Thomas 2017) that arose from the 'teacher talk' was the suggestion by Jana that, based on the idea of a writing frame, we develop a 'Viewing Frame' to develop and support our student teachers' noticing skills. This action was informed by listening to the voices of the teacher educators and hearing the voices of two student teachers who, having been asked about an instance of modelling in the peer-taught class, said:

Student Teacher 2:   "I'd have thought so but I didn't notice it".
Student Teacher 4:   "I didn't notice it until it was pointed out".

During the subsequent stimulated recall interview, Jana remarked: "We rely a lot on them thinking, "Oh, they must see it" – that you think that they are going to spot that we are doing this – but they don't." These voices reminded us of the danger of assuming student teachers notice the 'sayings, doings, and relatings' of teacher educators' practices.

Using Lunenberg, Korthagen, and Swennen's (2007) four forms of modelling, I designed and piloted a prototype Viewing Frame for my own class and then shared it with the team to use. Later I shared it with European teacher educators at a conference of the Association of Teacher Educators in Europe, where I invited four university-based teacher educators, from England, Poland, the Netherlands, and Israel, to use it in their country and teaching context to establish if it was transferable. The further education-based teacher educator team never found time to try it out in their teaching, they said, an instance of the material-economic arrangements shaping their practice, it would seem. However, feedback from the university-based ATEE teacher educators was that the Viewing Frame was a concrete tool for learning to teach because it developed student teachers' noticing skills and created an opportunity to make links between theory and practice (Powell 2016). It also turned on the student teachers' " 'student as teacher and learner' lens" (Taylor 2008, 78). The ATEE teacher educators felt that the use of the Viewing

Frame also contributed to their own professional learning as it allowed them to "see into" their own teaching as they reflected on the discussions they had with their student teachers (Powell 2016). This is another example of how collaborative research can support teacher educators' role as a 'teacher of teachers' (Lunenberg, Dengerink, and Korthagen 2014).

What shapes what happens?

There is a tendency to focus on and celebrate what happens in collaborative research, though it could be argued that it is as important for us to appreciate what might shape it if we are to navigate its ups and downs. Collaboration is shaped by the sayings, doings, and relatings of its co-labourers and the practice architectures of the site where it takes place (Pennanen et al. 2017). This study provides illustrative examples of what shaped its collaboration. For example, an organisational restructuring and changes within the teacher education team – some teacher educators left, others joined – and concerns about issues of power and with whom the findings of the study would be shared shaped which of the teacher educators participated and the nature of their participation. On reflection, some of my early collaboration was not as participatory as it could have been (Ball and Rundquist 1993). My own position – I was researching with teacher educators from a partnership I managed – might have contributed to some of the co-labourers' perceptions. For instance, Ben expressed their concerns about our first meeting: "I wasn't very happy. I think it was this whole idea that you had somehow got permission from the management here to do the study and that in some way that you were going to report back what was happening in our classrooms". Michael, who had been very keen to become involved in the study initially, stated in our first 'teacher talk' meeting: "It also made me think as well about power relationships because you're from the awarding body. It makes [me] feel a bit worried from that point of view". However, these voices need to be heard within the social-political arrangements of the site at the time (Kemmis et al. 2014). Jana, the team's leader, reflected towards the end of the study: "I think what people were worried about is that there was a host of competing and contradictory practices within so many people. I think [the start of] this research came at a moment where people were vulnerable in that respect". Ben agreed: "We were quite vulnerable", he said; and Christine, another who had been reluctant to participate, added: "We brought our baggage with us". The "human and contextual messiness" (Mockler 2017, xx) of a site and how it shaped this collaborative enquiry are audible here.

How we conduct our research can also become an enabling or constraining practice architecture in collaborative research (Pennanen et al. 2017). An example of this was my decision to film the classes. Kemmis et al. (2014, 224) assert that filming practices provide "better records" of the practice being studied and the practice architectures shaping them. However, Ben and Christine said they did not wish to be filmed. This surprised me. However, Segall (2002, 171) reminds us that, "regardless of how committed teacher educators might be, not everyone would relish the idea of having their practice open to external, critical scrutiny". My choice of filming classes as a data collection method had constrained participation in this instance.

This was my doctoral study. Understandably, I was protective of the data collection process at the start; I wanted to collect the data and be confident I was getting what I needed. After the first cycle of the data collection, I decided to introduce the 'teacher talk' meetings with the teacher educators. It was at this point that the study became more participatory and democratic. I was now confident about how things were going and so invited the teacher educators to make suggestions on the design of the second cycle of the study. There had been considerable discussion of the possible impact of my filming the classes. None of those who had been filmed in the first cycle felt it had affected how they taught, though we were unsure of the impact it may have had on their student teachers. Therefore, we discussed and agreed upon a different approach to the second cycle of the study:

1   We would invite one of the student teachers to film the class, with myself on stand-by if there was a problem with the filming.
2   The teacher educators who were filmed would lead the subsequent focus group instead of myself.

Here, the introduction of 'teacher talk' as a data collection instrument acted as an enabling practice architecture and changed some of the sayings, doings, and relatings and subsequent 'happenings' of the study.

To summarise, this instance of collaborative research supported these teacher educators' professional learning, in terms of being 'teachers of teachers' and 'researchers' (Swennen, Jones and Volman 2010; Lunenberg, Dengerink, and Korthagen 2014). It also resulted in an instance of praxis that produced a Viewing Frame which is now being used by other teacher educators. Finally, it suggests the site-specific forces that might shape teacher educators when collaborating and researching their practice.

Conclusions, thoughts, and reflections

This study asked the question: what happens when teacher educators work together to explore modelling and develop a pedagogy of teacher education? There seem to be two answers. first, these co-labourers had to learn to collaborate. Once this happened, they were able to use conversations and 'teacher talk' to turn on a modelling lens so they could explore, understand, and then develop their own pedagogies of teacher education. Second, teacher educator collaboration remains a valuable research approach and professional learning activity to support the skills, values, behaviours, and knowledge that underpin one or more of their professional roles.

As such, this study makes three contributions to what is known about teacher educators and their practices. First, it provides an account of the practices and practice architectures shaping the work of a group of rarely studied teacher educators:

further-education-based teacher educators. Second, it created and developed a new teaching resource – a Viewing Frame – that is being used by teacher educators in England and Europe. Third, it introduces practice architectures as a lens for studying the practices of teacher educator collaborative enquiry and allows researchers to focus on "the practice conditions" that "prefigure" (Pennanen et al. 2017, 202) practice and shape the research. It has illuminated how the practice architectures of a site and the practices of co-labourers are "enmeshed" (Mahon et al. 2017, 10) and how this shaped this instance of collaboration and, in turn, how the collaboration shaped the site and its co-labourers.

Invitations for future research into teacher education collaboration

There are two invitations to teacher educators arising from this research. First, they are invited to undertake collaborative research with other teacher educators on their practice and publish their findings so others might have examples of how to map and describe this "messy and complex terrain" (Berry 2008, 31). Second, teacher educators are invited to consider practice architectures as a conceptual lens when undertaking collaborative research and to document the practices and practice architectures that enabled and constrained it. This will provide other teacher educators with a better understanding of what shapes collaborative research and how they might work with and navigate any "fluidity and volatility" (Mahon et al. 2017, 10) that occurs in their own study.

Downloadable version of the viewing frame

The Viewing Frame is available for use by teacher educators and student teachers (www.go.herts.ac.uk/FLiTE) together with guidance on effective ways of using it: as a planning resource, you can consider your own practice and plan your use of modelling for a class; as a peer observation resource, you and other teacher educators can use it to focus on specific aspects of your practice; and as a resource to develop the noticing skills of your student teachers, you can invite your student teachers to notice your practice and record this.

References

Adamson, B., and E. Walker. 2011. "Messy Collaboration: Learning From a Learning Study." *Teaching and Teacher Education* 27: 29–36.

Ball, D., and S. Rundquist. 1993. "Collaboration As a Context for Joint Teacher Learning with Learning about Teaching." In *Teaching for Understanding: Challenges for Policy and Practice*, edited by D. Cohen, M. McLaughlin, and J. Talbert, 13–42. San Francisco: Jossey-Bass Publishers.

Berry, A. 2008. *Tensions in Teaching about Teaching: Understanding Practice as a Teacher Educator.* Dordrecht: Springer.

Boyd, P. 2014. "Using Modelling to Improve the Coherence of Initial Teacher Education." In *Teacher Educators and Teachers as Learners: International Perspectives*, edited by P. Boyd, A. Szplit, and Z. Zbróg, 51–74. Kraków: Libron.

Braun, V., and V. Clarke. 2006. "Using Thematic Analysis in Psychology." *Qualitative Research in Psychology* 3 (2): 77–101.

British Educational Research Association. 2014. *Research and the Teaching Profession: Building the Capacity for a Self-Improving Education System*. Final Report of the BERA-RSA Inquiry into the Role of Research in Teacher Education. London: BERA.

Chandler, D., and B. Torbert. 2003. "Transforming Inquiry and Action: Interweaving 27 Flavors of Action Research." *Action Research* 1 (2): 133–152.

Eliahoo, R. 2014. "The Accidental Experts: A Study of FE Teacher Educators, their Professional Development Needs and Ways of Supporting These." PhD, Institute of Education, University of London.

Eliahoo, R. 2017. "Teacher Educators: Proposing New Professional Development Models within an English Further Education Context." *Professional Development in Education* 43 (2): 179–193.

Hardy, I. 2010. "Teacher Talk: Flexible Delivery and Academics' Praxis in an Australian University." *International Journal for Academic Development* 15 (2): 131–142.

Heaton, R., and M. Lampert. 1993. "Learning to Hear Voices: Inventing a New Pedagogy of Teacher Education." In *Teaching for Understanding: Challenges for Policy and Practice*, edited by D. Cohen, M. McLaughlin, and J. Talbert, 43–84. San Francisco: Jossey-Bass.

Hoban, G. 1997. "Learning about Learning in the Context of a Science Methods Course." In *Teaching about Teaching: Purpose, Passion and Pedagogy in Teacher Education*, edited by J. Loughran, and T. Russell, 133–149. London: Falmer Press.

Kelchtermans, G., K. Smith, and R. Vanderlinde. 2018. "Towards an 'International Forum for Teacher Educator Development': An Agenda for Research and Action." *European Journal of Teacher Education* 41 (1): 120–134.

Kemmis, S., and C. Edwards-Groves. 2018. *Understanding Education: History, Politics, and Practice*. Singapore: Springer.

Kemmis, S., R. McTaggart, and R. Nixon. 2014. *The Action Research Planner: Doing Critical Participatory Action Research*. Dordrecht: Springer.

Kemmis, S., J. Wilkinson, C. Edwards-Groves, I. Hardy, P. Grootenboer, and L. Bristol. 2014. *Changing Practices, Changing Education*. London: Springer.

Korthagen, F. 2001. "Teacher Education: A Problematic Enterprise." In *Linking Practice and Theory: The Pedagogy of Realistic Teacher Education*, edited by F. Korthagen, J. Kessels, B. Koster, B. Lagerwerf, and T. Wubbels, 1–19. Mahwah, NJ: Lawrence Erlbaum Associates.

Lahiff, A. 2015. "Maximizing Vocational Teachers' Learning: The Feedback Discussion in the Observation of Teaching for Initial Teacher Training in Further Education." *London Review of Education* 13 (1): 3–15.

Livingston, K. 2014. "Teacher Educators: Hidden Professionals?" *European Journal of Education* 49 (2): 218–232.

Lofthouse, R., and U. Thomas. 2017. "Concerning Collaboration: Teachers' Perspectives on Working in Partnerships to Develop Teaching Practices." *Professional Development in Education* 43 (1): 36–56.

Loughran, J. 1997. "Teaching about Teaching: Principles and Practice." In *Purpose, Passion and Pedagogy in Teacher Education*, edited by J. Loughran, and T. Russell, 57–70. London/ Washington DC: Falmer Press.

Loughran, J. 2014. "Professionally Developing As a Teacher Educator." *Journal of Teacher Education* 65 (4): 271–283.

Loughran, J., and A. Berry. 2005. "Modelling by Teacher Educators." *Teaching and Teacher Education* 21 (2): 193–203.

Lunenberg, M., J. Dengerink, and F. Korthagen. 2014. *The Professional Teacher Educator: Roles, Behaviour, and Professional Development of Teacher Educators.* Rotterdam: Sense Publications.

Lunenberg, M., F. Korthagen, and A. Swennen. 2007. "The Teacher Educator As a Role Model." *Teaching and Teacher Education* 23 (5): 586–601.

Mahon, K., S. Kemmis, S. Francisco, and A. Lloyd. 2017. "Introduction: Practice Theory and the Theory of Practice Architectures." In *Exploring Education and Professional Practice Through the Lens of Practice Architectures*, edited by K. Mahon, S. Francisco, and S. Kemmis, 1–30. Singapore: Springer.

Mason, J. 2002. *Researching Your Own Practice: The Discipline of Noticing.* London: Routledge.

McNiff, J. 2014. *Writing and Doing Action Research.* London: Sage.

Menges, R. 1994. "Promoting Inquiry into One's Own Teaching." In *Informing Faculty Development for Teacher Educators*, edited by K.R. Howey, and N.L. Zimpher, 51–97. Westport: Ablex Publishing.

Mockler, N. 2017. "Foreword: Practical Theory for Complex Times." In *Exploring Education and Professional Practice Through the Lens of Practice Architectures*, edited by K. Mahon, S. Francisco, and S. Kemmis, xix–xxiv. Singapore: Springer.

Murray, J., and T. Male. 2005. "Becoming a Teacher Educator: Evidence From the Field." *Teaching and Teacher Education* 21 (5):125–142.

Nichol, C. 1997. "Learning to Teach Prospective Teachers to Teach Mathematics: The Struggles of a Beginning Teacher Educator." In *Teaching about Teaching: Purpose, Passion and Pedagogy in Teacher Education,* edited by J. Loughran, and T. Russell, 95–116. London: Falmer Press.

Noel, P. 2006. "The Secret Life of the Teacher Educator: Becoming a Teacher Educator in the Learning and Skills Sector." *Journal of Vocational Education and Training* 58 (2): 151–170.

Pennanen, M., L. Bristol, J. Wilkinson, and H. Heikinnen. 2017. "Articulating the Practice Architectures of Collaborative Practice Research." In *Exploring Education and Professional Practice Through the Lens of Practice Architectures*, edited by K. Mahon, S. Francisco, and S. Kemmis, 201–218. Singapore: Springer.

Powell, D. 2016. *"It's Not As Straightforward As It Sounds": An Action Research Study of a Team of Further Education-Based Teacher Educators and Their Use of Modelling During a Period of De-Regulation and Austerity.* EdD. University of Huddersfield.

Powell, D. 2017. "Collaborative Inquiry by Teacher Educators: Mess and Messiness." In *Teacher Educators and Teachers as Learners: International Perspectives*, edited by P. Boyd, A. Szplit, and Z. Zbróg, 239–262. Kraków: Libron.

Segall, A. 2002. *Disturbing Practice: Reading Teacher Education As Text.* New York: Peter Lang.

Simmons, R., and R. Thompson. 2007. "Teacher Educators in Post-Compulsory Education: Gender, Discourse and Power." *Journal of Vocational Education and Training* 59 (4): 517–533.

Swennen, A. 2015. "Weaverbirds and Twitter: Variety in the Landscape of Professional Learning of Educators." *Professional Development in Education* 41 (4): 597–601.

Swennen, A., K. Jones, and M. Volman. 2010. "Teacher Educators: Their Identities, Sub-Identities and Implications for Professional Development." *Professional Development in Education* 36 (1&2): 131–148. doi: 10.1080/19415250903457893.

Taylor, A. 2008. "Developing Understanding About Learning to Teach in a University-Schools Partnership in England." *British Educational Research Journal* 34 (1): 63–90.

Thurston, D. 2010. "The Invisible Educators: Exploring the Development of Teacher Educators in the Further Education System." *Teaching in Lifelong Learning: A Journal to Inform and Improve Practice* 2 (1): 47–55.

Tillema, H., and L. Kremer-Hayon. 2005. "Facing Dilemmas: Teacher Educators' Ways of Constructing a Pedagogy of Teacher Education." *Teaching in Higher Education* 10 (2): 203–217.

White, E., C. Dickerson, and K, Weston. 2015. "Developing an Appreciation of What It Means to Be a School-Based Teacher Educator." *European Journal of Teacher Education* 38 (4): 445–459.

6

"ARE WE DOING THE RIGHT THING?"

Challenges teacher educators face when taking the risk of opening up possibilities for students

Monique Leijgraaf

Introduction

Being lost in the misty forest, Pooh and Piglet are afraid. Piglet softly whispers "Pooh", and when Pooh asks him what is the matter, Piglet says, "Nothing, I just wanted to be sure of you" (Milne 2001, 209).

Piglet's reaction might be considered naïve and highly inaccurate: instead of asking for effective solutions resulting in the successful outcome of finding their way home, Piglet simply addresses his closest friend by whispering his name. However, the narrative gives no justification for interpreting both Piglet's action and Pooh's reaction as naïve or inaccurate. On the contrary, in the story their friendship is highly esteemed as one based on trust rather than control and measurable agreements, making this small conversation a kind of counter narrative of various private and public relations around the world.

For instance, the relationship between many national governments and institutions for teacher education has recently changed from trusting to controlling on the part of the governments. Due to the rising hegemony of a neoliberal ideology within both broader society and the field of education, on the one hand (see, for instance, Leijgraaf 2015), and, on the other hand, the "policy identification of a direct causal relation between teacher education, student teacher, school and pupil achievement" (Trippestad, Swennen, and Werler 2017, 8), governments have implemented accountability systems in their striving to control institutions for teacher education since the 1980s.

In the Netherlands, this striving for control revealed itself, among other things, in the government's interference in the content of the teacher education program, which had moved towards a competence-based curriculum. In response to concerns about the lack of knowledge in teacher education as expressed by the Dutch Educational Council (Onderwijsraad 2005), the Ministry of Education made available both money and a team of specialists to develop so-called knowledge bases for each subject, including tests to assess the student's knowledge (Swennen and Volman 2017). Besides this control-oriented intervention by the government, the overall demand for accountability in society influenced the way the notion of competences had been taken up in teacher education, confining it to highly controllable checklists of required skills (Kelchtermans 2012; Schuck and Buchanan 2012). It should also be mentioned that teacher educators themselves contributed to this atmosphere of accountability and control by creating and working with more or less scripted curricula that ensure the transmission of existing educational knowledge to students. Although teacher educators do not have externally created, scripted instructions at their disposal that direct "teachers to teach, even to talk, from standardized, written scripts, which allow teachers virtually no latitude to make their own instructional decisions" (Reeves 2010, 241), it might be said that teacher educators do limit their freedom to make situated judgements by making their self-created lesson plans the leading principle in their teaching. Gatti (2016) considers structured lesson planning and the deployment of scripted techniques as a materialisation of teacher educators' desire for certainty and predictability.

Whereas these knowledge bases, the accompanying tests, the checklists, and the more or less scripted curricula do contribute to the accountability of universities and the feeling of being certain and in control, they also reduce teacher education to a pure functional process determined by inputs and outputs.

This chapter focusses on this tension between being in control, certain, and accountable, on the one hand, and an open attitude of teacher educators to uncertainties, unexpected situations, and the risk that inevitably comes with (teacher) education (Biesta 2014), on the other hand. Based on a small-scale, qualitative study I conducted as a practitioner researcher (Cochran-Smith and Lytle 2009) working at a Dutch college of teacher education for primary education, this chapter aims to present 'risk-full' initiatives by teacher educators to improve their work with students by opening up the self-created lesson plans and supporting and challenging students to find their own route.

Conceptual framework

Despite the dominance of tendencies to consider good (teacher) education as risk-free, evidence-based, efficient, and functional, these ideas are being challenged by policy makers, advisory bodies, and academics as well. Within the academic debate, Joosten (2013) is one of the scholars who not only addresses the problematising attitude towards uncertainty and the accompanying search for ways to eliminate it from higher education, but also investigates ways to embed uncertainty in the educational practice of institutes of applied sciences. She undertook this investigation because today's "professionals have to deal with more uncertainties in their field than before" (Joosten 2013, 549), a statement that reveals the pragmatic origin of her plea (cf. Heck and Ambrosetti 2018). Other scholars relate their plea to embed uncertainty in teacher education to the teaching profession, underlining the complex and uncertain nature of teaching as well as the necessity to make student teachers aware of this (Helsing 2007; Schuck and Buchanan 2012). In Biesta's (2014, 2017) line of thought about uncertainties and education, however, more existential dimensions are at stake, since in his work one's view of the role of uncertainties in the educational process in the end also reflects the way one sees students: as empty buckets to be filled and trained, or as human subjects who try to exist in and with the world, being exposed to and addressed by others. In the former case, teaching is considered a risk-free process of transmitting knowledge from a teacher to students (cf. Freire's banking concept of education [Freire 2000]), whereby the appropriate input will guarantee the desired output. This presupposed causal connection between 'input' and 'output', between teaching and what it 'effects' is problematised by Biesta, who argues that causal connections in education are neither possible nor desirable because all educational connections are established through sense-making in the encounter with others. And this latter aspect explains why education always involves risk:

> The risk is there because education is not an interaction between robots but an encounter between human beings. The risk is there because students are not to be seen as objects to be molded and disciplined, but as subjects of action and responsibility.
>
> *(Biesta 2014, 1)*

Whereas the first argument in this quotation relates to the impossibility of risk-free education, the latter refers to the undesirability of this view on education, making it a normative argument. It might be said that Biesta's major concern in this normative argument is human freedom in the Arendtian sense of the word. According to Arendt (1998), one of the fundamental aspects of the human condition is the freedom of every human being to act and thereby to begin something new on his or her own initiative. However, human beings are unable to begin something new in isolation: on the contrary, to be of any consequence new words and deeds need to be taken up and responded to by others who are entirely free in their decision to respond to or ignore these new beginnings. This implies that all responses to our actions are not in our hands, making them highly unpredictable. What is more, these responses have to be out of our control, otherwise we would reduce the ones that respond to our actions to objects we possess and control and thereby deprive them of the opportunity to exist as subjects themselves and of their freedom. With regard to the field of education, these insights imply that teachers should not so much aim to control their students by transmitting things the students do not know yet, but should try to encourage students to use their own intelligence and make their own beginnings, thereby inviting them to appear as subjects in dialogue with what and who is other.

> Here, . . . teaching becomes concerned with opening up existential possibilities for students, that is, possibilities in and through which students can

explore what it might mean to exist as subject in and with the world. Along these lines teaching begins to appear as the very opposite of control, the very opposite of attempts at approaching students merely as objects, but rather takes the form of approaching students as subjects even . . . when there is no evidence that they are capable of it.

(Biesta 2017, 3)

Method

Like many other colleges of teacher education for primary education, the independent[1] college discussed in this chapter struggles to balance this desire and demand for control, and the idea of education as a dialogical process of which the outcomes can neither be guaranteed nor secured. Despite explicit attention to the student's personal professionalism, the college's curriculum and teaching practices are monopolised by long and detailed checklists of everything students should be (or become) competent in. More specifically, the standards and criteria, developed to make the grading efficient and transparent to students, dominate the teaching practices and stimulate students and teacher educators to focus only on the summative evaluation forms and the therein included predetermined outcomes of the educational process.

In order to decrease the hegemony of these checklists and to open up possibilities for students to find their own routes, the college started a process of redesigning the curriculum. During the first year of this redesign, a pilot programme was developed for a small group of bachelor's-degree students in their fourth and final year, opening up the almost scripted lesson plans and prioritising the students' curiosity, questions, and ideas. Partly based on the results of this pilot programme, a completely new spring semester programme was developed for all students in their third year of study, with a focus on the students' interests and creating room for the routes students want to take. From there on, the programme of the final year, in which students specialise in a domain that fascinates them, was redesigned and carried out during the third year of the curriculum redesign. The experiences with these initiatives by students and teacher educators have been researched in a small-scale, qualitative study. The overall aim of the research was to explore meanings that both teacher educators and students give to this redesign(ing) of the curriculum. The findings presented in this chapter consider the tension between feeling in control and the attitude towards uncertainties and risks.

For three years I collected data at the college where I was working both as researcher and teacher educator. During the first year, a group of ten full-time students in their final year and two teacher educators (one of whom was me) participated in the research, creating data via shared journals and focus group interviews. Throughout the second year of research, the focus was on three colleagues who developed a completely new programme for students in their third year of study; they participated in individual interviews, focus group interviews, and participant observations. The three students who participated in focus group interviews and participant observations during the third year of research were full-time students in their fourth and final year, and one of them was in my class. Whereas the inside perspective that comes with practitioner research gives the advantage of collecting data in a natural setting and great involvement on the part of the participants, the imbalance in power relations, especially between the participating students and me (as their teacher educator and researcher), may have affected the data.[2]

During the second and third year of research, all teacher educators taking part in the programme and all full-time students in their third and fourth year of study, respectively, were involved in a more indirect way: their written programme evaluations and the regular meetings regarding programme evaluations were included in the dataset. Besides that, my research and teaching journal was part of the data collection as well.[3]

The eight interviews and seven evaluation meetings were recorded (audio) and later transcribed. Besides that, full notes were constructed out of the field notes taken during the participant observations (Emerson, Fretz, and Shaw 2011). Together with my journal and the written programme evaluations, the transcripts and field notes were uploaded to Atlas.ti. The qualitative analysis of the data can be characterised as an iterative process of reading and rereading data, coding and writing memos. During this process, 'control', '(un)certainties', and 'risk' became the sensitising concepts that helped me to find "directions along which to look" (Blumer 1954, 7).

In an effort to overcome the risk of bias and tunnel vision that might arise out of practitioner research, the research process has been discussed with a critical friend working as a teacher educator and researcher in a different context.

Findings

Looking over the data, it is very hard not to notice the enthusiasm provoked by the redesigned programmes: teacher educators pleasantly surprised by the students' insights and students thrilled with teacher educators "who did keep their promise to actually set us free" (quoted from a student's evaluation). Besides this enthusiasm for the new programmes, both teacher educators and students also faced some challenges.

Quality of the program

For instance, teacher educators experienced feelings of insecurity about the quality of their redesigned programme and wondered whether the programme was good and well-balanced enough:

> I doubt whether it is enough; maybe it's too one-sided. Insecure . . . yeah, that's the right word. Not insecure about the effort we make, but whether it's OK what we're doing: are we moving in the right direction? Are we doing the right thing?
>
> *(Nadine, individual interview)*

Balance

In addition to this doubt about the quality of the programme, uncertainty existed about the balance between what teacher educators hold to be important and what students want to do and know:

> One of the difficulties is that I want to do quite a lot of things with them, but the idea behind this redesign is that it's the student who's in the lead and who's responsible. So how to implement this balance in our programme? That's quite a challenge to me, because there are so many things we want them to do and experience, but they also have to find out what it is they want to do, as a matter of fact.
>
> *(Nadine, individual interview)*

This means that teacher educators should avoid determining the entire educational programme in more or less scripted lesson plans; rather, they should open up possibilities for students to find their own route as well. As this teacher educator, being asked what 'being in the lead and being responsible as a student' means to her, explained:

> Well, that has several meanings to me: us not boarding up everything, not determining it in every detail, so students have the opportunity to choose their own path and to take a different direction.
>
> *(Nadine, individual interview)*

Despite good intentions, one of the students' comments illustrates the difficulty teacher educators sometimes experience in maintaining this good balance in what teacher educators hold to be important and what students want:

> In this programme, I feel like everything is going too fast. So many subjects came by and so much information that I'm really interested in. But you know, it goes on and on and on. It's like, well . . .
>
> [Researcher: An overload?]
>
> Yeah! Maybe the teacher educator could stop every now and then and ask: What do you think of it? And maybe not give another lecture and continue talking, but [ask] as well: what do you think you can do with all this? Give us some space to work on our portfolio, I'd like that very much.
>
> *(Ivy, focus group interview)*

Concrete tasks

Besides these uncertainties about the quality of the programme and maintaining the balance between students' and teacher educators' desires, concerns about the way students might handle uncertainties were brought up as well. One of the teacher educators, who defines herself as someone who loves to "have everything in hand" and who hates "to not know what's on my next week's lesson plan" (quoted from focus group interview), decided to give the students concrete tasks to fulfil, thereby avoiding doing all of the talking herself and making sure the students were actively involved in her programme instead of paralysed by insecurities they might experience in finding their own route:

> Everything I've been doing so far was focussed on the final exam of this pro-gramme. I give them very concrete tasks anyway, which they have to carry out instantly. There's no time to sit back and relax. I specifically chose to force them to go out of their depth. And I did give them inflatable armbands to help them float. After a while, I'll reduce my help. To me, it's important that to some extent the purpose of all is clear. At least the framework. So you'll be able to pick your own route [as a student], and your own ending, but without too many uncertainties.
>
> [Researcher: Exactly, to strike a balance. Because you did force them to go out of their depth, but with floaties.]
>
> Yes. I offered them enough supplies to not completely go blup–blup–blup [drown], I hope.
>
> *(Elise, individual interview)*

Despite the ambiguity towards uncertainties that can be derived from these words, this teacher educator also has an open attitude to things she is unfamiliar with:

> I told the students explicitly that I do not necessarily have to be the one who knows best. Especially during the second half of the semester, when they intensively study something they have an interest in, they'll probably know more about it than I do. I'm a bit nervous about it. I do like to have some control. But OK. [laughter] It's pretty exciting: maybe this all leads to some-thing I can learn from as well.
>
> *(Elise, individual interview)*

Trust

In line with this ambiguity, the data neither revealed an entirely negative attitude towards uncertainty nor disclosed attempts to eliminate it from the programmes. Discussing the possibility to appreciate uncertainties, one of the teacher educators argued that uncertainties are a fact of life:

> I think that uncertainties can help you to take the next step towards being a bit less insecure about certain issues. Students just have to accept that some issues are uncertain. They just have to accept that.
>
> *(Saskia, individual interview)*

Taking the uncertainty coming from a less scripted way of working with students as a starting point, one of the teacher educators related this uncertainty to the notion of trust and confidence:

> The way I see it, everything is a chaotic mess to them at the start of the year. But they did trust us, right from the start. We told them: be confident that things will work out well. This resulted in students relying on the process we were in together and on the judgements they made during that process. They learned to trust their own judgements, also because they knew they were not on their own in this: we were there as well, keeping an eye on what happened on the whole.
>
> *(Jacqueline, focus group interview)*

Freedom

On their part, students had to grow accustomed to the uncertainties that stem from the less scripted programmes:

> We had a say in everything. Every meeting, space was created for us to pose questions and thereby design the course. We sure did taste that kind of free-dom. In the beginning, it was tough: you long for freedom, but once given it's hard to decide what to do with it. During the first couple of meetings, everybody got kind of crazy and people were complaining: what am I sup-posed to do? Why this kind of freedom? But, well, we had to get out of our comfort zones, and then the ball started rolling.
>
> *(Student evaluation)*

It is noteworthy that, in this quotation, the feelings of insecurity are embedded in the freedom this student has experienced. Students recognised that the redesigned programmes bring forth a certain freedom to both create your own route and learn from routes other students create:

> It's no longer that you have to do something because the summative evalua-tion form tells you to. I'm so happy about that. We're quite free to conduct our research project the way we want to. Everybody has his own way of doing that; there are quite some different approaches. Some start teaching their pupils, some start reading, others start designing their sub-questions.
>
> *(Dahlia, focus group interview)*

> At the start [of class] we ask ourselves what it is we want to do today and what's up for discussion. That's what our class will be about. This is much better than having a teacher educator who has prepared a lesson about a sub-ject we don't take an interest in. Luckily our teacher educator knows a lot,

> so that's good. This way, we learn much more than working along the lesson plan prepared by the teacher educator.
>
> *(Abdullah, focus group interview)*

Challenging, encouraging, or even summoning students to find their route, instead of controlling them, can open up new and unexpected possibilities, as one of the students reported in the foreword to her written exam:

> To be honest, this was quite challenging to me, especially at the start. I happen to be a person who wants to know exactly what is being expected of her, and to have those expectations in black and white. I sure would have loved to have had a summative evaluation form to accompany my work.
>
> I learned a lot from this. I was challenged to see and think beyond the usual. Looking backward, I think it's been a good idea not to give out the summative evaluation form at the start. It challenged me to think deeper and to be more creative.
>
> *(Yvette – researcher's journal)*

Discussion and conclusion

This chapter has presented 'risk-full' steps teacher educators took in order to improve their working with students by decreasing the control of checklists over their teaching practices and at the same time opening up possibilities for students to find their own routes. The research presented in this chapter aimed to explore the significance of these steps to both students and teacher educators, thereby focussing on the tension between feeling in control and the attitude towards uncertainties and risks. In this discussion and conclusion section, the findings of the presented research, on the one hand, and theoretical insights concerning teacher education and uncertainties, on the other hand, will be brought together in a critical dialogue to identify challenging dilemmas teacher educators and students face in teacher educational practices. These dilemmas, defined by Helsing as a "common type of uncertainty . . ., where two or more values or commitments are pitted against each other" (Helsing 2007, 1318), will not be solved with recipe-like solutions but recognised as enduring challenges that ask for judgements about what is educationally desirable in this specific context (Biesta 2014, 2017) and engagement in reflection on these situated judgements in professional learning communities on a regular basis.

First dilemma

The first challenge that can be identified concerns the tension between teacher educators opening up new possibilities for students and (their fear of) students feeling paralysed by the insecurities they experience facing these new possibilities and finding their own route. As Rancière highlights, once the teacher (educator) no longer just transmits and explains knowledge that is in his or her control but challenges or even summons students to use their own intelligence and find their own route, it has to be taken into account that the "route the student will take is unknown" (Rancière 1991, 23), leading to an increase in uncertainty on the side of the student as well as the teacher (educator). In response to the uncertainties her students might face during their journey, one of the teacher educators tried to create a situation in which her students could partially evade these uncertainties, giving them concrete tasks to be undertaken instantaneously at the start of the pro-gramme. Although this same teacher educator also expressed a certain curiosity to see where the unknown routes her students take will lead to, it might be said that her initial response gives the impression that, at least at the beginning of a course, uncertainties can be a barrier to the students' journey.

Addressing teachers' attitude towards uncertainties in higher education, Joosten opposes this suggestion of uncertainties as a barrier and underlines the importance of stimulating students to make professional judgements:

> Teachers should encourage them [students] to manifest their truth in their actions, rather than eliminating uncertainty and discomfort. Teachers should create space to play and try out new forms of thinking and acting in order to expand the area of the possible, even when these new forms turn out to be different truths than the teachers expect or could imagine.
>
> *(Joosten 2013, 561)*

The research shows that efforts have been made to create spaces like these where students and teacher educators can explore new possibilities, and that some of these endeavours have been taken up as well: students finding their own routes in their research projects and learning from the various routes others created; classes that start with a shared exploration of the issues at stake; and students who realise that freedom involves responsibility to act as well.

Nevertheless, the concern raised by the teacher educator who feared the risk of 'drowning students' has to be taken into account as well. Even though, at the same time, the foreword of the written exam of one of the students revealed that 'the lack of floaties' did not automatically lead to drowning, but opened up new possibilities. In the end, the space that was created by not getting a detailed evalu-ation form at the start of the course turned out not to be so much a barrier as an interruption to what was familiar to this student, challenging her to start something that was new to her. The uncertainty that came with this interruption might have paralysed her in the beginning, but eventually this student took advantage of the liberty to use her own intelligence and find her own way instead of remaining within the bounds of the summative evaluation form developed by her teacher educators and living up to expectations she otherwise would had derived from that evaluation form.

The notion of confidence and trust, brought up by another teacher educator who was aware of the chaotic mess the students experienced at the start of the year, might be helpful to explore this first identified dilemma. This teacher educator expanded on the trustful relationship between students and teacher educators, which helped the students to bear their insecurities and uncertainties. In a way, this relationship of trust reminds me of the friendship between Pooh and Piglet in which Piglet, feeling uncertain and insecure, addresses his friend because he "just wanted to be sure" of him (Milne 2001, 209). Tightly connected to the uncertainties and risks that come with education, Biesta finds in the concept of trust one of the appropriate concepts to capture what is special about educational relationships. Elaborating on this concept, he argues that trust is needed only in situations where people have no secure and certain knowledge of how someone else will act, since there would be no need for trust if somebody else's action was already known or predictable. Moreover, he underlines that giving trust always involves a risk:

> From the side of the trust-giver, trust . . . always entails a risk, particularly the risk that the other person will act differently from what we expected or hoped for. Rather than attempting to capture this in moral terms, . . . the risk that comes with trust is better to be seen as an acknowledgement of human freedom: the freedom we all have to act in this way or that, to say yes or no, to go with the flow or against it. . . . What is important from an educational point of view is that trust precisely opens up a "space" where the child or student encounters its freedom and where they need to figure out what to do with this freedom. Trust, in other words, puts their subject-ness at stake.
>
> *(Biesta 2017, 92)*

The research presented here finds its limitations in precisely this more existential dimension in Biesta's thoughts on education: whereas the research does show that efforts have been made to open up possibilities and even that some of them have been taken up, the current study was not designed to explore the existential significance of these endeavours. Whether, for example, the interruption due to the absent summative evaluation form actually was experienced as an opening up of a space where the student encountered her freedom to begin something new (in the Arendtian sense of the word) remains to be seen. Future and more in-depth case studies might be able to explore the meaning of the renewed educational practices related to the students' and teacher educators' existence in and with the world.

In an indirect way, however, this research did reveal what might be referred to as some hesitation or uncertainty in the teacher educators' vocabulary concerning these existential dimensions of education in general and an ambivalent attitude towards risks and uncertainties in particular. Although no signs can be traced of a purely moulding and objectifying attitude towards students, only implicit indications can be found that teacher educators consciously try to approach their students as subjects by, for instance, encouraging them to make their own beginnings. The discourses hardly show any traces of the notion that, in the end, human freedom is at stake in educational relationships, and that by opening up possibilities for students to find their own routes, teacher educators create room in which students can encounter their freedom and figure out what to do with it. Therefore, it is recommended to discuss issues related to these existential dimensions of education explicitly in professional learning communities, thereby empowering teacher educators in their drive to open up new possibilities for students under the acknowledgement of the first identified challenge.

Second dilemma

The second dilemma that can be identified concerns teacher educators' desire to 'not board up everything in every detail' and their serious worries about the quality of the newly designed programme, summarised in the ultimate question: are we doing the right thing? Whereas Helsing (2007) addresses uncertainties like these as an inevitable by-product of school reform, Ball explicitly enlarges this issue to a question on a macro level, emphasising that today's era of accountability makes the teacher (educator) subject to a myriad of judgements, measures, comparisons, and targets, creating self-doubt and personal anxieties rather than public debate:

> Within all this, there is a high degree of uncertainty and instability. A sense of being constantly judged in different ways, by different means, according to different criteria, through different agents and agencies. There is a flow of changing demands, expectations and indicators that makes one continually accountable and constantly recorded. We become ontologically insecure: unsure whether we are doing enough, doing the right thing, doing as much as others, or as well as others, constantly looking to improve, to be better, to be excellent.
>
> *(Ball 2003, 220)*

To illustrate the devastating repercussion of this accountability discourse on the confidence teachers have in their own judgement, he quotes an English primary school teacher:

> Every time I do something intuitive I just feel guilty about it. "Is this right; am I doing this the right way; does this cover what I am supposed to be covering: should I be doing something else: should I be more structured; should I have this in place; should I have done this?"
>
> *(Ball 2003, 221)*

Unless governments choose a more trusting relationship over their attempts to control institutions for teacher education, teacher educators will find that working with students on a basis of trust instead of control, with all the risks and uncertainties this entails, will be very demanding. Therefore, teacher educators as a community need to seek their place and open up a public debate about what education is really about, transforming the onerous question of whether we are doing the right thing into the existential one merited by the students and the world they live in.

Notes

1 Whereas in the Netherlands "teacher education and other institutes of higher vocational education, like medical, technical, economical studies, merged into large non-academic HEIs [Higher Educational Institutions]" (Swennen and Volman 2017, 122–123) during the 1990s, the college discussed in this chapter remained an independent college of teacher education for primary education. The college's regular four-year programme leads to a qualified primary school teacher status.
2 In an effort to reduce this effect, I choose to have focus group interviews with the students instead of individual interviews. During those interviews, I encouraged them to speak freely.
3 All participants were informed of the aims and methods of the research, and gave written consent. The participants' names used in this chapter are fictional.

References

Arendt, H. 1998. *The Human Condition*. 2nd ed. Chicago and London: University of Chicago Press.

Ball, S. 2003. "The Teacher's Soul and the Terrors of Performativity." *Journal of Education Policy* 18 (2): 215–228.

Biesta, G. 2014. *The Beautiful Risk of Education*. Boulder, CO: Paradigm Publishers.

Biesta, G. 2017. *The Rediscovery of Teaching*. New York: Routledge.

Blumer, H. 1954. "What is Wrong with Social Theory?" *American Sociological Review* 19: 3–10.

Cochran-Smith, M., and S. Lytle. 2009. *Inquiry as Stance: Practitioner Research for the Next Generation*. New York: Teachers College Press.

Emerson, R., R. Fretz, and L. Shaw. 2011. *Writing Ethnographic Fieldnotes*. 2nd ed. Chicago: University of Chicago Press.

Freire, P. 2000. *Pedagogy of the Oppressed* (30th Anniversary ed.). Translated by M. Bergman Ramos. New York: Continuum International Publishing Group.

Gatti, L. 2016. *Toward a Framework of Resources for Learning to Teach: Rethinking US Teacher Preparation*. New York: Palgrave Macmillan US.

Heck, D., and A. Ambrosetti. 2018. *Teacher Education in and for Uncertain Times*. Singapore: Springer.

Helsing, D. 2007. "Regarding Uncertainty in Teachers and Teaching." *Teaching and Teacher Education* 23: 1317–1333.

Joosten, H. 2013. "Learning and Teaching in Uncertain Times: A Nietzschean Approach in Professional Higher Education." *Journal of Philosophy of Education* 47 (4): 548–563.

Kelchtermans, G. 2012. *De Leraar als (On)Eigentijdse Professional: Reflecties Over De "Moderne Professionaliteit" van Leerkrachten. [The Teacher Being a (Non-) Contemporary Professional: Reflections on the "Modern Profession" of Teachers]*. Leuven: Centrum voor Onderwijsbeleid, -Vernieuwing en Lerarenopleiding.

Leijgraaf, M. 2015. "Education Contributing to Social Justice." In *Social Justice and Diversity in Teacher Education*, ATEE 2014 Winter Conference Proceedings, 16–27. Brussels: ATEE.

Milne, A. 2001. *Winnie-the-Pooh: The Complete Collection of Stories and Poems*. London: Egmont Books Limited.

Onderwijsraad. 2005, November. "Kwaliteit en Inrichting van de Lerarenopleiding" [Quality and Design of Teacher Education Colleges]. Accessed on 26 June 2019 at www.onderwijsraad.nl/publicaties/2005/kwaliteit-en-inrichting-van-de-lerarenopleiding/volledig/item573

Rancière, J. 1991. *The Ignorant Schoolmaster: Five Lessons in Intellectual Emancipation*. Stanford, CA: Stanford University Press.

Reeves, J. 2010. "Teacher Learning by Script." *Language Teaching Research* 14 (3): 241–258.

Schuck, S., and J. Buchanan. 2012. "Dead Certainty? The Case for Doubt in Teacher Education." *Australian Journal of Teacher Education* 37 (8). http://dx.doi.org/10.14221/ajte.2012v37n8.7

Swennen, A., and M. Volman. 2017. "Dutch Teacher Educators' Struggles over Monopoly and Autonomy." In *The Struggle for Teacher Education: International Perspectives on Governance and Reforms*, edited by T. Trippestad, A. Swennen, and T. Werler, 115–129. London: Bloomsbury.

Trippestad, T., A. Swennen, and T. Werler. 2017. "The Struggle for Teacher Education." In *The Struggle for Teacher Education: International Perspectives on Governance and Reforms*, edited by T. Trippestad, A. Swennen, and T. Werler, 1–16. London: Bloomsbury.

7

OLD LEARNING, NEW LEARNING

Teacher educators as enquiring professionals

Mhairi C. Beaton

Introduction

Teacher education is considered fundamental to improving educational systems and the experiences of pupils in schools internationally. Indeed, teacher education often becomes a highly politicised issue to which governments devote time and money considering how best it might be undertaken. Cochran-Smith (2016) refers to it as a policy problem and Mourshed, Chijioke, and Barber (2010) note the intense scrutiny that teacher education undergoes of the relationship between teacher education, teacher quality, and learning in schools.

One issue which is often contentiously debated is where the teacher education, or in some national settings teacher training, should take place: in the schools in which the teachers will eventually work or in universities or colleges where theoretical understandings of teaching and learning first might be examined. Many countries provide a blended model with student teachers spending time learning theory prior to time in practicum in schools supervised by classroom teachers and, in some instances, in collaboration with university tutors (Conroy, Hulme, and Menter 2013).

A commonality in all international settings is that the responsibility for the education of student teachers entering the profession lies within the profession. In much literature, teacher educators are considered to be a group of professionals based in universities and colleges and adopting one or more of the identities outlined by Swennen, Jones, and Volman (2010): school teacher, teacher in higher education, teacher of teachers, or researcher. Nevertheless, with many countries moving towards making initial teacher education courses more practical, such as Australia (Morrison 2016), towards a more school-based overall model, such as England (White 2014; Jackson and Burch 2019), or a blended model in which the university tutors and the school classroom mentors may have equal standing in assessment during practicum, such as Scotland (Conroy, Hulme, and Menter 2013), one must include both those who are based in colleges and universities and those who are student mentors or co-operating teachers in schools as teacher educators, as all have influence on the development of student teachers' professional knowledge and understanding, skills and abilities, and values and attitudes. Therefore, it might be argued that teacher educators in the broadest sense include those in university and college settings and those based in school settings.

McMahon, Forde, and Dickson (2015) confirm that pupil learning is strongly influenced by what and how teachers teach. Therefore, it is essential to consider how student teachers are prepared to engage in the decision making that is essential for their pupils to learn effectively and to attain the high standard of teacher quality and learning in schools aspired to by governments. Swennen, Jones, and Volman (2010, 145) assert that we have "limited understanding of the professional development of teacher educators", noting a number of research questions which are outstanding and must be answered if we are to better support teacher educators in university/college settings who have made the transition from schools to a new role – and, it might be argued, those who adopt the equally important role of student teacher mentor or cooperating teacher during practicum in schools (Burns et al. 2006).

This chapter seeks to shed light on one of those questions, posed by Swennen, Jones, and Volman (2010), who query what knowledge teacher educators bring with them to teacher education. The research presented in this chapter was undertaken in Scotland. It is acknowledged that this research focuses on only one policy context and indeed on only one case: a primary school classroom. However, in the spirit of Stake's (1995) notion of an instrumental case study, it is suggested that this particular case and the findings from the study provide insight into one troubling element of the knowledge that teacher educators seem to bring to their role preparing student teachers. It is suggested that the findings from this study are enlightening to those in other policy contexts when considering how we prepare and continue to support teacher educators in their role.

First, we provide a brief description of teacher education in Scotland. It should be noted that Scotland, although part of the United Kingdom, has always maintained a separate educational system from England. Consequently, educational policy and practice in each of the two countries has been shaped by a slightly different "mix of social, economic, political and historical concerns formed within shifting national and international landscapes" (Beaton and Black Hawkins 2014, 341); and indeed it has been noted that the current Scottish government promotes a discourse that emphasises the differences between Scottish and English policy (Riddell and Weedon 2014; Beaton and Spratt 2019).

Scotland

All pre-service education of teachers in Scotland is conducted in a university setting within designated schools of education. Schools of education are expected to work closely with primary and secondary schools to ensure coherence between theoretical knowledge from university-based elements of the programme and its implementation in classrooms during practicum (Mtika, Robson, and Fitzpatrick 2014). Much continuing professional development is also provided for qualified practitioners by those same schools of education. The General Teaching Council for Scotland, the professional body tasked with oversight of the teaching profession in Scotland, has accreditation powers over all pre-service training. Therefore, all university providers of teacher education in Scotland must be accredited and subsequently reaccredited with the General Teaching Council for Scotland every five years.

There are currently two routes to achieving teacher status in Scotland. Primary or elementary teachers can opt for a four-year undergraduate degree in education which combines theoretical study with qualified teacher status or a one-year professional diploma in education following the successful completion of an undergraduate degree. Secondary students must first complete a relevant undergraduate degree in their chosen subject prior to a one-year professional diploma in education. The content of both these routes is prescribed and overseen by the General Teaching Council for Scotland with clear rules relating to the time that student teachers must spend in practicum, supervised and assessed by both the school mentor and university tutor, and the standards that must be achieved to gain Provisional Teacher Status (www.gtcs.org.uk).

All teachers must then complete an induction year during which they are supervised by a mentor teacher appointed within their first school setting (Shanks and Robson 2012). Following completion of their induction year, the mentor teacher is tasked with assessment of whether the new inductee teacher has met the Standard for Full Registration with the General Teaching Council for Scotland. A recent development in Scotland is that all teachers, through a process of professional review and update, must self-evaluate professional values and attitudes, knowledge and understanding, and skills and abilities against the Standard for Career-Long Professional Development or the Standard for Leadership and Management. This process must be conducted annually within schools, and the evidence to support the process must be uploaded to the General Teaching Council for Scotland website every five years. Teacher educators working in universities preparing student teachers must also undertake this process, often in conjunction with annual university self-evaluation processes.

One of the General Teaching Council for Scotland requisites for the accreditation of initial teacher education programmes is that teacher educators working on teacher preparation programmes must be qualified and registered as qualified practitioners with the General Teaching Council for Scotland; that is, they must have trained as teachers and achieved full registration through the General Teaching Council for Scotland within Scotland.

Therefore, teacher educators in Scottish universities will have been trained in schools of education within those same university providers. Those same teacher educators will also have worked, some for a significant length of time, in schools in Scotland. This system is viewed as providing a rigorous education for all student teachers in Scotland, which is informed by university-level studies in education by teacher educators who can speak to their practical experience in Scottish schools. This is advantageous for those students wishing to learn from qualified and experienced teacher educators who are able to speak with authority to both the theory and practice of teaching.

There are, however, also potential disadvantages to the requirement for all teacher educators in Scotland to be registered with the General Teaching Council for Scotland. It can mean that the teacher educators may have operated within only one system of education, and the possibility arises that there is a recycling of understandings and assumptions about teaching and learning processes as one generation of teacher educators imparts its own knowledge and skills to the next who, in turn, may become the next generation of teacher educators. There is potential for this to occur in the training of teachers, as in all professions, across many countries, as experienced professionals are often expected to prepare the future workforce. However, it might be suggested that the General Teaching Council for Scotland's strong regulatory control of teacher education can exacerbate this potential challenge.

The Scottish government and General Teaching Council for Scotland are aware of this challenge. In a report considering the future of the teaching profession in Scotland commissioned by the Scottish government, Donaldson (2011) suggests that teachers, and by implication this applies to teacher educators also, must become enquiring professionals. This language and aspiration for teachers and teacher educators has been adopted by the General Teaching Council for Scotland in its professional standards. The definition of an enquiring professional is not included in either the Donaldson report (2011) or the General Teaching Council for Scotland standards (www.gtcs.org.uk). However, one possible interpretation would require the teaching profession to engage critically with research evidence to inform practice. It certainly implies that all teachers and teacher educators must approach their work with an openness and curiosity to learn and act in new ways to ensure that the teaching workforce is prepared to meet the many challenges of the 21st-century.

Adopting the stance of an enquiring professional is certainly a complex process that requires ongoing reflection and critical awareness of beliefs and attitudes that underpin the professional work undertaken by teachers in classrooms and teacher educators preparing the next generation of classroom teachers. This chapter describes findings from a research project that, although not entirely aimed at consideration of the role of teacher educators, highlights an ongoing issue of which many teacher educators may not be fully cognisant.

The findings originated in an ethnographic research project that sought to explore the complexity of primary school pupils' identities – their understanding of themselves as learners within the school community. Nevertheless, as the data was collected and analysed, findings emerged about the roles of teachers and teacher educators, their values and beliefs about their pupils, and how this may lead to potential challenges. This will be of interest to those seeking to improve teacher education in Europe and beyond.

Project background

The ethnographic project was based in a primary school in the north of Scotland. Working with a group of seven- and eight-year-old pupils, it sought to explore the complexity of those pupils' identities and how developing identities influence pupil career (Pollard 1985). It sought to answer the question: what are the children's perceptions of the influences on the development of their learner identities? The research project was underpinned by a belief in the necessity of listening to the opinions of children and young people to fully understand classroom processes, teaching, and learning with the underpinning belief that when

> the objective of the investigation is to improve teaching and learning, then it is only the testimony of pupils and teachers themselves that can provide essential, first-hand evidence.
>
> *(Flutter and Rudduck 2004, 2)*

Flutter and Rudduck (2004) helpfully list the benefits to learning and teaching if student voice is implemented effectively in three strands – for pupils, for teachers, and for schools. It should be noted that all classroom teachers in Scotland are expected by their professional body, the General Teaching Council for Scotland, to adopt the role of mentor to student and inductee teachers. For the purposes of this chapter, the most interesting section lies in those benefits for teachers and the teacher educators who work with them to enhance practice through professional learning opportunities.

In this study, the belief in children as incompetent "becomings" was assumed to be socially constructed and the study was based on the idea that children are competent social agents whose views and beliefs have value. Indeed, as with the "tribal child" described by James, Jenks, and Prout (1998), children were seen as experts in their own culture and therefore valuable contributors to research; in this case, experts on their experience of school, teaching, and learning. It was proposed that the pupils had information of importance to how educational processes might be enhanced and teachers prepared more effectively for their work. Indeed, when the author first introduced the project to the pupils in the class, the purpose of the project was to assist teacher educators at the nearby university to prepare student teachers more effectively; a purpose that the pupils embraced both seriously and enthusiastically.

Project methodology

The project was therefore underpinned by ontological and epistemological beliefs that all pupils in the classroom were knowledgeable and active agents in their own lives. As the underpinning theoretical notions of the research project were based on a constructivist understanding of the complexity of the meaning making of each of the participants, it was decided that a mixed methods methodology was necessary to ensure the fullest possible understanding of the complexity of what was occurring in the classroom – to understand exactly what interactions were occurring in the classroom and how the pupils were responding to them. This would, it was hoped, provide valuable information to better inform teacher educators as they prepared student teachers for the task of classroom practice.

The project was undertaken over an academic year with the researcher being present in the classroom on at least one day per week. Participant observation was a primary source of data, and the researcher took copious notes during her time in the classroom of her observations in addition to participating in the life of the classroom. In addition, video footage was collected both with a wide-angle-lens camera that was left running during class time and video footage taken by the pupils with a small hand-held camera when they judged that something interesting to the researcher was occurring.

Finally, to ensure that the classroom teacher and pupils' interpretations of the video and participant observation data collected was accessed, semi-structured interviews with the students were conducted. During these interviews, the pupils were given the opportunity to articulate their interpretation of a number of events and their understanding of classroom interactions. During and after the data collection process, the researcher engaged in ongoing thematic analysis of all collected data.

Findings

The main research question focussed on the children's understandings of the development of their learner identities. In response to one of the research sub-questions (*What factors do the children in the study attribute to the construction of their learner identities?*), the pupils could clearly identify the interactions that they utilised to construct this learner identity or sense of self as a learner. In addition to discussions they had with other pupils and a range of adults, including their parents and some adults within the school setting, to inform their learner identity, they chose to identify a range of classroom practices such as ability grouping and provision of textbooks. However, the response by the pupils of relevance to teacher educators and how they might be prepared to work effectively with student teachers lies not in what the pupils chose to utilise to construct their learner identity but in those interactions they chose to reject.

Some of the pupils further explained that they believed that the root issue lay in the fact that the teachers did not seem to view them as valid partners in the process of learning or assessment. This was one of the most surprising findings of the project, as Assessment for Learning was embedded deeply within the Scottish government legislation and was expected to be implemented in all schools (Hutchison and Hayward 2005). Assessment for Learning as a process advocates the facilitation of dialogue about learning progress between teachers and pupils. This understanding of the Assessment for Learning is deeply rooted in socio-constructivist learning theory that requires all participants, teachers and pupils, to be collaboratively involved in the process (Black and Wiliam 1998).

Much current educational policy and accompanying rhetoric in European educational policy and practice are based on definitions of childhood and children as proposed by the "new sociology of childhood" theories. In particular, the idea of children as knowledgeable and active agents in their own lives underpins much teaching and learning theory that is currently espoused and disseminated within our teacher education and training institutions.

Despite the rhetoric surrounding the potential role of children and young people to be involved as knowledgeable and active agents in their education (UNCRC 1989), the pupils in this study articulated the belief that their voices were not being authentically heard or valued. The pupils articulated that teachers retained traditional beliefs that the pupils were not yet capable of participating in this manner.

It must be acknowledged that the teachers hold professional knowledge about children, childhood, and education that the pupils do not yet possess. Many of the teachers' actions and comments in class, which the pupils interpreted as disregarding their ability to contribute, may actually be the result of exerting their professional understanding. A key element of their traditional, professional role is to facilitate the smooth organisation of the classroom and planned learning activities based on their professional knowledge and skill. However, what was significant in the pupils' responses was that they believed the teachers were not willing to work collaboratively with them to make decisions about their learning.

Certainly, when the initial findings were shared with the staff of the school, they were surprised, but, following reflection, they acknowledged that there was an element of truth in the pupils' comments. The teachers acknowledged their underpinning attitude that their pupils were often, as yet, not developmentally able to contribute to decisions about their learning. This seems indicative of the teachers holding views similar to Rousseau and his 'tabula rasa' (James, Jenks, and Prout 1998). Piaget's (1926) theories also, although extensively critiqued (Donaldson 1978), remain influential in primary education. The teachers acknowledged holding implicit theoretical assumptions dictated by a belief that pupils are subject to sequential and maturational progression through fixed stages of development that limit their ability to contribute to discussions about their learning. This was based on their training, some during the 1980s, when Piaget's work underpinned much initial teacher education, and it still influences their attitudes and practices in the 21st century.

However, many of our educational policies and current educational rhetoric centre on the pupil as a valid contributor. Certainly the notion of formative assessment requires this. The comments by the pupils highlighted a tension in the teachers' practice based on their training but one of which they had not been cognisant. Indeed, it might be suggested the implicit retention of a 'traditional' view of childhood by some teachers may actually be a factor in the failure to enact many of these policies effectively.

The findings have relevance for the classroom practitioners' role as teacher educators as they must be aware of both the tensions between their practices and the theoretical underpinnings of much new educational theory. Classroom practitioners who have adopted the role of student mentor must be able to demonstrate research-informed practice and be able to articulate their reasons for the decisions they make.

The findings also have relevance for teacher educators working in universities and colleges. Student teachers also may bring with them traditional views of children and childhood, and therefore teacher preparation courses must include sessions examining student teachers' underpinning values and attitudes relating to children and childhood.

It should be noted that teacher educators who have left the classroom and now work in research-informed university courses were also noted as having practices which did not align with current research. As the author continued to reflect on the findings, her manner of interacting with the pupils was not one that would be advantageous to model to student teachers.

As mentioned previously, during the interviews, the pupils had stated they did not view most teachers as valid sources of information to construct their learner identities. The pupils stated that in addition to not viewing them as collaborative partners in the learning process, they believed that the teachers were under pressure to provide them with only positive feedback in the form of praise statements.

As an experienced classroom practitioner of more than 20 years with a deeply held commitment to hearing the voices of the students in her classes, the author believed that she was an expert in listening to the voices of young people. She was acutely aware that her role had changed and that she no longer acted in the role of classroom practitioner but as a researcher who was seeking to enhance the teacher education provided for her students through rigorous research activity.

When making the decision to analyse the data thematically, the author decided that in order to immerse herself in the data, she would transcribe the interviews herself. This was a time-consuming task, but one that she felt was necessary to authentically and meaningfully immerse herself in the data. As she did not have touch typing skills, she engaged in a lengthy process in which she listened to short sections of the interview, wrote these down in pencil on a notepad, and later typed them up on her laptop. Originally, she had planned to interview between six and eight students, but when a request was put to the class, all the pupils requested to be interviewed. This resulted in 24 interviews, some longer than half an hour, that had to be transcribed. This was a time-consuming process but one that proved to be most fruitful. Committing the time to listen intently to the pupils as they articulated deeply meaningful elements of their lives, facilitated the opportunity to hear and respond to, at times, surprising views and opinions.

During the subsequent data analysis, however, as she listened to the interviews, she became increasingly uncomfortable to hear herself acting in ways the pupils said that they did not appreciate their classrooms teachers enacting. Increasingly, the author became aware that she was experiencing what McIntyre, Pedder, and Rudduck (2005) refer to as "uncomfortable learnings"; she was using meaningless non-contingent praise in an effort to ensure the pupils' self-esteem was not damaged by the interview process and indeed was unconsciously seeking to enhance it. The author's constant response of "great", "marvellous", and brilliant" was in direct contrast to what the pupils were actually saying:

MB: Right. And what about maths, are you in groups for maths?
BA: Sometimes. Like, there's the squares, the circles, and the triangles.
MB: Aha. And do they get different work?
BA: Yeah, sometimes, the circles, they're the highest and the squares are the middle and the triangles are the lowest.
MB: Right, so which one are you in?
BA: The squares.
MB: In the squares, so you're getting on.
BA: I'm always the middle!
MB: You're always the middle, that's a good place to be!

This fragment of the interview data illustrates that the author's actions, although she was confident that she had made the transition from classroom practitioner to teacher educator, were still underpinned by values and attitudes held by herself and many other classroom practitioners rather than research which advocates contingent feedback that allows pupils to build an accurate understanding of themselves as learners (Dweck 2000, 2012; Robins 2012).

Discussion

Although this research study was not solely designed to inform the teacher educator role, the pupils contributed some important thoughts for consideration. The findings of this research project would seem to confirm the potential for teacher educators to recycle the knowledge and understandings that were either explicitly taught as part of their own training or implicitly transmitted in the profession during their time in the classroom. Indeed, potentially the most problematic knowledge and understandings held by professionals are those which are so deeply embedded within their values and practices that the teacher educators are not aware of their presence or the influence they have on daily decision making. When this professional knowledge and understanding is so embedded within practice that it is no longer questioned, this may cause issues.

It has been widely acknowledged that society has changed in fundamental ways during the past 30 years, with changes including technological advances, in the ways children and young people are viewed, and how power is shared between different sectors of society (James, Jenks, and Prout 1998; Gallagher 2008). There have also been fundamental changes in our understanding of teaching and learning in recent times, as outlined by Lunenberg, Korthagen, and Swennen (2007). Zeichner and Ndimande (2015) note the need for teacher education to respond and adapt to rapid advancements in knowledge and communication.

Zeichner and Ndimande (2008) note that it can be challenging to engage teachers in educational reform if they feel uncomfortable about the underpinning ideas of these reforms. This research highlights that often teachers are actually unaware of this discomfort. The classroom teachers in this study who acted as teacher educators for student teachers on practicum had been unaware of their somewhat traditional view of their pupils and their ability to participate in the decision making about classroom learning until the pupils voiced their views. They were also unaware of how this created challenges for the implementation of new ideas and policies on teaching learning and assessment.

In the same manner, the author as teacher educator had been unaware of the values and attitudes she has brought with her from her previous role as classroom teacher to her new role as teacher educator and how these embedded and unchallenged views on the use of praise were influencing her interactions with pupils. Because classroom teachers and the author, as a former classroom teacher and then teacher educator, were unaware of these values, attitudes, and practices which did not jibe with new theories of learning, they were also unaware of how these might be transmitted to the student teachers in their charge, thereby unwittingly transferring them to another generation of teachers.

Lunenberg, Korthagen, and Swennen (2007, 586) note that most educationalists believe that there is a need for 'new visions of learning' that should affect teaching in our schools and advocate that an effective method of communicating these new ideas to student teachers is through modelling them in their own practice. However, they also express doubt as to where this approach is currently fruitful, as they have serious doubts about the competence of teacher educators to serve as those role models. This research highlights a potential issue that underpins this role of model for teacher educators and so must be addressed. First, we must note that teacher educators' outdated, enculturated assumptions about knowledge, skills, and attitudes may not match the new understandings of teaching and learning requiring them to be challenged and informed by new research.

Czerniawski, Guberman, and MacPhail (2017) note ongoing lacunae in current research knowledge about the professional development needs of teacher educators. They also highlight that the needs of teacher educators working in school-based settings may differ from those working in universities. Van der Klink et al. (2017) note that teacher educators new to the remit of teacher educator have different priorities to experienced teacher educators. Nevertheless, despite these differences, Czerniawski, Guberman, and McPhail further note the common need for both higher education institutions and government policy makers to "allocate designated time for proper induction and professional learning" (2017, 137), informed by the most recent relevant research, for all teacher educators, so that they may create their own "distinct and coherent professional identity" (138).

To return to the context of Scotland, the recommendation made by the Donaldson report (2011) advocated exactly this requirement for all those in education: not only to be given this opportunity but for research-informed learning to become fundamental to the profession. As stated previously, Donaldson (ibid) recommended that all classroom teachers must be encouraged to adopt an enquiring professional stance. One interpretation was that all classroom teachers should be encouraged to engage with research evidence critically to inform their work. Although this was a challenging goal, it was certainly expected that they would approach their work in an informed manner, allowing them to make changes to their practice and align with the many societal and educational changes which had taken place since their initial training.

It might also be suggested that teacher educators, whether physically located at universities, colleges, or schools, might also benefit from this approach. For all teacher educators, it is essential to remain open to "new visions of learning" (Lunenberg, Korthagen, and Swennen 2007) and ensure that they become aware of instances where these new understandings misalign with previously held knowledge and understanding, particularly common knowledge and understanding which has built up over time but is not based on research evidence. Introducing student teachers to this critical, inquiring approach to all elements of professional practice is key to this endeavour.

Additionally, if teacher educators are to model practice that they wish student teachers to adopt, whilst acknowledging the extensive theoretical and experiential knowledge and skills that teacher educators possess, it may be worthwhile to consider how to model a collaborative teaching, learning, and assessment context between teacher educators and student teachers. This would require teacher educators to acknowledge that they must not simply impart knowledge but that teacher education must be a collaboration between teacher educators and student teachers as they jointly explore how best to provide education for all pupils. Only once these new socio-constructive ideas about learning and assessing have been deeply embedded within teacher education will they be reliably embedded within our new teachers' practice in schools with their pupils.

It is however acknowledged that this is not easily accomplished. Many teacher educators in universities are employed on scholarship contracts with no contractual obligation to engage in research. Instead, their working time is extensively taken up with teaching and assessing student teachers. Likewise, those in schools who have mentoring roles find little time for engaging with research publications as their mentoring role is often in addition to full-time employment as a classroom teacher. Nevertheless, if teacher education is to adequately prepare student teachers for their career, through many more changes to society and to our understanding of learning and teaching, then perhaps what is most required is an attitude of renewed and continual professional critical enquiry – be it individual or collaborative action research or availability of accessible research findings that have relevance to teachers and teacher educators.

Conclusion

Teacher educators must prepare the future workforce to meet educational needs related to these challenges and future ones that are as yet unknown. A primary purpose of this research study was to permit pupils to articulate views on how teacher education might be improved. The pupils engaged in this study have highlighted that to achieve improvements in teacher education, it is essential that teacher educators themselves, whether based in universities as tutors or in schools as student mentors, must make themselves aware of tensions between 'new visions of learning' and their values, attitudes, knowledge, and understandings developed either through education they received in their early career or through enculturation within the profession. Only by continual, critically informed professional reflection or enquiry can this be addressed to ensure these tensions are not communicated and perpetuated within the values and practices of succeeding generations of student teachers entering the profession.

References

Beaton, M., and K. Black-Hawkins. 2014. "Changing Legislation on Inclusive and Special Education: Perspectives Across the Four Nations of the UK." *British Journal of Special Education* 41 (4): 340–343.

Beaton, M., and J. Spratt. 2019. "Inclusion Policies in Two UK Countries – Vernacular Responses to Global Influence." In *Including the North: A Comparative Study of the Policies on Inclusion and Equity in the Circumpolar North*, edited by M. Beaton, D. Hirschberg, G. Maxwell, and J. Spratt, 71–88. Rovaniemi: University of Lapland Press.

Black, P., and D. Wiliam. 1998. *Inside the Black Box: Raising Standards through Classroom Assessment.* London: King's College.

Burns, C., M. Beauchesne, P. Ryan-Krause, and K. Sawin. 2006. "Mastering the Preceptor Role: Challenges of Clinical Teaching." *Journal of Paediatric Health Care* 20 (3): 172–183.

Cochran-Smith, M. 2016. "Foreword." In *Teacher Education in Times of Change*, edited by G. Beauchamp, L. Clarke, M. Hulme, M. Jephcote, A. Kennedy, G. Magennis, I. Menter, J. Murray, T. Mutton, T. O'Doherty, and G. Peiser, x–xvi. Bristol: Policy Press.

Conroy, J., M. Hulme, and I. Menter. 2013. "Developing a 'Clinical' Model for Teacher Education." *Journal of Education for Teaching* 39 (5): 557–573.

Czerniawski, G., A. Guberman, and A. MacPhail. 2017. "The Professional Developmental Needs of Higher Education-Based Teacher Educators: An International Comparative Needs Analysis." *European Journal of Teacher Education* 40 (1): 127–140.

Donaldson, G. 2011. *Teaching Scotland's Future.* Edinburgh: Scottish Government.

Donaldson, M. 1978. *Children's Minds.* London: Harper Perennial.

Dweck, C. 2000. *Self-Theories: Their Role in Motivation, Personality and Development.* Philadelphia: Psychology Press.

Dweck, C. 2012. *Mindset: The New Psychology of Success.* London: Constable and Robinson.

Flutter, J., and J. Rudduck. 2004. *Consulting Pupils: What's in It for Schools?* Abington, Oxon: Routledge.

Gallagher, M. 2008. "Foucault, Power and Participation." *The International Journal of Children's Rights* 16 (3): 395–406.

Hutchison, C. and L. Hayward. 2005. "The Journey So Far: Assessment for Learning in Scotland." *The Curriculum Journal* 16 (2): 225–248.

Jackson, A., and J. Burch. 2019. "New Directions for Teacher Education: Investigating School/University Partnership in an Increasingly School-Based Context." *Professional Development in Education* 45 (1): 138–150.

James, A., C. Jenks, and A. Prout. 1998. *Theorizing Childhood*. Cambridge: Polity Press.

Lunenberg, M., F. Korthagen, and A. Swennen. 2007. "The Teacher Educator as Role Model." *Teacher and Teacher Education* 23: 586–601.

McIntyre, D., D. Pedder, and J. Rudduck. 2005. "Pupil Voice: Comfortable and Uncomfortable Learnings for Teachers." *Research Papers in Education* 20 (2): 149–168.

McMahon, M., C. Forde, and B. Dickson. 2015. "Reshaping teacher Education through the Professional Continuum." *Educational Review* 67 (2): 158–178.

Morrison, C. 2016. "Purpose, Practice and Theory: Teacher Educators' Beliefs about Professional Experience." *Australian Journal of Teacher Education* 41 (3): 105–125.

Mourshed, M., C. Chijioke, and M. Barber. 2010. *How the World's Most Improved School Systems Keep Getting Better*. London: McKinsey & Company.

Mtika, P., D. Robson, and R. Fitzpatrick. 2014. "Joint Observation of Student Learning and Related Tripartite Dialogue during Field Experience: Partner Perspectives." *Teaching and Teacher Education* 39: 66–76.

OECD. 2011. *Lessons from PISA for the United States, Strong Performers and Successful Reformers in Education*. Paris: OECD Publishing.

Piaget, J. 1926. *The Language and Thought of the Child*. London: Routledge and Kegan Paul.

Pollard, A. 1985. *The Social World of the Primary School*. London: Holt, Rinehart and Winston.

Riddell, S. and E. Weedon. 2014. "Changing Legislation and its Effects on Inclusive and Special Education: Scotland." *British Journal of Special Education* 41 (4): 363–381.

Robins, G. 2012. *Praise, Motivation and the Child*. London: Routledge.

Shanks, R., and D. Robson. 2012. "Apprenticeship of New Teachers during their Induction Year." *Higher Education, Skills and Workbased Learning* 2 (3): 256–270.

Stake, R. 1995. *Multiple Case Study Analysis*. London: The Guilford Press.

Swennen, A., K. Jones, and M. Volman. 2010. "Teacher Educators: Their Identities, Sub-Identities and Implications for Professional Development." *Professional Development in Education* 36 (1–2): 131–148.

United Nations. 1989. "Convention on the Rights of the Child." Accessed on 30 July 2019 at www.globaldetentionproject.org/wp-content/uploads/2016/06/Convention-on-the-Rights-of-the-Child.pdf.

Van der Klink, M., Q. Kools, G. Avissar, S. White and T. Sakata. 2017. "Professional Development of Teacher Educators: What Do They Do? Findings From an Explorative International Study." *Professional Development in Education* 43 (2): 163–178.

White, E. 2014. "Being a Teacher and a Teacher Educator – Developing a New Identity?" *Professional Development in Education* 40 (3): 436–449.

Zeichner, K., and B. Ndimande. 2008. "Contradictions and Tensions in the Place of Teachers in Educational Reform: Reflections on Teacher Preparation in the USA and Namibia." *Teachers and Teaching: Theory and Practice* 14 (4): 331–343.

Zeichner, K., K. Payne, and K. Brayko. 2015. "Democratizing Teacher Education." *Journal of Teacher Education* 66 (2): 122–135.

8

A PROFESSIONAL SOCIAL NETWORK AS A PLATFORM FOR TEACHER EDUCATORS' PROFESSIONAL DEVELOPMENT

Tami Seifert and Smadar Bar-Tal

Introduction

Teacher education has a long-term effect on the teachers' professionalism and knowledge, and affects pre-service teachers' influence on their pupils' achievements (Smith 2003; Nevin, Thousand, and Villa 2009). The teacher educator's role, therefore, is complex and requires unique knowledge and skills, such as professional expertise regarding curricular content and pedagogical knowledge. However, in most teacher education institutions there is no organised preparation or professional development for teacher educators (Lunenberg and Hamilton 2008; Grossman, Hammerness, and McDonald 2009; Van Velzen et al. 2010). It is important to support teacher educators to create high-quality professional communities (Shagrir 2012). Teacher educators need to connect with their colleagues, share their experiences and their world perceptions, promote professional discussions, continually deal with learning and reflection, and serve as experts in their profession (Koster and Dengerink 2008; Murray, Swennen, and Shagrir 2008; Nevin, Thousand, and Villa 2009). Teacher educators should be able to use their experiences, theories and conceptualisations, and practical experiences and personal history to support the development of pre-service teachers (Korthagen, Loughran, and Lunenberg 2005; Lunenberg and Hamilton 2008). Teacher educators also need to be able to explain the principles of teaching to pre-service teachers and be a model of good teaching and reflection (Loughran 2006; Helterbran 2008; Swennen, Lunenberg, and Korthagen 2008; Martin and Russell 2009). Their professional responsibility includes the construction of a pedagogy that enriches the understanding of good teaching and teacher education (Furlong et al. 2000; Loughran 2006(.

Teachers are the most important influential factor for the quality of learning in school. Therefore, teacher educators – those who educate teachers – should have high-level qualifications (European Commission 2012; Czerniawski, Guberman, and MacPhail 2017). A survey of 1158 teacher educators in academic teacher education institutes in different countries (Belgium, UK, the Netherlands, Ireland, Israel, and Norway) showed that the participating teacher educators were not a homogenous professional population, and the professional contexts in which they worked were not uniform. Despite this heterogeneity, most participants expressed a preference for continuous professional learning opportunities based on collaborative experiential learning (Czerniawski, Guberman, and MacPhail 2017). This suggests teacher educators have a preference for learning in an online, collaborative, and non-hierarchical environment without limitations of time and place. This can offer them 'meetings' with their colleagues, wherever they reside and work as teacher educators in a wide range of disciplines. Such meetings can enable them to share knowledge and professional information which in turn contribute to the development of their professional identity. In order to promote these processes, education policy-makers and teacher education institutions should assign time for professional learning of teacher educators. They should also encourage teacher educators to acquire and develop a balanced, varied, and integrated professional profile, without expecting that teacher educators can do this independently (Czerniawski, Guberman, and MacPhail 2017).

Online professional communities

The accelerated development of technology and its increased use in daily and professional life facilitates the development of educational communities (Lock 2006). Educational communities have the potential to build and support ongoing professional development needs of educators and help them to construct a professional identity. Also, professional learning communities are groups of professionals that inter-relate to examine and discuss knowledge and practice. This helps them to improve their professional work (Birnbaum 2009). When these communities are on-line, they may also support teacher educators to adopt innovation and become familiar with and implement new pedagogies while maintaining close communication. This raises the level of technology literacy among the members of the on-line community. Online communities expand the time and location of learning beyond physical limitations (Greenhow, Robelia, and Hughes 2009; Mazman and Usluel 2010). They constitute platforms for discussion, interaction, and sharing between their members (Wilson et al. 2009; John 2012; Boyd 2014). On-line communities are meeting places where collective knowledge is constructed by the participants in a collaborative and democratic manner with the intention to distribute this knowledge.

On-line communities perform better when structural and cultural components contribute to the creation of a rich network of trustful relations between their members, a sense of a common purpose, cooperation, and reciprocity (Amin and Roberts 2008; Hemmasi and Csanda 2009). In such an encouraging atmosphere, the community enables the participants to join a group of colleagues and experts to share information, to improve their performance, and to collect and construct knowledge for future use (Lave and Wenger 1991).

The community may also include members who are not regularly active, although they still constitute significant potential for participation in shared activities. Lev-On (2015) described the important factor of the size of an online community. The number of participants in online communities can grow unlimitedly, permitting different types of interaction by those who know something about an issue raised by one of the community's members. One of the members may supply different and helpful viewpoints to solve problems and to help those who join the community to become more professional. Thus, a 'reservoir of skills' is formed through a community of 'professional amateurs', enjoying mutual enrichment and growing professionalisation. By using advanced learning communities for on-line collaborative activities, teacher educators can also encourage global interactions between educators, groups of students, schools, and other learners who are geographically dispersed and, by doing that, learn from others outside their daily environment (Ran and Sperling 2016).

Teacher educators may feel that they lack suitable technological skills and that this constitutes an obstacle when they need to integrate technology in their work. Consequently, they feel that technological training should be an important aspect of their professional development (Kopcha 2012). Teacher educators who feel less confident about working with technology can overcome their anxiety with the help of personal support and guidance, high levels of interaction with personal feedback forms, instructors, and activities in a supportive online environment (Eaton et al. 2015; Seifert 2017). Learning about and being able to use technological environments requires time, patience, and practice.

As in any other digital space, there is usually a characteristic power system in a social network, and it is possible to identify various roles fulfilled by its members. The strength of the social network stems from the number of its members and their commitment and contribution to their professions. The members build the community and are the basis for the existence of the network. Without them, there will be no community and no activity on the social network (Seifert and Bar-Tal 2017). A certain level of participation is essential for the existence of the network, for its richness of materials, and for its attraction to the members. Activities performed in the online community constitute a sort of 'glue' connecting the different participants and providing support for various issues that interest them (Cruickshank, Edelmann, and Smith 2010; Huysman and Wulf 2005). People can participate in online communities publicly and visibly by publishing and reacting to published materials, but they can also read the materials without reacting or publishing anything themselves. This manner of participation is known as 'lurking'. Lurkers constitute approximately 90% of online community members (Marett and Joshi 2009). They contribute passively but essentially to the existence of social networks and other online communities (Preece, Nonnecke, and Andrews 2004). The division into types of lurkers is based on members' expectations regarding the online community's goals, their attitudes towards participation in the network, areas of interest and expertise, and their consideration of information and awareness concerning the presence of others (Takahashi, Fujimoto, and Yamasaki 2003; Preece, Nonnecke, and Andrews 2004; Shafie, Yaacob, and Singh 2016). Today there is a tendency to see lurking as a type of listening. Looking at lurking that way means that teacher educators' lurking on PSNs can be seen as an important form of listening to the discourse and as devoting time and attention to what others have to say, to think about what has been said, and to advance the personal, professional, emotional, and sometimes even didactic discourse (Crawford 2009).

Studying the Shluvim Network

The context of this research is the Shluvim network. This network is an innovative attempt to establish a professional social network (PSN) for educators in Israel. In 2010 the MOFET Institute established, for teacher educators and for all those dealing with education in Israel, a PSN by the name of Shluvim (meaning 'integrated' in Hebrew) (http://shluvim.macam.ac.il). This project enables educators at various levels to interact under a single, professional online 'roof'. The network aims to provide teacher educators, teachers, and other educational leaders in Israel in different institutions with a platform on which they can present initiatives at national and international levels. In Israel, the Shluvim network is considered unique, since it is in Hebrew, the language spoken in Israel, which makes it easier for Israeli educators to use, especially for a large segment of educators who are not sufficiently fluent in English. To support the network members, a pedagogical manager and a technical consultant (who receive payment for their work) guide the network's activity. The contribution of this network is expressed in the creation of an educational and pedagogical professional discourse, discussing dilemmas and various issues relating to educational professions and disciplines.

The visual presentation of groups according to name and logo creates a sense of cohesion and pride among group members and a sense of belonging to a large network. The groups may fluctuate between being open and closed, enabling members to enjoy flexibility and the confidence to write without fear. Additionally, to write and publish in a closed group prevents the participation of outsiders, and only members of the group can see the materials and participate. Moreover, there may be some network members who, for religious, personal, or ideological reasons, or due to time limitations, are not active on massive, mainstream social networks such as Twitter or Facebook. One of the helpful characteristics of Shluvim is that members can join Shluvim groups without any connection with other groups. The professional focus of the Shluvim network enables everyone to be active professionally, with no need to expose details of their private lives or to waste their time on their colleagues' reports on subjects in which they are not interested.

The data in Figure 8.1 show that in general, educators join the Shluvim network out of their intrinsic personal motivations, such as curiosity about innovation. They have a desire to receive information and to publish personal and professional information and want to participate in a well-valued site. Joining the network was also extrinsically motivated, by invitations from colleagues or compulsory membership as a condition of participation in an academic course.

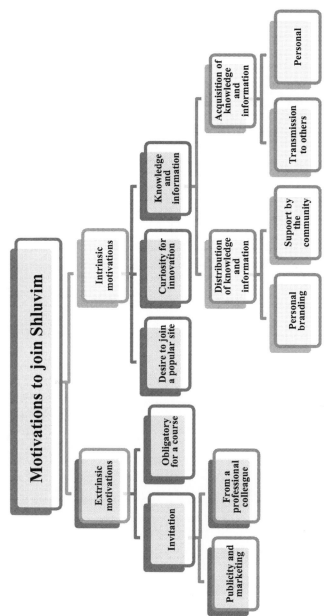

FIGURE 8.1   Intrinsic and extrinsic motivations to join the network (Seifert and Bar–Tal 2017)

The research questions

The contribution of the Shluvim PSN to the professional development of teacher educators was investigated through the following two questions:

1   What are the patterns of activity of members on the Shluvim network?
2   What are the patterns of activity of groups on the Shluvim network?

Methodology

The research boundaries of this case study were defined as all the participants in all the years of the network's activity. The research paradigm was a mixed methods model, combining both quantitative and qualitative methods (Johnson and Onwuegbuzie 2004). The research focussed on identification of users' patterns of activity as individuals and also of the groups on the Shluvim PSN after four years.

The research tools

To obtain data we employed four research tools. First, data for the years of the network's activity were drawn from the network using the Google Analytics tool, in order to obtain the profiles of use by the different groups of the network. Data were obtained regarding the number of visits to the network during different periods of time. Since all the activities of the network's members were conducted within the network, there was full documentation of these activities. Based on this, a non-participatory 'observation' of the network materials was conducted (Wisker 2008) in order to learn about the participants' patterns of activity on the network.

Second, a researcher's journal was written up over the period of the research (Ely et al. 2001) in order to record ideas, insights, and questions that arose while conducting interviews, surfing on the network, and discussions between the researchers during the research.

Third, a questionnaire was issued to members of the Shluvim network, with the aim of examining participants' reasons for use of the network, their satisfaction from the use of the network, and reasons for non-use of the network. The validity of the questionnaire content was tested by two colleagues, experts in the studied field.

And fourth, 15 in-depth semi-structured interviews were held with network members and with the pedagogical manager of the network (Seidman 1998; Wisker 2008; Yin 2008) in order to go deeper into the knowledge collected in the questionnaire. The research was administered with suitable consideration for ethical rules concerning the network and after obtaining the informed consent of all informants. Pseudonyms are given to the network members in the presentation of the findings.

Data analysis

The qualitative data were read several times by two external judges and divided into repetitive 'units of analysis' that were defined as categories. The collected data were analysed with the assistance of software (Atlas.ti 7.1) using thematic content analysis, in order to enable the identification of patterns through repeated readings and a cautious examination of the documents (Neuendorf 2002). Then comparisons were drawn between the categories that were unique for different participants in order to characterise common and individual patterns of active and passive participation (Yin 2008) and the value of using the network.

Findings

Members' patterns of activity on the Shluvim network

Members take part in activities on the Shluvim network in two main channels: individual participation in the general network space and/or within a specific group.

Individual participants' patterns of activity

There are three groups of participants: active participants, inactive participants, and those who choose to become lurkers, whose activities focus on the collection of materials. The last group do not contribute anything concrete to the online professional community that has grown over the years. However, the lurkers' passive activity has contributed to the empowerment of the groups, the group managers, and some of the other members as they have increased the number of views and helped the groups which they chose to join to be seen as 'successful' groups. As Miki noted, "All the time I go in and upload materials. . . . I go in at least once every two days, in order to see if there is a request".

Group managers' patterns of activity

Obvious group managers' styles of activity include: (1) the 'lone runner' style whereby the manager is almost the only one who conducts activities in the group; (2) the 'participatory style' whereby the manager is active with other active members of a learning group, or where the manager is active and 'consumers' who are not group members are 'connected' to her or him. An example of this style might be a training course for supervisors who direct the teachers under their supervision to download materials; (3) a 'new leader' may emerge from among the members who receives or takes the leadership from a manager who is less active; or (4) the 'chameleon' – a group manager who is active but with changing styles (Bar-Tal and Seifert 2019).

The life duration of a group within the PSN depends on the type of activity that it conducts and the group's goals (Bar-Tal and Seifert 2019). There are groups that accompany specific learning activities over an academic degree course in a teacher education college, or groups that exist solely for a particular course or seminar. Short-term groups may be used to lead a course or seminar, to supplement an area of knowledge, or to discuss an innovative idea.

Examples of ways the network can be used

The following two examples are illustrative of patterns of activity of members and groups on the Shluvim network. They demonstrate how the PSN can be used as a tool for professional development.

Example 1

This example relates to a teacher educator who led an activity on the PSN in a master's degree course for pre-service teachers (Lotan 2012): the teacher educator harnessed the PSN as a learning environment for the course. The PSN enabled the teacher educator to redefine the learning method and to facilitate autonomous learning, allowing both the teacher educator and the pre-service teachers to express their voices equally, and to plan their studies. Thanks to these possibilities, new knowledge concerning learning and teaching methods was constructed in this environment. The strength embodied in the sharing of knowledge, its publication on a social network, and collaborative learning helped to empower the teacher educator as well as each of the learners. The activities implemented during the course enhanced the teachers' presence, which was expressed in an authentic, professional, and reflective manner.

It is clear from the findings that the teacher educator should support the learners' appeals and messages to the community, cultivate the members' sense of community, and encourage others to do the same. The teacher educators should be pro-active, and instead of merely identifying with the personal and group learning process, they should engage in the community to create activity and dynamism both formally (by giving assignments) and informally (as a participant in the activities). They should support the creation of content and support people who advance the community and its members.

Example 2

The second example is that of a live journal transmitted during an international academic conference on teacher education (Bar-Tal, Shonfeld, and Orad 2016). In preparation for the conference, a live journal was created within the network. The journal remained active over the three days of the conference. It provided the conference participants with a wide range of perspectives during the conference and enabled a dialogue to be conducted with the content of the conference materials and lectures and with other participants. It also transmitted the conference contents to those who were unable to attend the sessions. The journal helped to develop collective knowledge, as happens in blog communications (Orad 2011). The activity on the live journal showed potential to assist in the construction of a professional community, to act as a motivator for professional development, and to enable connections between professionals in this field.

These examples demonstrate that the Shluvim network provides a response to educators' academic and administrative needs, so that the uses of the network are very broad and varied. The creativity and possibilities offered by the PSN enable teacher educators to redefine their pedagogy and create a new and diverse environment which provides various opportunities for learning. Analysis of the activities on the network shows that the implementation of the network dictates the pattern of activities by both the members of the network and the different groups. In the case of course teaching on the network, the activities of the participating students are intensive and so is that of the group over the period of the course. Similarly, the group that created the live journal (Bar-Tal, Shonfeld, and Orad 2016) was a group that lasted for the duration of a conference, creating professional contacts between the participants, who in many cases continued this contact beyond the space of the PSN.

The contribution of the PSN to the teacher educators' professional development

A PSN enables the teacher educators to overcome their isolation as lonely professionals (Flinders 1988; Ostovar-Nameghi and Sheikhahmadi 2016) and to shape their knowledge and beliefs concerning content, pedagogy, and learners' understanding (Darling-Hammond 1999). In this way, they are able to improve their teaching knowledge and practice (Darling-Hammond and Richardson 2009). The network enabled its members to build a strong professional identity and to form connections with colleagues at various levels of management and research.

Brody and Hadar (2015) indicated how complex it is for teacher educators to implement pedagogical changes. They found that new teacher educators more easily learn to use pedagogical innovations when they are involved in constructing their new professional identity. PSNs can accelerate this process and open up many opportunities for teacher educators that could not otherwise be realised. As a result of this research, we recommend that it is important to:

- Assist teacher educators in developing their professional identity via access to teacher educator PSNs.
- Give teacher educators an opportunity to enjoy support, and to share and rethink their practices among a community of teacher educators. It allows them to engage in collaborative work with experienced teacher educators and researchers, on whom they can model their practice.

- Manage and lead the network by introducing high-quality content and enabling interactive openness. Ways should be found to create a community that is both empathetic and supportive, enhancing trust and facilitating the development and growth of its members.
- Support teacher educators on PSNs to embrace innovation and to use new technologies. However, the transition to new media or unfamiliar technologies may not be simple and is often accompanied by fear.

Over the years of the PSN's activities, the network has been used for various learning and professional development purposes. This research highlighted the strength, importance, and contribution of the PSN as a platform that provides teacher educators with a space for shared activity. The activities of a PSN should be planned, professional initiatives with a professional group leader who has the vision and ability to lead a learning community for a short or longer period according to the subjects discussed in the group and the needs of the group members. Additionally, there should continually be a supply of new 'oxygen' from group members to ensure rich, continuous activity that contributes to the group and to empower the group members' professional development.

One way to ensure a significant contribution to teacher educators' professional development is through their belonging to a specially dedicated PSN for teacher educators. This affiliation creates not only commitment but also an opportunity for professional development. This is reinforced by the fact that lurkers, who do not contribute materials of their own, still contribute to the development and popularity of the group (Preece, Nonnecke, and Andrews 2004). Lurkers' 'passive' participation in the group, downloading materials, increased the number of views in the group and improved its reputation as a leading network group.

This chapter highlights the contribution of individual network participants, through sharing materials and taking an active part in activities on the PSN in general and in its dedicated groups, but also the contribution of 'lurkers' to the perceived popularity of a group. It also enhances knowledge and understanding concerning the role of the group manager leading a learning community for professional development. The chapter clarifies that a PSN can have both direct and indirect influences on teachers' practices and can augment the direct effects of teacher educators' professional development in promising ways and directions.

References

Amin, A., and J. Roberts. 2008. "Knowing in Action: Beyond Communities of Practice." *Research Policy* 37 (2): 353–369.

Bar-Tal, S., and T. Seifert. 2019. "The Identified Characteristics of Group Members and Managers of the 'Shluvim' Groups." *Time for Education*, Ohalo Teacher Training College in press. [Hebrew]

Bar-Tal, S., M. Shonfeld, and Y. Orad. 2016. "Live Journal – An Initiative to Enrich a Teacher-Educators' Conference." *Journalism and Mass Communication* 6 (9): 523–541.

Birnbaum, M. 2009. "Evaluation for Learning and Characteristics of a Professional School Community and the Classroom Culture That Empowers It." In *Evaluation, Jewish Education and the History of Education: An Anthology in Memory of Professor Arieh Levy*, edited by I. Kashti, 77–100. Tel Aviv: University of Tel Aviv, School of Education and Ramot Publishers. [Hebrew]

Boyd, D. 2014. *It's Complicated: The Social Lives of Networked Teens*. New Haven, CT: Yale University Press.

Brody, D., and L. Hadar. 2015. "Personal Professional Trajectories of Novice and Experienced Teacher Educators in a Professional Development Community." *Teacher Development* 19 (2): 246–266.

Crawford, K. 2009. "Following You: Disciplines of Listening in Social Media." *Continuum: Journal of Media & Cultural Studies* 23 (4): 525–535.

Cruickshank, P., N. Edelmann, and C. Smith. 2010. "Signing An E-Petition as a Transition from Lurking to Participation." In *Electronic Government and Electronic Participation,* edited by J. Chappellet, O. Glassey, M. Janssen, A. Macintosh, J. Scholl, E Tambouris, and M. Wimmer. 275–282. Linz, Austria: Trauner.

Czerniawski, G., A. Guberman, and A. MacPhail. 2017. "The Professional Developmental Needs of Higher Education-Based Teacher Educators: An International Comparative Needs Analysis." *European Journal of Teacher Education* 40 (1): 127–140.

Darling-Hammond, L. 1999. *Professional Development for Teachers: Setting the Stage for Learning from Teaching*. Santa Cruz, CA: Center for the Future of Teaching and Learning.

Darling-Hammond, L., and N. Richardson. 2009. "Teachers Learning, What Matters?" *Educational Leadership* 66 (5): 46–53.

Eaton, S., R. Dressler, D. Gereluk, and S. Becker. 2015. *A Review of the Literature on Rural and Remote Pre-Service Teacher Preparation with a Focus on Blended and E-Learning Models.* Calgary: University of Calgary. Accessed on 11 August 2019 at https://prism.ucalgary.ca/bitstream/handle/1880/50497/Lit_Review_-_Pre-service_Teacher_Ed.pdf;jsessionid=3C7BA18CEF3ED0A6A8370032B02D9A72?sequence=6

Ely, M., R. Vinz, M. Downing, and M. Anzul. 2001. *On Writing Qualitative Research: Living By Words*. London: Falmer Press.

European Commission. 2012. "Supporting the Teaching Professions for Better Learning Outcomes." *Commission Staff Working document* 374, Strasburg, France: EC.

Flinders, D. 1988. "Teacher Isolation and the New Reform." *Journal of Curriculum and Supervision* 4 (1): 17–29.

Furlong, J., L. Barton, S. Miles, C. Whiting, and G. Whitty. 2000. *Teacher Education in Transition*. Buckingham: Open University Press.

Greenhow, C., E. Robelia, and J. Hughes. 2009. "Research on Learning and Teaching with Web 2.0: Bridging Conversations." *Educational Researcher* 38 (4): 280–283.

Grossman, P., K. Hammerness, and M. McDonald. 2009. "Redefining Teaching, Re-Imagining Teacher Education." *Teachers and Teaching: Theory and Practice* 15 (2): 273–289.

Helterbran, V. 2008. "The Ideal Professor: Student Perceptions of Effective Instructor Practices, Attitudes, and Skills." *Education* 129 (1): 125–138.

Hemmasi, M., and C. Csanda. 2009. "The Effectiveness of Communities of Practice: An Empirical Study." *Journal of Managerial Issues* 21 (2): 262–279.

Huysman, M., and V. Wulf. 2005. "The Role of Information Technology in Building and Sustaining the Relational Base of Communities." *The Information Society* 21 (2): 81–89.

John, N. 2012. "Sharing and Web 2.0: The Emergence of a Keyword." *New Media and Society*. 152: 167–182.

Johnson, B., and A. Onwuegbuzie. 2004. "Mixed Methods Research: A Research Paradigm Whose Time Has Come." *Educational Researcher* 33 (7): 14–26.

Kopcha, T. 2012. "Teachers' Perceptions of the Barriers to Technology Integration and Practices with Technology under Situated Professional Development." *Computers & Education* 59 (4): 1109–1121.

Korthagen, F., J. Loughran, and M. Lunenberg. 2005. "Teaching Teachers – Studies into the Expertise of Teacher Educators: An Introduction to This Theme Issue." *Teaching and Teacher Education* 21 (2): 107–115.

Koster, B., and J.J. Dengerink. 2008. "Professional Standards for Teacher Educators: How to Deal with Complexity, Ownership and Function." Experiences from the Netherlands." *European Journal of Teacher Education* 31 (2): 135–149.

Lave, J., and E. Wenger. 1991. *Situated Learning: Legitimate Peripheral Participation*. Cambridge, UK: Cambridge University Press.

Lev-On, A. 2015. "Introduction: Online Communities – Their Functioning and Uses." In *Online Communities*, edited by A. Lev-On, 7–25. Tel Aviv: Rassling. [Hebrew]

Lock, J. 2006. "A New Image: Online Communities to Facilitate Teacher Professional Development." *Journal of Technology and Teacher Education* 14 (4): 663–678.

Lotan, Z. 2012. "Learning Patterns of Student-Teachers on a Social-Professional Network." *Dafim* 54: 248–280. [Hebrew]

Loughran, J. 2006. *Developing a Pedagogy of Teacher Education: Understanding Teaching and Learning about Teaching*. London: Routledge.

Lunenberg, M., and M. Hamilton. 2008. "Threading a Golden Chain: An Attempt to Find Our Identities as Teacher Educators." *Teacher Education Quarterly* 35 (1): 185–205.

Marett, K., and K. Joshi. 2009. "The Decision to Share Information and Rumors: Examining the Role of Motivation in an Online Discussion Forum." *Communications of the Association for Information Systems* 24 (1): 4.

Martin, A., and T. Russell. 2009. "Seeing Teaching as a Discipline in The Context of Preservice Teacher Education: Insights, Confounding Issues, and Fundamental Questions." *Teachers and Teaching: Theory and Practice* 15 (2): 319–331.

Mazman, S., and Y. Usluel. 2010. "Modeling Educational Usage of Facebook." *Computers and Education* 55 (2): 444–453.

Murray, J., A. Swennen, and L. Shagrir. 2008. "Understanding Teacher Educators' Work and Identities." In *Becoming a Teacher Educator: Theory and Practice for Teacher Educators*, edited by A. Swennen and M. van der Klink, 29–43. Dordrecht: Springer.

Neuendorf, K. 2002. *The Content Analysis Guidebook*. Thousand Oaks, CA: Sage.

Nevin, A., J. Thousand, and R. Villa. 2009. "Collaborative Teaching for Teacher Educators – What Does the Research Say?" *Teaching and Teacher Education* 25 (4): 569–574.

Orad, Y. 2011, January. "Physics Teacher Training Blog: Use of Blogs to Train Physics Teachers in the David Yellin College." *Journal of Educational Circles* 1.

Ostovar-Nameghi, S., and M. Sheikhahmadi. 2016. "From Teacher Isolation to Teacher Collaboration: Theoretical Perspectives and Empirical Findings." *English Language Teaching* 95: 97.

Preece, J., B. Nonnecke, and D. Andrews. 2004. "The Top Five Reasons for Lurking: Improving Community Experiences for Everyone." *Computers in Human Behavior* 20 (2): 201–223.

Ran, A., and D. Sperling. 2016. *Trends and Future Challenges in Education*. Edited by L. Yosefsburg Ben-Yehoshua. Tel Aviv: Mofe"t Institute. [Hebrew]

Seidman, I. 1998. *Interviewing As Qualitative Research*. New York: Teachers College Press.

Seifert, T. 2017. "Training the Teachers of Tomorrow in an Era of Rapid Technological Advancement." *i-Manager's Journal of Educational Technology* 14 (1): 35–46.

Seifert, T., and S. Bar-Tal. 2017. "Participants in a Social-Professional Network for Educators." *i-Manager's Journal of Educational Technology* 13 (4): 22–37.

Shafie, L., A. Yaacob, and P. Singh. 2016. "Lurking and L2 Learners on a Facebook Group: The Voices of the Invisibles." *English Language Teaching* 9 (2): 1–12.

Shagrir, L. 2012. "How Evaluation Processes Affect the Professional Development of Five Teachers in Higher Education." *Journal of the Scholarship of Teaching and Learning* 12 (1): 23–35.

Smith, K. 2003. "So, What About the Professional Development of Teacher Educators?" *European Journal of Teacher Education* 26 (2): 201–215.

Swennen, A., M. Lunenberg, and F. Korthagen. 2008. "Preach What You Teach! Teacher Educators and Congruent Teaching." *Teachers and Teaching: Theory and Practice* 14 (5–6): 531–542.

Takahashi, M., M. Fujimoto, and N. Yamasaki. 2003. "The Active Lurker: Influence of an In-House Online Community on Its Outside Environment." In *Proceedings of the 2003 International ACM SIGGROUP Conference on Supporting Group Work*, 1–10. ACM.

Van Velzen, C., M. van der Klink, A. Swennen, and E. Yaffe. 2010. "The Induction and Needs of Beginning Teacher Educators." *Professional Development in Education* 36 (1–2): 61–75.

Wilson, C., B. Boe, A. Sala, K. Puttaswamy, and B. Zhao, 2009. "User Interactions in Social Networks and Their Implications." In *Proceedings of the 4th ACM European Conference on Computer Systems*, 205–218.

Wisker, G. 2008. *The Postgraduate Research Handbook*. 2nd ed. Basingstoke: Palgrave. Palgrave Study Guides.

Yin, R. 2008. *Case Study Research: Design and Methods*. 4th ed. London: Sage Publications.

9

INTERNATIONAL SEMI-COLLABORATIVE RESEARCH INITIATIVE

A critical reflection of the research process

Leah Shagrir

Introduction

Teacher educators are called upon to continue learning and developing professionally throughout their careers (Lewis and Young 2013; Solbrekke and Sugrue 2014).
Research literature focussing on the professional development of teacher educators
emphasises, amongst others, the importance of research undertakings carried out in
collaboration with colleagues (Sargent and Waters 2004); Griffiths, Thompson, and
Hryniewicz 2010; McGregor et al. 2010; Jones et al. 2011. Professional interactions
that exist within the framework of collegial communities influence the professional
development of each partner (Wenger 1998; Hadar and Brody 2017; APA–American
Psychological Association 2019), and in a fruitful collaboration each participant
takes an active part in the process and contributes from his/her knowledge, experience, and expertise (Jones et al. 2011; Shagrir 2017a; APA–American Psychological Association 2019). In examining the areas in which teacher educators prefer to
collaborate for the sake of academic development, a collaborative research project
found a clear preference for initiating, planning, and carrying out research under
joint leadership. It encourages more collaborative professional activities even after
completing a particular research project (Shagrir 2017a).

Based on these studies and wishing to bring about professional development
and improve the image of teacher educators, an international semi-collaborative
research project was born as an initiative of the members of the Research and
Development Community (RDC) called the Professional Development of Teacher
Educators (PDTE). The PDTE RDC operates in the framework of the Association
for Teacher Education in Europe. The RDCs are the core of this organisation, creating a backbone for social coherence within the association. They provide the first
platform for dialogue, exchange, and joint international activities between individuals and institutions (ATEE – Association for Teacher Education in Europe 2019).

This chapter presents a critical reflection of the semi-collaborative research project, referring to different actions taken at every stage of the research. Together with a description of these actions, the results achieved at each stage will be examined, distinguishing between contributions and advantages and revealing weaknesses that emerged.

An in-depth presentation of a collaborative international research process critically provides a clear and comprehensive picture of a unique initiative that is likely to be a model for researchers who are interested in initiating and participating in similar initiatives. Reflection shows a clear picture of the challenges facing researchers in working with others, and different variations for carrying out collaborative research. Revealing research work stages, including a description of benefits and problems, teach us that every stage must be adapted to the goals of researchers, their timetable, their availability to work together, and ways of communication.

The process of the initiative

As part of the PDTE RDC's activities and initiatives over the past two decades, there have been a number of joint collaborative projects, including putting together panels for international conferences with representatives from different countries (Vaz-Rebelo et al. 2015), joint research undertakings, and presenting research findings at international conferences and in academic publications such as books and articles (Swennen and van der Klink 2009) and more.

At the RDC's sessions during the 2014 ATEE annual conference, there were several discussions and considerations in both the plenum and teams, addressing a new and large-scale initiative. In the end, several decisions were reached, by majority vote, with regard to the first and basic stage of a new initiative of the PDTE RDC:

- To conduct an international semi-collaborative research;
- The nature and means by which the research would be executed;
- The research questions, topic, goals and tools.

Because RDC members had previously investigated the professional characteristics of *novice* teacher educators (Shagrir 2010; Swennen, Shagrir, and Cooper 2009; Van Velzen et al. 2010), it was decided that the group would address the professional characteristics of *expert* teacher educators using collaborative research.

International collaborative research has become very popular (Wary 2006) and is actively supported by states, institutions, bodies, and organisations such as APA (APA-American Psychological Association 2019), ATEE (ATEE – Association for Teacher Education in Europe 2019), EU (European Commission 2013), and others. To encourage such studies, grants are available to researchers and various bodies offer themselves as hosts and provide guidelines, tools, and training to accompany international collaborations.

Researchers found that this research format is very important in countries generally, and is especially supported in countries where higher education systems are small and where international collaboration is essential to promote higher education staff (Iglic et al. 2017; APA-American Psychological Association 2019). Collaboration in international studies helps researchers develop connections with colleagues from different countries and institutions, potential and relevant partners because of similar interests and/or area of expertise (Birnholtz 2007; Heinze and Kuhlmann 2008). Through international collaborative studies, groups of researchers are actively involved in the generation of knowledge that they could not achieve alone (APA-American Psychological Association 2019), and the dissemination of this knowledge to a range of populations (Heinze and Kuhlmann 2008). International collaboration provides opportunities to extend the range of applicability of research and develop mutually beneficial relationships across national boundaries (APA-American Psychological Association 2019).

One can find in research literature proposals for models and frameworks presenting the processes included in the development of collaborative research (e.g., Sargent and Waters 2004). These models teach how a group of researchers become a professional community where everyone acts together as a collection of people with skills and competences in areas of knowledge, everyone chooses the research topic and how the research will be conducted, everyone carries out the research in practice until conclusions are deduced, and research success depends on all (Wagner and Leydesdorff 2005).

Collaborative research in the framework of a community of practice such as PDTE RDC creates opportunities for the members to support one another, it encourages research work that cannot always be carried out independently (Griffiths, Thompson, and Hryniewicz 2010; Shagrir 2014), and it supports development of thought and creativity. It was found that collaborative research also contributes to the development of the collaborators' professional identity as teacher educators and professional researchers (Griffiths, Thompson, and Hryniewicz 2010; McGregor et al. 2010; Shagrir 2010; Dinkelman 2011).

Stage I: determining the research topic, research goals, and research tools

Researchers emphasise that research goals must be determined in advance, collaboratively by all researchers. It is important to make these decisions at the joint project planning stage because agreeing on goals in advance is likely to encourage the researchers' collaboration (Stokols et al. 2008).

At the first stage of our work, the research topic and research conduct were determined collaboratively. It was determined that the research question would examine how teacher educators perceive the characteristics of expert teacher educators and the nature of their professional development.

It was also determined that the research coordinator will be the RDC's chair. Studies have shown that in research in which a number of researchers are partners, the role of the coordinator is a key role, and only if this role is carried out well will a study be conducted properly and results achieved. The role of the coordinator is to lead all research activities throughout the study and be concerned with meeting research demands (Sooryamoorthy and Shrum 2007; Cummings and Kiesler 2007). The research coordinator is required to use his/her authority to resolve problems arising during the research, to coordinate between researchers, and ensure that each one contributes their part to the collaboration (Walsh and Maloney 2007). In any collaborative research, the coordinator is the person who sees that the research gets done, and in international research, his/her responsibility is even greater because of the geographic distance between researchers (Stokols et al. 2008) and the need for them to communicate mainly through technological media. In conclusion, the success of international collaborative research is largely dependent on the coordinator and his/her way of coordinating (Sooryamoorthy and Shrum 2007).

Other decisions taken at the session addressed research tools and the main stages according to which the study would be conducted. The chosen research tool was an online self-completion research questionnaire that would be constructed using the Google Forms platform. This is a user-friendly tool for both the questionnaire builder and respondents that provides a clear picture of the data acquired from the answers, in the format of an Excel spreadsheet, diagrams, and pie charts.

With regard to the next collaborative research stages, it was agreed that there would be four more stages: at the second stage, the coordinator would construct the online self-completion research questionnaire to collect responses to the research questions as determined by the members (two months were allocated to this stage). During the third stage, the online questionnaire would be distributed by email to all RDC members for self-completion. In addition, every member would distribute the questionnaire to at least two teacher educators among their work colleagues, for them to complete as well (the questionnaire would appear as a web page for a month). At the fourth stage, the coordinator would collect the completed questionnaires and enter the data into an accessible for use Excel file (two months were allocated to this stage). We decided that research execution would maintain reciprocity and data sharing (Jones et al. 2011; Santagata and Guarino 2012), and therefore at the fifth stage, the collected data would be distributed to all members for data analysis and identifying findings according to the needs and wishes of each member.

This collaborative research model allows data transparency and gives researchers access to all data obtained from questionnaires. This model ensures that the work outcomes will allow each researcher to benefit from the research and exploit it for their own professional development needs while emphasising the uniqueness that he/she wants to emphasise and considering local limitations required in the country or institution in which he/she works (APA-American Psychological Association 2019). Researchers could use all the data, or parts thereof, to construct findings and conclusions from their own point of view and areas they wish to explore. This model prevents any dispute between researchers about intellectual property issues and does not require addressing the issue of co-authorship, which is an acute issue when a large group of researchers work together.

In conclusion, it can be seen that at the first stage of research, researchers agreed on a number of issues, such as research aims and questions, research design, research tools, how researchers would work, coordinator's areas of responsibility, and level of data transparency and access to it. These agreements served as a sort of terms of agreement between researchers and helped prevent arguments at a later stage of the process and delays in progressing the research.

Stage II: constructing and disseminating an online self-completion questionnaire

In discussions among RDC members, it was decided to use an anonymous online self-completion questionnaire as the research tool. An online questionnaire is a convenient tool, allowing access to a wide range of participants living in different geographical regions and working in diverse teacher education institutions. It is available as an internet page and participants can answer it when they have time to do so and at their own pace. The online questionnaire is also user-friendly for researchers interested in collecting a large amount of data within a short period of time. Software packages and web-based services provide assistance for questionnaire design and collecting and analyzing data (Wright 2017).

To gather useful and relevant information, the questionnaire design comprised four sections. The first section asked for information about the academic and professional backgrounds of the respondents, their current job, and activities in which they engage for their professional development.

The second section of the questionnaire asked respondents to express their thoughts about teacher educators' professional development and how their ideas emerged in their own development. They were asked, for example, to express their opinions on the frequency at which teacher educators are meant to undertake professional development activities, both in general and specific activities such as participating in conferences, membership in professional associations, writing academic publications, and more. Participants were asked to rank the level of contribution of each professional development activity appearing in a list. In addition, they were asked to point out how they expressed their worldview in their choices of professional development activities.

The third section asked respondents to rank a list of characteristics of experts from most to least important. This list included statements describing different attributes of teacher educators. The statements in the questionnaire were in fact a sentence or two quoted from published articles concerned with teacher educators' professional development. The statements were divided into four areas of expertise as expressed in every profession: knowledge, skills, abilities, and personality traits.

The knowledge area comprised seven statements referring to knowledge of content being taught as well as teacher education knowledge. The skills area included 13 statements referring to the skills teacher educators require and their work skills with students. In the area of abilities, there were 19 statements referring to teacher educators' abilities to educate the next generation of teachers and acquiring and maintaining a professional identity. In the section dealing with the professional area, 11 statements were included referring to professional worldviews and perceptions of the role of teacher educators and higher education faculty members. A ranking of 1 indicated that the statement was not fitting for an expert, while a ranking of 6 indicated that the statement was a very important and essential part of an expert's identity.

The final section of the questionnaire included open-ended questions for comments and remarks about subjects discussed in the questionnaire and for adding suitable statements, expressing opinions and comments addressed to the researchers.

To examine the reliability of the questionnaire, three teacher educators with rich experience completing questionnaires were asked to complete it. Thereafter, they expressed their opinions on the questionnaire structure and parts, its contents, types of questions, and suitability to obtain a response to the research question. Following the feedback received, several changes both in content and structure were made to the questionnaire, resulting in a final document. The anonymous questionnaire appeared for four weeks as a clearly designed and user-friendly web page in English.

This stage was carried out by the coordinator leading the research, while other members of the research group waited for it to be completed. The decision that this stage would not be jointly conducted by all researchers derived from the fact that a questionnaire being prepared by one person has a noticeable time-saving advantage. With a large group of researchers participating in collaborative research and spread over many countries, it was decided that the research coordinator would construct the questionnaire and have it examined by experts and teacher educators experienced in conducting research with similar research tools. Hence, there were no discussions about the structure and content of the questionnaire while building it, to avoid any arguments between researchers.

However, it is important to consider the fact that using research tools prepared by one researcher are likely to preclude other researchers from understanding its composite parts, identifying its validity, and having a sense of belonging to the research group. If a decision had been reached to share the second stage of work among all researchers, each one of them would have been able to make proposals about the questionnaire's structure and suggest items. Collaborative work at this stage of the research is likely to be more interesting, but it demands a long, challenging process needing patience and restraint on the part of the coordinator, who has to collate many people's suggestions and clarify which are suitable. Another risk of this type of working is that researchers whose suggestions are not accepted may feel disappointed and let down by the common initiative.

Stage III: distributing the online self-completion questionnaire

The research group decided together what the target population of the research would be, which included three groups of participants. The first group was the researchers themselves – in other words, all those who took part in the annual meeting and shared in the decision to implement the research initiative. The second group included all those registered as members of the ATEE and who had participated once or more in PDTE RDC activities, including those who were absent from the conference at which the research was determined. Since all members are teacher educators who willingly joined the community, and their main professional interest was examining the characteristics of teacher educators and their professional development, they were found to be a suitable population to participate. To expand and increase the research population, it was decided that a third group of participants would include colleagues of the first two groups mentioned.

All those who received questionnaires for completion would pass them on by email to two teacher educator colleagues of their choice. Hence, participants were added whose focus of concern was not necessarily researching professional development and its characteristics among teacher educators. Choice of colleagues was limited to those concerned with the teacher education profession, and no restrictions were determined such as years of experience in the profession, gender, age, academic degree, position, and so on. This decision came from a desire to increase the number of participants and thus improve chances of the questionnaire being completed, thereby providing a larger sample of respondents.

This collection of three groups was found to be a population suitable for the research needs because it included people from different countries, places of work, cultures, and stages in their professional careers. It is important to note that, although the research addresses the characteristics of expert teacher educators, the preference was that the research population would include novice, experienced, and long-serving teacher educators as one, with an objective of obtaining information about worldviews on the question of expert teacher educators from professionals at every stage of the career.

While at the second research stage the issue of the size of the groups of participants prevents collaboration in constructing the research tool, at this stage the size of the group constitutes an advantage because the researchers also served as some of the participants. Since the researchers are teacher educators exploring their own and their colleagues' professional development, and as they were not associated with the construction of the research tool, it was proper for them to be part of the sampled research population.

At this stage all PDTE members took an active part in completing the questionnaire and disseminating it to other teacher educators. It can be said that the most noticeable advantage was access to a large number of participants (Heinze and Kuhlmann 2008), especially in light of the fact that the research design and preparation of the research tool allowed adding the researchers themselves as part of the research population.

Stage IV: collecting the research data

The research coordinator collected the data from the completed questionnaires. The questionnaire was constructed using Google Forms, a software enabling receipt of respondents' answers collectively. Data was retained in an Excel format, an easy platform for presenting data that interfaces with a wide range of statistical software packages that carry out analysis processes speedily, crosscheck and segment data, and lead to the emergence of research findings. The Excel file included texts written by respondents as answers to open questions in the last part of the questionnaire. The data from the closed questions and texts of answers to open questions were collected in a data document to enable researchers to conduct both statistical and content analyses and arrive at rich findings.

In total, the questionnaire was completed by 105 teacher educators from 18 countries: Austria, Belgium, Croatia, Czech Republic, Denmark, England, Estonia, Finland, Israel, Japan, Latvia, Malaysia, the Netherlands, Norway, Poland, Portugal, Turkey, and the United States. All respondents declared they were teacher educators, and more than half had previous experience teaching at schools. They included 72 women and 33 men, of whom two-thirds were over the age of 50, and approximately one-third each had up to 10 years of experience, 10–20 years' experience, and more than 20 years of experience. The data on participants' education was as follows: 46% of respondents had a doctoral degree, 47% a master's degree, and 7% a bachelor's degree.

Unlike the previous stage, when all the researchers had an important role in progressing the research as participants who completed and distributed the questionnaire, at this stage responsibility again transferred to the research coordinator (Cummings and Kiesler 2007). Having one single person collating data into one central document allows accuracy in dealing with the questionnaires and prevents confusion. Adding additional researchers at this stage is not an advantage because they are located in different places around the world and their correspondence is conducted by email. Dividing work between a number of researchers, each one dealing with a group of questionnaires, is likely to confuse and disrupt the work.

Stage V: distributing data to the members of the RDC for analysis

At this stage of the collaborative research, an email was sent to participating researchers informing them of the completion of the database created from the questionnaire answers. The email advised participating researchers who were interested in getting the database to request it. The database was sent to about 20 researchers who requested it to use for their own professional development in diverse ways, such as presentations, studies, research, publications, and more. The entire database and an example of analysis were presented to the group members at a conference taking place a year after the one at which the research initiative was decided upon.

According to advance planning, the fifth stage is the final stage of the joint research arrangement. The researchers received a file of data and had to decide how to use it. The advantage of this stage is that it allows every researcher to analyse the data in line with their areas of interest, focus on what they wish to explore, and uncover new ideas (Jones et al. 2011; Santagata and Guarino 2012). A large database was available to researchers and therefore many options were created to analyze and construct research findings from different points of view, and from these, to reach conclusions and make recommendations.

This type of collaborative research work is very advantageous because it allows researchers to choose how they work with the research data. Each researcher can choose whether to continue to explore independently or with a group of researchers that may include people who had participated in the research or others. Each researcher can choose how to analyse the data and different angles on which to concentrate. Researchers can focus on the entire database or on parts, according to their interests, to produce diverse findings from the same database, and present them in different ways.

At this stage, researchers moved from collaborative work with a large group of researchers to independent work or work with smaller groups where each one can put his/her own mark on it and turn the shared research data into academic publications. This arrangement can serve as a springboard for continued professional development, each one from the stage of development he/she had so far reached.

Conclusions and recommendations

To turn the semi-collaborative research that we conducted into a tool that is likely to serve other researchers, a model was constructed including the five stages, emphasising the areas in which collaborative work was done and those in which only the coordinator carried out the work (Figure 9.1):

A rational analysis of the initiative's contribution and benefits for the professional development of the RDC members provides recommendations for teacher educators at different stages of their professional career development.

The initiative enabled a large number of people to be involved in different stages of the research. At the basic stage, involvement was expressed in the design and construction of the research and research question, determining how the research would be structured and choosing the research population. At the final stage, all those who had been involved at the basic stage, and other members, received the data to utilise for academic advancement needs such as writing academic publications and/or integrating them into presentations. In previous initiatives of the group, who were part of the RDC activity framework, such an opportunity was given only to research leaders and a small number of people because of location and time constraints among researchers. In the current initiative, we overcame this issue and had an objective that every group member would be able to be recruited and exploit the initiative for their own professional development needs.

Another advantage of the shared initiative for professional development is the opportunity to process data collected from a diverse sample of participants originating in different countries – in other words, an opportunity to participate in international research. In international research it is possible to examine differences and generics in professional worldviews of people from the same profession. This type

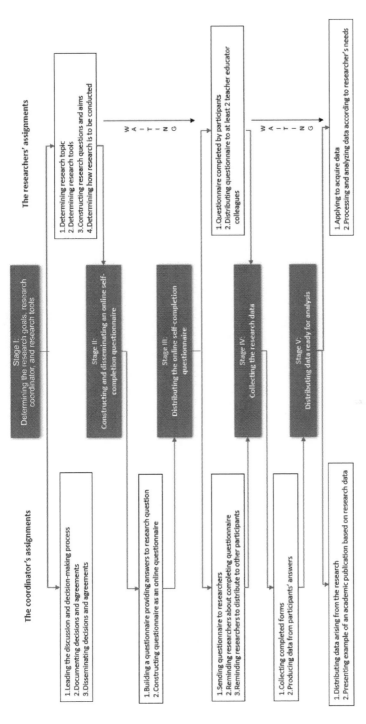

FIGURE 9.1   International semi-collaborative research model

of research expands knowledge and professional dialogue between researchers and allows them to use findings, terms, and concepts that are not restricted to locality.

The initiative has another benefit for researchers' professional development and that is the opportunity to use an online questionnaire research tool, both as participants completing the questionnaire and as researchers analysing the answers and deducing conclusions from them that contribute to the professional body of knowledge.

Higher education faculty members are required to continue their professional development throughout their careers. Some of them are unsuccessful in taking initiative themselves and leading in-depth research, so the opportunity for them to collaborate partially and be part of a group of researchers is an opportunity to devote time and effort to their development and deepen the culture of collaboration in research undertakings (Shagrir 2017a).

To critically discuss the research initiative, we will mention a number of key difficulties learned during the research. One difficulty comes from the fact that a number of research stages were carried out by the lead researcher without the participation and collaboration of all researchers. As such, it seems to be right to refer to such an initiative as semi-collaborative, research in which only some stages were carried out in partnership.

Another difficulty derived from how the research tool was built. The online questionnaire was built by the coordinator, and it should be noted that this is a complex task and more researchers should have shared in it. In such cases it is recommended to explore the possibility of establishing a group comprising some of the people working together to build the research tool. Because researchers are residents of different countries and communication will only be digital, one must take into account that such a work format will necessitate delays during the research.

A further problem was discovered in the last research stage. With the distribution of the research data to members who were interested in it, there was no possibility of monitoring to what extent the data was used. To date, one academic article has been published based on a basic analysis of the data arising from this research and was written by the research coordinator (Shagrir 2017b), and one presentation of the research findings was made by the chair and co-chair to RDC members at the ATEE conference in 2015, a year after the shared research work began. Apart from this, no notice has been received or any information sent from researchers regarding any use made of the data, and it was never predetermined that researchers had any obligation to notify the group about the essence and extent of use of the data. Some of the researchers provided notice that they intended to utilise the data, but it is unclear whether they did so. This fact reveals the weak link of the work on this initiative. With the end of the fifth stage, the joint work ended. It is possible that it would have been better to pre-plan additional stages such as predetermining the makeup of working groups to analyze the data and document the findings that arose, where each group of researchers would examine the data from a specific predetermined point of view, and according to the level of interest of members of the group.

Despite the previously -mentioned difficulties, the initiative was well received and garnered the cooperation of many people, who stated that joint work contributed much to their professional development and opened channels for collaborative work.

The conclusions presented here are likely to encourage teacher educators to lead similar and other initiatives whose basis is collaboration among colleagues and whose main goal is professional development, improvement, and enrichment of teacher educators. This method of presenting semi-collaborative research steps will enable readers to know the details and significance of its execution and is likely to help those who are interested in adopting it.

References

APA-American Psychological Association. 2019. "Engaging in International Collaborative Research." Accessed on 20 February 2019 at https://www.apa.org/international/resources/publications/research.

ATEE – Association for Teacher Education in Europe. 2019. "The Association." https://atee.education/.

Birnholtz, J. 2007. "When Do Researchers Collaborate? Toward a Model of Collaboration Propensity." *Journal of the American Society for Information Science & Technology* 58 (14): 2226–2239.

Cummings, J., and S. Kiesler. 2007. "Coordination Costs and Project Outcomes in Multi-University Collaborations." *Research Policy* 36 (10): 1620–1634.

Dinkelman, T. 2011. "Forming a Teacher Educator Identity: Uncertain Standards, Practice and Relationships." *Journal of Education for Teaching* 37 (3): 309–323.

European Commission. 2013. "Supporting Teacher Educators for Better Learning Outcomes." Accessed on 27 April 2019 at http://ec.europa.eu/assets/eac/education/policy/school/doc/support-teacher-educators_en.pdf.

Griffiths, V., S. Thompson, and L. Hryniewicz. 2010. "Developing a Research Profile: Mentoring and Support for Teacher Educators." *Professional Development in Education* 36 (1–2): 245–262.

Hadar, L., and D. Brody. 2017. "Professional Learning and Development of Teacher Educators." In *Handbook of Research on Teacher Education*, edited by J. Clandinin and J. Husu, 1049–1064. Thousand Oaks: Sage.

Heinze, T., and S. Kuhlmann. 2008. "Across Institutional Boundaries? Research Collaboration in German Public Sector Nanoscience." *Research Policy* 37 (5): 888–899.

Iglic, H., P. Dorien, L. Kronegger, and A. Ferligoj. 2017. "When Do Researchers Collaborate? Toward a Model of Collaboration Propensity." *Scientometrics* 112 (1): 153–174.

Jones, M., G. Stanley, O. Mcnamara, and J. Murray. 2011. "Facilitating Teacher Educators' Professional Learning Through a Regional Research Capacity-Building Network." *Asia-Pacific Journal of Teacher Education* 39 (3): 263–275.

Lewis, D., and V. Young. 2013. "The Politics of Accountability: Teacher Education Policy." *Educational Policy* 27 (2): 190–216.

Mcgregor, D., B. Hooker, D. Wise, and L. Devlin. 2010. "Supporting Professional Learning Through Teacher Educator Enquiries: An Ethnographic Insight into Developing

Understandings and Changing Identities." *Professional Development in Education* 36 (1–2): 169–195.

Santagata, R., and J. Guarino. 2012. "Preparing Future Teachers to Collaborate." *Issues in Teacher Education* 21 (1): 59–69.

Sargent, L., and L. Waters. 2004. "Careers and Academic Research Collaborations: An Inductive Process Framework for Understanding Successful Collaborations." *Journal of Vocational Behavior* 64 (2): 308–319.

Shagrir, L. 2010. "Professional Development of Novice Teacher Educators: Professional Self, Interpersonal Relations and Teaching Skills." *Professional Development in Education* 36 (1–2): 45–60.

Shagrir, L. 2014. "Patterns and Characteristics of the Professional Development of Teacher Educators." In *Through the Lens of Professional Identity: Collaborative Research as a Multi-Method Approach in Teacher Education*, edited by H. Ezer, 87–108, Tel Aviv: Mofet Institute.

Shagrir, L. 2017a. "Collaborating with Colleagues for the Sake of Academic and Professional Development in Higher Education." *International Journal for Academic Development* 22 (4): 331–342. doi: 10.1080/1360144X.2017.1359180.

Shagrir, L. 2017b. "The Professional Characteristics and Nature of Professional Development of Experts." In *Research on University Teaching and Faculty Development: International Perspectives*, edited by O. Alegre De La Rosa, 139–153. New York: Nova Science Publishers.

Solbrekke, T., and C. Sugrue. 2014. "Professional Accreditation of Initial Teacher Education Programmes: Teacher Educators' Strategies – Between 'Accountability' and 'Professional Responsibility'?" *Teaching and Teacher Education* 37: 11–20.

Sooryamoorthy, R., and W. Shrum. 2007. "Does the Internet Promote Collaboration and Productivity? Evidence from the Scientific Community in South Africa." *Journal of Computer-Mediated Communication* 12 (2): 733–751.

Stokols, D., S. Misra, R. Moser, K. Hall, and B. Taylor. 2008. "The Ecology of Team Science – Understanding Contextual Influences on Transdisciplinary Collaboration." *American Journal of Preventive Medicine* 35 (2): S96–S115.

Swennen, A., L. Shagrir, and M. Cooper. 2009. "Becoming a Teacher Educator: Voices of Beginning Teacher Educators." In *Becoming a Teacher Educator: Theory and Practice for Novice Teacher Educators*, edited by A. Swennen and M. van der Klink, 91–102. Dordrecht: Springer.

Swennen, A., and M. van der Klink, eds. 2009. *Becoming a Teacher Educator: Theory and Practice for Novice Teacher Educators*. Dordrecht: Springer.

Van Velzen, C., M. van der Klink, A. Swennen, and E. Yaffe. 2010. "The Induction and Needs of Beginning Teacher Educators." *Professional Development in Education* 36 (1&2): 61–75.

Vaz-Rebelo, P., A. Swennen, M. Golan, M. van der Klink, C. van Velzen, M. Pedroso De Lima, J. Vermel, C. Barreira, T. Pessoa, and C. Gomes, eds. 2015. *Professional Development of Teacher Educators: Bringing Together Policy, Practice and Research*. Brussels: ATEE (Association for Teacher Education in Europe).

Wagner, S., and L. Leydesdorff. 2005. "Mapping the Network of Global Science: Comparing International Co-Authorships from 1990 to 2000." *International Journal of Technology and Globalisation* 1 (2): 185–208.

Walsh, J., and N. Maloney. 2007. "Collaboration Structure, Communication Media, and Problems in Scientific Work Teams." *Journal of Computer-Mediated Communication* 12 (2): 712–732.

Wary, B. 2006. "Scientific Authorship in the Age of Collaborative Research." *Studies in History and Philosophy of Science Part a* 37 (3): 505–514.

Wenger, E. 1998. *Communities of Practice Learning, Meaning, and Identity.* Cambridge: Cambridge University Press.

Wright, K. 2017. *Researching Internet-Based Populations: Advantages and Disadvantages of Online Survey Research,* Online Questionnaire Authoring Software Packages, and Web Survey Services. *Journal of Computer-Mediated Communication* 10 (3). doi: 10.1111/j.1083-6101.2005.tb00259.x.

10

LEARNING FROM STORIES ABOUT THE PRACTICE OF TEACHER EDUCATORS IN PARTNERSHIPS BETWEEN SCHOOLS AND HIGHER EDUCATION INSTITUTIONS

Elizabeth White, Miranda Timmermans, and Claire Dickerson

Introduction

Institute-based teacher educators (IBTEs) experience little opportunity for (formal) professional development (Livingston 2014), whilst for school-based teacher educators (SBTEs) there is usually nothing beyond a course on coaching and supervising student teachers. Also, the professional development of teacher educators depends on their own initiative; there is no structure for professional development of teacher educators, and from small-scale research we learn that managers of teacher educators hardly play a role in their professional development (Swennen 2012). That is why it is important to cultivate ways of professional development for teacher educators that support the informal nature and the direct use of the activities they engage in, like using narratives. This chapter illustrates a research-based initiative led by two teacher educators, who used insightful stories, contributed by teacher educators from partnership schools and higher education institutions, to develop tools with and for teacher educators in both settings. Teacher educators' stories about challenges they experience in practice were explored, with the aim of using the stories to support professional learning and development. The tools developed from the stories were designed to help SBTEs and IBTEs better understand and value their different perspectives and contributions to initial teacher education, and to support them to find ways to discuss and develop collaborative working practices, explore new possibilities, and enhance the quality of school-based teacher education. The tools could be employed in schools, in higher education institutions, and in partnerships, with teacher educators from both settings, and with others involved in initial teacher education, including mentors, student teachers, school leaders, and managers. A similar approach may be effective in supporting professional learning and development in other contexts where stakeholders are crossing boundaries between and within institutions.

Rationale for the focus on teacher educator professional learning and development

Even though teacher educators have actively facilitated the formal learning of student teachers and teachers for many years, the teacher educator profession is at an early stage of development across Europe (European Commission 2013). Policy-driven changes to teacher education in many countries have led to diversification of teacher educators as an occupational group, and increased the number of SBTEs (Musset 2010; Tatto and Furlong 2015). In the Netherlands, about 30% of student teachers are educated in partnerships between schools and higher education institutions, with shared responsibility for student teachers' education and assessment (Auditdienst Rijk 2018). This form of teacher education is known as *Opleiden in de school* (school-based teacher education); several schools and higher education institutions work together in school-led initial teacher education. The SBTEs guide the student teachers' development in the schools, working with the teacher mentors and sometimes teaching at the higher education institution (Van Velzen and Volman 2008, 2009).

In England, more than 50% of student teachers are in school-led teacher education, where there may be little or no involvement of IBTEs (Department for Education 2017). Structures are decided locally for these partnerships. SBTEs have differing roles, including supervising the student teachers' school-based experience; supporting teacher mentors; liaising between partnership schools; teaching student-teachers; and quality assurance. For some, this role is in addition to teaching pupils (White 2013, 2014). Many of these supervising SBTEs do not have a traditional mentoring role with student teachers, but rather have a mentoring and coaching role for the mentors within their partnerships.

Research evidence indicates:

* The importance of recognising the roles of SBTEs in initial teacher education and the value of their contributions;
* The need to develop new ways of working in collaborative partnerships that suit the new terrain;
* The importance of providing for the professional learning and development of SBTEs (White 2013, 2014; White, Dickerson, and Weston 2015; Boei et al. 2015).

According to Fullan and Hargreaves (2016), professional learning involves learning something new that has potential value, whereas professional development comprises growth in terms of who you are and what you can do as a professional. Combining professional learning and development "is at the heart of an effective and continuously growing teaching profession" (Fullan and Hargreaves 2016, 2). The current project embraces the need for both professional learning and development for effective teacher education, quality, and sustainability of initial teacher education partnerships. The organisation and structure of school-led teacher education is becoming well established in the new partnerships (Akker-man and Bruining 2016; Mutton et al. 2018), and a priority is to find optimal, and agreed, ways of achieving high-quality initial teacher education in these new contexts (Van Velzen and Timmermans 2017; Mutton et al. 2018). Jackson and Burch (2019, 2) report on third-space working, where "the school and the university work *together*, rather than *in parallel*", as a step towards a new way of envisioning teacher education. New opportunities are available for partners to work closely to design programmes and activities that use workplace learning opportunities more fully. Akkerman and Bruining (2016) draw attention to the brokers who enable boundary-crossing activity to facilitate this change. SBTEs who co-ordinate student teachers' training within the partnership schools and IBTEs adopt this brokering role. This study focussed on challenges in practice in the context of developing partnerships between schools and higher education institutions, and how teacher educators working in those partnerships are manag-ing their ever-changing role. In response to the research evidence in the bulleted list, the current project was designed to help to address the need for specific pro-fessional development and resources for SBTEs around their work with student teachers in the context of school-based practice, and to support collaboration between partners. It is crucial to meet SBTEs' professional learning and develop-ment needs because of their role in high-quality education of student teachers. It is also important for the IBTEs who work alongside them, as the context of their work has changed and they have new professional learning and development needs. This is essential for raising pupil learning and attainment (Murray and Kosnik, 2011; Lunenberg, Dengerink, and Loughran 2014) and for the wider development of teaching both now and for the future (Timmermans 2012).

Recent research on professional development of experienced IBTEs (n = 1158) in different countries identified a range of professional development issues and activities (Czerniawski, Guberman, and MacPhail 2017). These researchers found that participants had a strong preference for professional learning opportunities that are continuous and based on experiential learn-ing; for example, working collaboratively, observing colleagues or experienced researchers, being mentored, and being part of a team. Dengerink, Lunenberg, and Kools (2015) reported that Dutch teacher educators (SBTEs and IBTEs) (n = 268) preferred intentional informal learning, such as reading literature, attending conferences, intentionally experimenting, and undertaking peer con-versations rather than formal courses, again suggesting that teacher educators learn a lot in informal learning situations. The SBTEs and IBTEs in their study looked for different things in their professional development: SBTEs focussed predominantly on partnership and coaching skills, and IBTEs on the pedagogy of teacher education. There is less in-depth understanding about the profes-sional development of SBTEs in school-based teacher education (White, Dick-erson, and Weston 2015), or about IBTEs who are working closely with SBTEs in these partnerships.

The current chapter reports on an international research project around the work of teacher educators working in partnerships, which draws on the acknowledged benefits of a co-operative learning approach for teacher educators in differing settings (Boei et al. 2015). Greater insight is required around what happens in practice within partnerships at grass-roots level in order to identify the professional development needs of SBTEs, and the IBTEs who work alongside them. An extra dimension to this professional development is the work across boundaries between higher education institutions and schools, where types of knowledge, curricula, and pedagogy differ depending of the needs of learners in the different contexts. In reality, there are differences between guiding learning in the workplace and in the higher education institution, leading to different professional development requirements (Timmermans and Van Velzen 2017). Coherence is needed across initial teacher education programmes, necessitating co-operation and communication within and across organisations.

This project focussed on designing resources to support the professional learning and development of teacher educators who work in complex situations within partnerships. It may also contribute to a greater understanding of the experience and interactions that comprise informal learning in partnerships between schools and higher education institutions by answering questions on the challenges that teacher educators identify in their practice, the key themes of the challenges, and how teacher educators learn from them.

Rationale for the 'stories about practice' approach

A story is a narrative with a specific shape: a beginning, a plot, and an ending; or a before, a transformation, and an after (Scholes 1981; Pauw et al. 2017). 'Storying' has been used in the field of professional development (Jarvis 2005) and stories have been used in research to analyse the professional knowledge of teachers and teacher educators for more than two decades (Carter 1993). In this project, teacher educators' stories were collected for several reasons: they enable or encourage the projection of personal values onto the content (Scholes 1981); they allow complexity of the phenomena being dealt with to be captured; and they allow for "ambiguity and dilemma as central figures or themes" (Carter 1993, 6). In addition, when stories are told, communication is different to the formal language in research publications and professional literature, so the language of stories may be easier to understand (Jarvis 2005).

The challenges or dilemmas that teacher educators experience in practice can provide a useful trigger for teacher-educators to reflect on their thinking and actions. In this project, these challenges or dilemmas were captured as stories. A challenge was taken to mean a "task or situation that tests someone's abilities" and a dilemma as "a difficult situation or problem" (Oxford Dictionary 2018). The rationale for using the terms *challenge* and *dilemma*, when working with teacher educators, was to encourage participation without judging whether a situation described was 'severe' enough to warrant attention. Tillema and Kremer-Hayon (2005) collected dilemmas from teacher educators around their teaching. They suggested that dilemmas may be a useful tool for professional learning to help teacher educators to articulate their practice and examine their beliefs, and to bring to the surface strategies that they used to manage inconsistencies between beliefs and practice. The stories collected in the current project may trigger a discussion and examination of beliefs around school-based practice, when they are employed as professional learning and development tools.

Collecting and preparing the stories

Teacher educators from a range of European countries, attending a workshop of the Research and Development Community on Professional Development of Teacher Educators at the conference of the Association for Teacher Education in Europe (ATEE) were invited to write a story (see Text Box 1).

Most stories written during the workshop were not focussed on current school-based practice in initial teacher education because of the work the participants were engaged in. However, the process and feedback was used to sharpen the framework and make the task clearer. A number of participants reported that the experience of writing a story alone, and then sharing in small peer groups, was very helpful and affirming, and the activity helped to confirm that using dilemmas and challenges would be useful to teacher educators' professional learning.

Twenty Dutch and 15 English teacher educators supplied their stories of a challenge or dilemma following a personal invitation from the authors (see Table 10.1). These teacher educators, ten IBTEs and 25 SBTEs, work in the partnership institutions the authors engaged with, or attended conferences and workshops when the authors presented. They were provided with a form for writing their story and consented to its use in the research project. Some teacher educators were inexperienced in the practice of writing reflectively about a story of practice, and needed prompts, examples, and guidance. Two examples were

---

TEXT BOX 1   INVITATION TO WRITE A STORY

Please write a brief story below of a specific challenge or dilemma you have faced in your recent practice (using pseudonyms). Please include a beginning and a plot and an ending (if you had one!). You could start 'When I was . . .'

What was the real challenge for you?	*Where did the challenge arise?*
How did you deal with it?	*How did that work?*

TABLE 10.1 Location and settings where the teacher educators were working

	England		Netherlands		Totals
Setting	SBTE	IBTE	SBTE	IBTE	
Primary	1		8	2	11
Secondary	12	2	1	6	21
Vocational*			3		3
Totals	13	2	12	8	35

* Vocational education in the Netherlands is a form of secondary education and can be a part of the partnerships for initial teacher education. In England, further education embraces vocational education (usually for pupils over age 14) and is less likely to be included in initial teacher education partnerships.

used from Pauw et al. (2017). The Dutch stories were transcribed into English using Google Translate, and then checked by a native speaker to ensure that the true sense of the stories had been captured through face-to-face discussions with teacher educators. Identifiers were removed and the stories were read, amended, abbreviated if necessary, and proofread to ensure the translations were meaningful. Wherever possible, personal idiosyncrasies in the stories were retained. Both SBTEs and IBTEs used the stories in workshops to make sure they were 'understandable'.

About the stories

The teacher educators' stories were content-analysed (e.g., Patton 2002) by each researcher separately, and then through dialogue an agreement was reached. Initially 16 different aspects of practice were identified by repeatedly reading the stories and by drawing on feedback within workshops. These aspects were divided into four main themes (see Table 10.2).

Whilst both IBTEs and SBTEs provided stories around assessment, professionalism, growth and well-being, and collaborative working, only SBTEs provided stories around quality assurance. Although the 35 stories may not cover the full range of challenges currently being experienced in school-based practice, they provide a useful sample to trial as tools for teacher educators' professional learning and development.

Using the stories

The stories were used in five workshops and included about 100 teacher educators altogether. The workshops included groups of IBTEs alone, groups of SBTEs alone, and mixed groups of IBTEs and SBTEs. One workshop was with Dutch teacher educators, one with an international group, and three with English teacher educators. The aim was to create co-operative spaces where teacher educators

TABLE 10.2 Themes relating to the content of the stories

	Number of incidences
1 Guiding and assessing student teachers	30; in 26 of 35 stories
a Assessment (judgements around pass/fail)	10
b Guiding student-teachers' teaching	9
c Providing learning opportunities for student teachers	5
d Teaching student teachers	6
2 Professionalism, growth, and well-being	11; in 9 of 35 stories
a Professionalism (teacher educator)	3
b Professionalism (student teacher)	3
c Personal growth/identity (SBTE)	1
d Personal growth/identity (student teacher)	2
e Well-being (student teacher)	2
3 Collaborative working	12; in 10 of 35 stories
a Communication in partnership	3
b Working in partnership across institutions	6
c Working with school leadership	1
d Roles of teacher educators in the partnership	2
4 Quality	5; in 5 of 35 stories
a Quality assurance	3
b SBTE training	1
c Mentor training	1

could explore aspects of school-based practice with the goal of improving the quality of prospective teachers' education, an approach advocated by Boei et al. (2015) and Jackson and Burch (2019). Encouraging teacher educators from different settings and countries to share their stories, and then using the stories with mixed groups of SBTEs and IBTEs, might provide an opportunity to flatten hierarchies and develop a sense of equality and mutual responsibility between participants in teacher education. Workshop participants were informed about the research project and consented to any of their materials from the workshop being used for tool development. Different ways of using the stories were explored in the workshops (see Table 10.3). Two examples are provided to illustrate the nature of the stories and how they were used.

Two examples of using the stories

Slicing: what would you do?

This story is sliced into two parts (see Text Boxes 2 and 3) with questions to guide the use of the stories between the text boxes.

TABLE 10.3 How the stories were used

Activity	Prompt	Action
Key issue	What's it all about? Give the story a title.	Discuss a story in pairs or triplets. What do you think are the key issues that it highlights?
Slicing	What would you do?	Read the first part where the challenge is introduced. What would you advise the teacher educator to do? Read the second part of the story and compare your solution with what happened.
Perspective taking	Suppose you were in their shoes. . .	Who are the participants in the story? Look at the story from their perspectives. What does each person have to gain or lose?
Positive feedback	It was helpful when you . . .	How do you think this teacher educator feels? What positive feedback would you give them?
Dealing with challenges	Do you recognise the challenge?	Is this also a dilemma for you? In what way do you identify with this incident? Have you experienced anything similar? What are the warning signs in the story? What did you do in the situation? What choice did you make?

TEXT BOX 2   PART 1: THE CHALLENGE

I am a qualified secondary teacher and a school-based teacher educator (SBTE), supervising the school-based training of all the student teachers in our school and working with a number of different initial teacher education providers.

Amanda had a strong academic record; her main initial teacher education placement was at my school. Soon after starting her placement, it became quite evident there were a number of issues relating to her development as a trainee teacher. It was reported that Amanda was quite abrasive towards her mentor, department colleagues, and support staff. She was overly critical in observing the lessons of experienced teachers, reluctant to accept advice and guidance, and had difficulty in accepting feedback on her classroom practice. In addition, it became apparent that Amanda was very critical of her department colleagues and the school at university and with her peers on social media although she raised very few specific issues with her teacher mentor or myself.

What would you advise the SBTE to do?

Compare your plan of action to what actually happened (see Text Box 3). What are the similarities? What are the differences?

TEXT BOX 3   PART 2: THE SOLUTION

After discussions, Amanda's teacher mentor and I agreed to take on different but complementary roles in supporting and developing Amanda. Her mentor continued to be supportive, positive, and encouraging with Amanda, particularly focussed on developing her classroom practice, which had shown some improvement, and I, in close liaison with university staff and school colleagues, gave Amanda time and opportunity to voice her concerns while making clear and reinforcing our expectations of professional behaviour. Amanda's teaching practice did make enough improvement that enabled her to pass her first assessment point, but her relationship with colleagues and the school remained difficult at times and [she] even became abrasive with her fellow trainee teachers. Amanda remained adamant that problems were caused by the school and her department and that things would be better in her second school placement, which she started in the new year. Her mentor and I continued our dual roles, supporting each other as well as the department. Regular contact and support from university staff also helped.

Amanda found her second school placement extremely challenging. She quickly fell out with her professional mentor and department colleagues, missed nearly two weeks of a six-week placement due to illness, and seriously considered leaving the course. As a result, she was at risk of failing her assessment point 2. Prior to her return to the school, Amanda met with her mentor and myself to give her the opportunity to off-load some of her feelings, to set realistic expectations for her return, and to offer advice and support. Amanda returned to the school and successfully completed her placement, securing a newly qualified teacher post in a school outside the local area. As Amanda's confidence in her own practice grew and she accepted the clear professional expectations we had of her, then [her] problems . . . with colleagues diminished.

Looking back, the key factors which enabled Amanda to successfully complete her teacher training were patience; a focus on the positives but at the same time clear expectations of professional behaviour; collaboration and teamwork between all concerned; clear delineation of roles.

Perspective taking: Story Two – Suppose I was in your shoes . . .

This story is recorded (see Text Box 4), with the provocations following the text box, for learning from the story.

TEXT BOX 4   THE STORY

For many years I worked as a teacher in secondary education and a school-based teacher educator (SBTE) overseeing the placement of students in my school. Four years ago I started to work as an institute-based teacher educator (IBTE).

Somewhere mid-October I go to the first meeting of the team with SBTEs of different teaching schools with whom I work as an IBTE. This SBTE team had already had several meetings this academic year. Only recently had I received the invitation to attend this meeting. I notice that I'm somewhat nervous. The reason is that I know that this SBTE team has had an unpleasant experience with a colleague IBTE of mine who attended the meetings in the past. The SBTE would rather train the student teachers alone, without cooperation of a colleague IBTE of the teacher education institute. But that isn't what the partnership is about, so an IBTE must join with the SBTE team. That IBTE is me! My assignment – especially directed by my institute – is to join and to NOT be the all- or better-knowing IBTE. OK – that's the role I must play. I'm a little nervous, and ask myself: will I be accepted by them?

After the introductions (who is who, and the goal of the meeting), I receive the material that's going to be used by the students in the upcoming weeks. Just to get insight into the process of how this material is developed, I ask for the minutes of the last meetings. It turned out there are none, but they seem to like the idea to make notes during every meeting and add it to a list of agreements made. So, would they live up to expectations? I'm feeling a little bit awkward, and am thinking "I hope they don't think that I think that they aren't professional".

While they are talking about several things that were nothing to do with me I browse the material the SBTE team made for the students. Coincidentally the references get my attention because they didn't conform to referencing that we require the students to use, so this referencing system should also be used correctly in teaching materials for students developed by SBTEs. Realising that I'm instructed not to be the wise IBTE, I hesitate to mention it. I am waiting for the right moment, so I'm glad that one of the SBTEs brings up some minor things that should be changed. During tea break I tell the SBTEs, "While you have to make some changes as asked, perhaps you could also take a look at the references. A couple of books aren't referred to properly, using the referencing system. I just noticed". One of the SBTEs says thanks. It seems OK.

After the break we discuss the material, especially the themes and content concerning the first meeting for the student teachers at their schools. Listening to what is said, I realise that they don't consider the authentic context of the school as a valuable input to learn from. That is a pity; that is one of the main reasons for workplace learning. What to do? How to act? Gosh . . .!! I decide to tell them how I as an IBTE work with students at the institute when these themes are on the timetable and how jealous I am of the SBTEs because they have their own authentic and rich environment (that is also the environment of the student teacher) to refer to whilst discussing the themes. One of the SBTEs gets the point and reacts: "We could ask the students to do some observations and afterwards we can discuss what they saw with them and their mentors". All of a sudden the SBTEs have a lot of interesting new ideas about connecting the themes to the context and the learning opportunities that the school can provide. They write them down. Their enthusiasm does take me along. . . . The meeting ends. The SBTEs thank me. I am invited to come again. Phew!

Who are the participants in the story? Look at the story from their perspectives. What does each person have to gain or lose?

Early observations of teacher educators learning from using the stories

In each workshop, after carrying out an activity with a story, the teacher educators were asked to consider what they had learned personally, and to give feedback on how they found the activity. Ideas were gathered from the participants of how they would use the stories themselves. The personal learning that they identified is summarised in Table 10.4.

Some participants felt that using a story to explore a challenge or dilemma had an authenticity that might not have been apparent in a descriptive case study, and that they were able to respond emotionally to the power of the story. It helped them to identify personally with the situation. They appreciated the time and space provided by the workshops to be able to reflect on an aspect of school-based practice with other teacher educators. Using the story of another person made it easier to talk about what was really going on rather than directly talking about his or her own situation. Discussing the stories in a mixed group of teacher educators helped them to see different perspectives and understand their own partnerships better. This view was repeated by mixed groups (SBTEs and IBTEs) and by homogenous groups (all IBTEs or all SBTEs). They could resonate with the stories as they illustrated real issues, even if the contexts were different. Where stories were used at international conferences, the participants reported that they could understand and relate to the stories, even to the extent that they were not sure which stories had originated in England and which in the Netherlands. Teacher educators from across international boundaries (England, Germany, India, Israel, the Netherlands, Wales, and the USA) and across institutional boundaries recognised the challenges and dilemmas in practice.

During the discussions it became clear that some words have different meanings between countries and within countries, and between different partnerships,

TABLE 10.4 Personal learning from an activity using a story in the workshops

It raises questions in a bigger issue

It raises more questions

It helps to see beyond your own context

It makes clear that we all have our opinion on people

You start to get to know your biases

It pictures the students and all the people involved

Interestingly, there can be different interpretations of the same story – such a variety in the way a story can be understood and spoken about. The role you have colours the narrative

It helps in perspective taking

It helps to discuss in heterogeneous groups (of SBTEs and IBTEs)

Why do the exact same issues come up repeatedly? Why aren't we learning? Why aren't we passing on our learning?

It makes more clear that it is all about asking the right questions

More explanation is needed to understand some stories

Stories can be carefully chosen for when you want to address specific issues

---

especially with respect to the complexities of how functions and roles are shared between teacher educators. When using the stories in specific settings, workshop leaders might decide to change the terminology from IBTE, SBTE, mentor, and student teacher into terms used in their setting, so that the terms do not distract from the desired learning. IBTEs and SBTEs may use different language to articulate their practice within their settings and misunderstandings can arise. Using stories in workshops may provide opportunities for a real meeting of minds, avoiding superficiality where teacher educators in a partnership do not realise they have miscommunication. This is one of the many benefits of learning from one another and taking time to understand one another's perspective.

Significance of this project

The challenges in practice that were identified by teacher educators working in the initial teacher education partnerships in this research expand our understanding of current experiences in the field, where there has been a rebalancing of responsibilities between schools and higher education institutions. Dilemmas were experienced in guiding and assessing student teachers; working collaboratively; and in the areas of quality of provision, professionalism, growth, and well-being. It is not possible, with such a small data collection, to draw conclusions about whether this is a typically representative distribution of challenges, especially as the sample of participants was self-selecting. New and experienced SBTEs and IBTEs identified helpful professional learning from using the tools developed from the stories. Dialogue around stories of practice may "allow for an understanding of different perspectives and for an understanding of how our own stories have developed in personal and cultural contexts" (Jarvis 2005, 10). Using stories in workshops provided opportunities to challenge practices, understand power relationships, and consider what learning can be transferred between contexts. A story may bring participants in a workshop closer because it "may allow us to reveal part of ourselves, either because we include ourselves as characters, or because we show personal perspectives on events" (Jarvis 2005, 7). Using stories in this way may enhance the quality of initial teacher education by recognising and valuing the unique contributions made by the teacher educators in the partnership, supporting effective cooperation within partnerships and the development of the teacher educators' professional identity. Stories of practice can be viewed through different lenses to understand cultural and institutional assumptions and teacher educators can critically analyse them together in relation to appropriate literature and apply different theoretical models.

Where teacher educators came from the same setting, the tools did not provoke the same level of discussion. Jarvis (2005) warns that some discussion groups may be too homogeneous to be able to see beyond their own professional or cultural frames and may silence minority views. For this reason, using the stories in mixed groups of teacher educators from schools and higher education institutions could help support the understanding of different perspectives in order to enable smoother boundary transitions for all involved in initial teacher education.

Planned further research and development

A further larger-scale study of the variety of challenges and dilemmas that teacher educators are facing in initial teacher education partnerships would provide useful data to identify where specific professional development needs exist for IBTEs and SBTEs, and what problem-solving strategies are being employed, in order to provide for these needs and to enhance the quality of partnership working and student experience.

These workshops have helped in understanding that SBTEs and IBTEs value learning collaboratively, across institutions both within their partnerships and between partnerships. This way of working helps to make the boundaries seamless, and to enable a greater understanding of the complexity of school-based practice. In the stories of teacher educators that focus on a challenge in their school-based practice, there is the potential to look more deeply at the formation and development of teacher educator identities and to consider how the current context can be affecting them. Further research could focus on the values the teacher educators express through the way they narrate their stories and explore how to open these up for discussion.

Feedback from teacher educators during this project indicated that the process of writing the stories and using them as an autobiographical self-study tool for critical reflection on practice could also be beneficial for professional learning. A similar approach was used by Jasman (2010) for her own continuing professional learning as a teacher educator; she examined her involvement in five practice-based research projects where border-crossing between different professional knowledge contexts enabled her professional learning. Writing stories about challenges and dilemmas in practice and sharing them with peers also surfaced as beneficial for professional learning.

The learning from these sessions has informed the production of a collection of stories in Dutch (Timmermans, 2020) and in English (www.go.herts. ac.uk/FLiTE), together with guidance on effective ways of using the stories and guidance on writing them. They are available for use by teacher educators and others involved in initial teacher education, and evaluative feedback would be valued. Those subscribing to the authors' mailing list will be kept informed of further research-informed resources that become available for the professional learning and development of SBTEs and IBTEs working in school-based teacher education.

Acknowledgements

This work was funded by a grant from the University of Hertfordshire. We are grateful to all the teacher educators who contributed their stories and participated in workshops to refine resources that will be freely available to teacher educators internationally for professional learning and development.

References

Akkerman, S., and T. Bruining. 2016. "Multi-Level Boundary Crossing in a Professional Development School Partnership." *Journal of the Learning Sciences* 25 (2): 240–284. doi: 10.1080/10508406.2016.1147448.

Auditdienst Rijk. 2018. "Financing School-based Teacher Education. Final report. 's Gravenhage: Ministerie van Financiën." Accessed on 6 August 2019 at https://www.rijksoverheid.nl/documenten/rapporten/2018/10/17/onderzoeksrapport-naar-financiering-opleiden-in-de-school.

Boei, F., J. Dengerink, J. Geursen, Q. Kools, B. Koster, M. Lunenberg, and M. Willemse. 2015. "Supporting the Professional Development of Teacher Educators in a Productive Way." *Journal of Education for Teaching* 41 (4): 351–368. doi: 10.1080/02607476.2015.1080403.

Carter, K. 1993. "The Place of Story in the Study of Teaching and Teacher Education." *Educational Researcher* 22 (1): 5–18. doi: 10.3102/0013189X022001005.

Czerniawski, G., A. Guberman, and A. MacPhail. 2017. "The Professional Developmental Needs of Higher Education-Based Teacher Educators: An International Comparative Needs Analysis." *European Journal of Teacher Education* 40 (1): 127–140. doi: 10.1080/02619768.2016.1246528.

Dengerink, J., M. Lunenberg, and Q. Kools. 2015. "What and How Teacher Educators Prefer to Learn." *Journal of Education for Teaching* 41 (1): 78–96. doi: 10.1080/02607476. 2014.992635.

Department for Education. 2017. "Initial Teacher Training: Trainee Number Census – 2017 to 2018." Accessed on 6 August 2019 at www.gov.uk/government/statistics/initial-teacher-training-trainee-number-census-2017-to-2018.

European Commission. 2013. "Supporting Teacher Educators for Better Learning Outcomes." Accessed on 6 August 2019 at http://ec.europa.eu/dgs/education_culture/repository/education/policy/school/doc/support-teacher-educators_en.pdf

Fullan, M., and A. Hargreaves. 2016. *Bringing the Profession Back In: Call to Action*. Oxford, OH: Learning Forward.

Jackson, A., and J. Burch. 2019. "New Directions for Teacher Education: Investigating School/University Partnership in an Increasingly School-Based Context." *Professional Development in Education* 45 (1): 1–13. doi: 10.1080/19415257.2018.1449002.

Jarvis, J. 2005. "Telling Stories in Class: An Exploration of Aspects of the Use of Narrative In a Higher Education Context." *Journal for the Enhancement of Learning and Teaching* 2 (1): 6–13.

Jasman, A.M. 2010. "A Teacher Educator's Professional Learning Journey and Border Pedagogy: A Meta-Analysis of Five Research Projects." *Professional Development in Education* 36: 307–323. doi: 10.1080/19415250903457521.

Livingston, K. 2014. "Teacher Educators: Hidden Professionals?" *European Journal of Education* 49 (2): 218–232.

Lunenberg, M., J. Dengerink, and J. J. Loughran. 2014. *Professional Teacher Educator: Roles, Behaviour, and Professional Development of Teacher Educators*. 1st ed. Rotterdam: Sense Publishers.

Murray, J., and C. Kosnik. 2011. "Academic Work and Identities in Teacher Education." *Journal of Education for Teaching* 37 (3): 243–246. doi: 10.1080/02607476.2011.587982.

Musset, P. 2010. "Initial Teacher Education and Continuing Training Policies in a Comparative Perspective: Current Practices in OECD Countries and a Literature Review on Potential Effects." *OECD Education Working Papers* 48. doi: 10.1111/ejed.12074.

Mutton, T., K. Burn, H. Hagger, and K. Thirlwell. 2018. *Teacher Education Partnerships. Policy and Practice*. St Albans: Critical Publishing.

Oxford Dictionary. 2018. "Definitions of Challenge and Dilemma in English." Accessed on 6 August 2019 at https://en.oxforddictionaries.com/definition/

Patton, M. 2002. *Qualitative Research and Evaluation Methods*. 3rd ed. Thousand Oaks, Ca: Sage.

Pauw, I., P. van Lint, M. Gemmink, W. Jongstra, and M. Pillen, 2017. *Een Leraar als Geen Ander. Ontwikkeling van Professionele Identiteit van Leraren door Verhalen*. [A Teacher Like No Other. Developing Teachers Professional Identity through Narratives]. Garant: Antwerpen-Apeldoorn.

Scholes, R. 1981. "Language, Narrative, and Anti-Narrative." In *On Narrative*, edited by W. Mitchell, 200–208. Chicago: University of Chicago Press.

Swennen, A. 2012. "Van Oppermeesters tot Docenten Hoger Onderwijs: De Ontwikkeling van het Beroep en de Identiteit van Lerarenopleiders" [The Development of the Profession and Identity of Teacher Educators]. Amsterdam: Vrije Universiteit Amsterdam. Accessed on 6 August 2019 at http://dare.ubvu.vu.nl/handle/1871/38045.

Tatto, M., and J. Furlong. 2015. "Research and Teacher Education: Papers from the BERA-RSA Inquiry." *Oxford Review of Education* 41 (2): 145–153. doi: 10.1080/0305 4985.2015.1017404.

Tillema, H., and L. Kremer-Hayon. 2005. "Facing Dilemmas: Teacher-Educators' Ways of Constructing a Pedagogy of Teacher Education." *Teaching in Higher Education* 10 (2): 203–217. doi: 10.1080/1356251042000337954.

Timmermans, M. 2012. "Kwaliteit van de Opleidingsschool: Over Affordance, Agency en Competentieontwikkeling" [Quality of the Opleidingsschool: On Affordance, Agency and Competence Development]. Doctoral dissertation, Tilburg University, the Netherlands.

Timmermans, M. 2020. *Het grote verhalenboek. Een professionaliseringstool voor school- en instituutsopleiders* (The Big Storybook. A Professionalization Tool for School-Based and Institute-Based Teacher Educators). Platform Samen Opleiden & Professionaliseren Utrecht.

Timmermans, M., and C. van Velzen. 2017. "Samen in de School Opleiden." [Teaching Together in School-Based Partnerships]. *Kennisbasis Lerarenopleiders* (Knowledge Base of Teacher Educators), Katern 4. Breda: Vereniging Lerarenopleiders Nederland (Velon).

Van Velzen, C., and M. Timmermans. 2017. "Opleiden in de School/in de School Opleiden: de Blik Vooruit!" [Teacher Education in Schools/In School Teacher Education] In *Samen in de School Opleiden* [Teacher Education in Schools in Partnership]. *Katern 4. Kennisbasis Lerarenopleiders*, edited by M. Timmermans, and C. van Velzen, 147–150. Vereniging Lerarenopleiders Nederland (Velon).

Van Velzen, C., and M. Volman. 2008. *School-Based Teacher Education in The Netherlands and the Opportunities of the School as a Learning Place.* Paper presented at the ISCAR, San Diego.

Van Velzen, C., and M. Volman. 2009. "The Activities of a School-Based Teacher Educator: A Theoretical and Empirical Exploration." *European Journal of Teacher Education* 32 (4): 345–367. doi: 10.1080/02619760903005831.

White, E. 2013. "Exploring the Professional Development Needs of New Teacher Educators Situated Solely in School: Pedagogical Knowledge and Professional Identity." *Professional Development in Education* 39 (1): 82–98. doi: 10.1080/19415257.2012.708667.

White, E. 2014. "Being a Teacher and a Teacher Educator – Developing a New Identity?" *Professional Development in Education* 40 (3): 436–449. doi: 10.1080/19415257.2013.782062.

White, E., C Dickerson, and K Weston. 2015. "Developing an Appreciation of What it Means to be a School-Based Teacher Educator." *European Journal of Teacher Education* 38 (4): 445–459. doi: 10.1080/02619768.2015.1077514.

11

TEACHER EDUCATOR AS RESEARCHER

Striving towards a greater visibility for teacher education

Ann MacPhail

Teacher educator as researcher

It has been proposed for some time now that if teacher education is to be taken seriously, it must be research-based, with teacher educators as active researchers and perceived as 'public intellectuals' (Cochran-Smith 2005; European Commission 2015). This re-positioning of the teacher educator results in associated teacher education programmes that are expected to be 'research driven', developing a research disposition among teacher educators as well as preparing consumers and producers of research (Tack and Vanderlinde 2014). Such a focus is accompanied by pressure from university leadership for teacher educators to focus on securing research funding and increase publication output (Furlong 2013; Stern 2016). In mapping the field of teacher education research in the UK, Menter et al. (2010) commented that teacher education research remains a young sub-field of education research more generally. The notion of a 'dual economy' in the teacher education space has become more evident, where some academic staff are primarily teacher educators and others are primarily researchers, with some teacher educators experiencing tension between the two forms of academic activity (Christie and Menter 2009; Munn and Baron 2008).

A special edition of the *Journal of Education for Teaching* (Menter and Murray 2009) focused on building research capacity in teacher education. They shared some major challenges facing teacher educator research communities as they positioned themselves for a national assessment framework that focused on research outputs, research impact, and research environment as quality indicators for academic promotion and retention. Engaging teacher educators in research continues to gain exposure (Livingston, McCall and Morgado 2009) and the common thread across many such studies is that teacher educators' engagement in conducting research is referred to as a necessity rather than an advantage (Hadar and Brody

2016). This message is evident in studies that provide personal perspectives on undertaking the role of teacher educator as researcher (Kane 2007; Kosnik 2007). It is this personal perspective that I favour in this chapter in approaching the 'teacher educator as researcher' topic. This aims to complement the premise of the book being to provide research-based illustrations from the lives and professional development of experienced teacher educators. In doing so, the intention is to foster the voice of the teacher educator and support teacher educators to strive towards a greater visibility of their (research) contributions to high-quality teacher education and education in general. I am conscious of the related challenges that may arise for teacher educators whose role is to predominantly focus on their 'educational capacities' (such as curriculum development and assessment) at the expense of 'scholarly activities' (such as reviewing and publishing peer-reviewed papers) that appear to be more aligned with progressing in an academic career (Czerniawski et al. 2018). To appreciate the positioning of teacher educators in Irish higher education, it is imperative to understand the changing expectations and challenges facing higher education after a decade of austerity and a global financial crisis. Such expectations and challenges, as well as a more thorough overview of teacher education in the Irish context and teacher educators in the Irish education system than is allowed in this chapter, have been published previously (MacPhail and O'Sullivan, 2019).

Teacher educators in Ireland

The dominant professional pathway to working in teacher education in Ireland has been, until recently, that those with professional experience as teachers (along with a Master's degree) would have been initially seconded to a teacher education post for a period of up to ten years and the secondment would have been perceived as a positive career move (Waldron et al. 2012). Over time, most of these teachers secured permanent posts and opted to stay in the university. These teacher educator recruits would not have been expected to have a doctoral qualification. While they would have been expected to be research-informed as to best practices in teacher education, they would not have been expected to be research active, i.e., conducting and publishing research.

The role of teacher education and research in Ireland

The recent policy context in Ireland has re-framed the role of teacher education and research. Significantly, the joint influence of the more complete universitisation of teacher education recommended in the recent Sahlberg Report (2012), along with increased rankings pressure on universities, has meant that there is more pressure on teacher education academics as they work in higher education institutions to acquire a PhD and publish in peer-reviewed research outlets. Contextualising this recent policy reframing is important in terms of patterns of research practice in teacher education. While there have been no studies or reviews as such related to this, trends can be identified. First, there has been recent growth of research outputs on teacher education in Ireland over the past decade, with publication of peer-reviewed journal articles, reports, and small-scale collaborations providing evidence in terms of associated outputs. Much of the research on teacher education has comprised small-scale studies within individual programmes or sometimes small-scale studies between programmes in different institutions (e.g., Standing Conference on Teacher Education, North and South). There have been a small number of larger-scale studies as well as commissioned reports on teacher education which have provided more system-level insights on teacher education. Third, the focus of research has been mainly on initial teacher education, with some focus on continuing professional development and very little, until more recently, on induction (Conway et al. 2009). Taken together, these observations indicate that the opportunities to learn and experience research as a teacher educator are typically studies within one's own institution. We do not know the proportion of staff involved, the duration of involvement, the types and foci of studies, nor the extent to which such research is seen as central (or not) to teacher educators' professional institutional profiles. Anecdotal evidence would suggest significant differences between institutions in the standing and profile of research on teacher education.

Teacher educators as researchers in Ireland

Gleeson et al. (2012) explored the potential for research capacity building in initial teacher education programmes in Northern Ireland and the Republic of Ireland, reporting an identifiable tension between the identity of initial teacher education faculty as 'teacher educators' and 'educational researchers'. They noted the requirement to critically unpack the meaning of initial teacher education-based research and what it means to be 'research-active' as a teacher educator. They also reported that a significant minority of initial teacher education staff rated their own research experience as satisfactory or poor and that they would like more time to devote to educational research activity. Teacher educators working in the Republic of Ireland noted that pressure to publish emanated "mainly from competitive individualism alongside changing institutional cultures particularly in the universities . . . [and] noted the influence of and the increasing importance being attached to research profiles both for academic appointments and subsequent promotions" (Gleeson et al. 2012, 6). In a more recent study conducted with a sample of teacher educators working in the Republic of Ireland, it was reported that the top three professional learning activities valued by teacher educators all related to research: (1) personal reading, (2) role of research when studying one's own practice in teacher education, and (3) the extent to which research is essential to inform teacher education practice (Czerniawski et al. 2018). This presents a challenge to the individual teacher educators who require upskilling in the identified research-related professional learning activities. It also presents a challenge to a predominantly higher-education-based teacher education profession that is looking to compete in research-driven universities on who to recruit into teacher education – that is, recruitment of teachers from schools and/or the recruitment of teachers from a predominantly research background.

Author's positioning

In striving towards a greater visibility for teacher education from the perspective of teacher educator as researcher, I present three considerations. I revisit the three considerations towards the end of the chapter to reinforce the extent to which teacher educators can develop a capacity to engage with academic and institutional 'research' changes in productive, proactive ways.

I draw predominantly on my time as a teacher educator for the past 16 years in the same Irish university setting. On beginning my role as a teacher educator, I had completed a four-year undergraduate physical education honours degree programme, undertaken physical education teaching in schools and completed a research PhD investigating the social construction of knowledge within a specific physical education curriculum development initiative. Following graduation from the PhD programme, and prior to entering the teacher education profession, I had spent the previous three years as a research associate, a privileged position that provided me a solid grounding in conducting research and writing for publication, both of which I have strived to maintain. I have chronicled my story of becoming a teacher educator and researcher elsewhere (MacPhail 2014).

My experience to date supports the belief that engaging in research serves as a powerful motivator for teacher educators to participate in the teacher education community (Hadar and Brody 2016). I have been fortunate to be an integral member of a department-level subject-discipline-driven teacher education community (MacPhail et al. 2014; Tannehill et al. 2015). This has consistently provided me with a critical mass of research-active physical education teacher educators with whom I have conducted and disseminated research. In addition, as a member of the International Forum for Teacher Educator Development (InFo-TED) (Kelchtermans, Smith, and Vanderlinde 2018), I have gained access into a more generic teacher education and teacher educator research space. This has provided me the opportunity to be active in research with teacher educator colleagues from multiple disciplines and multiple jurisdictions and to subsequently be involved in research targeted at the international teacher education community. Indeed, my involvement in both communities illustrates the engendered reciprocal contributions of the community to the individual and of the individual to the community (Hadar and Brody 2016). I do not take for granted the extent to which both communities provide safe, enquiry-orientated and collaborative spaces for me to sustain my interest and passion in contributing to the teacher educator knowledge base.

Acknowledging that our academic and career biographies are inextricably linked to our work and life practices, my aim throughout this chapter is to prompt the reader to consider the extent to which my experience as teacher educator as researcher aids consideration on how to strive towards a greater visibility for teacher education. My experiences are captured under three considerations. The first consideration will share my experiences in researching my own practices with pre-service teachers as well as my engagement in self-study that captures my ongoing journey as a teacher educator. The second consideration will focus on increasing exposure in the higher institute of credible teacher educators who can connect with the university's strategic positioning. The third consideration will focus on opportunities to contribute to interdisciplinary/multidisciplinary research.

Researching and disseminating teacher education practices

I share two personal scenarios here. The first is related to researching my own teacher education practices. The second is ensuring that as teacher educators we are providing pre-service teachers with appropriate and relevant research reference points, as well as educating them on how to access relevant research for themselves.

I research my own teacher education practices in a bid to educate teacher education colleagues, teachers, and other practitioners and academics about the work that teacher educators undertake in preparing effective pre-service teachers. This has included practices such as examining what pre-service teachers' teaching metaphors tell us about their developing beliefs about teaching and learning (Tannehill and MacPhail 2014), preparing pre-service teachers to design instructionally aligned lessons through constructivist pedagogical approaches (MacPhail, Tannehill, and Goc Karp 2013) and helping pre-service teachers and beginning teachers examine and reframe assumptions about themselves as teachers and change agents (MacPhail and Tannehill 2012).

Aligned with researching my own teacher education practices is focussing on my experiences of being a teacher educator, specifically through self-study research. Such research openly interrogates and conveys the space in which I operate and, in turn, educates readers about the reality of enacting 'teacher educator as researcher'. This has predominantly been conducted with the acknowledgement that our academic and career biographies are inextricably linked to our work and life practices. Self-study has led me to explore my positioning as an apprentice, academic, and administrator within the teacher education space (MacPhail 2017), examine the experiences and challenges I faced as I strove towards investing in a professional teacher education community that resided within a university department (MacPhail 2014) and consider how I support pre-service teachers in their endeavours to identify and sustain their own professional learning requirements and contribute to developing a pedagogy of teacher education (MacPhail 2011). Self-study has also encouraged me to interrogate my position as a member of a teacher education learning community (MacPhail et al. 2014; Tannehill et al. 2015; Lunenberg in press). Targeting different outlets, such as teacher education scholarly journals, other professional journals, blogs, Twitter, and conference presentations, has increased the exposure of my use of teacher education practices and my experiences as a teacher educator as well as increasing access to the teacher education community. The challenge for me has been to appreciate that, while what we do in the name of teacher education may be effective in and of itself in preparing caring and passionate pre-service teachers, our role includes a significantly increasing responsibility to share our practices and research. In doing so, the intention is to educate a wide audience on the reality, challenges, experiences, and study of doing teacher education and being a teacher educator as researcher.

The second scenario I share revolves around ensuring we are providing appropriate research-informed reference points for pre-service teachers that allow them to engage with, understand, and strive to enact teaching practices, initially during school placement and later as a practising teacher. This has resulted in my choosing to write specifically for an audience of pre-service teachers when I have been unable to find a resource that captures what I wish them to understand. One such example was addressing the gap in denoting the considerable changes that were being considered and subsequently enacted as regards assessment in Irish school physical education (MacPhail and Murphy 2017).

Related to the concern of ensuring pre-service teachers can access appropriate research outlets/reference points is the concept of 'teacher as researcher'. The teacher as professional, reflective practitioner and researcher is a mandatory element of all initial teacher education programmes in Ireland, with provision for the development of pre-service teachers as researchers and lifelong learners (Teaching Council 2017). I teach a module that assists pre-service teachers to access pertinent research to support their 'learning about' and their 'teaching of' physical education in post-primary-school contexts and consider how the research they read can be applied immediately in the planning priorities for school placement. Based on pre-service teachers' reading of selected research articles and discussions of relevant topics as an early-career teacher, pre-service teachers develop their own strategy on how best to use this research analysis process. The process is intended to assist pre-service teachers in their planning decisions, selecting their teaching and assessment practices, and increase their understanding of physical education and the nature of student learning in physical education. While research findings do not ensure results, in all settings and with all students, they can provide insight into how things might be adapted or revised to improve practice or learning. It is hoped that instilling a level of confidence, engagement, and appreciation for research in pre-service teachers will allow them to maintain such a skill set when they enter the teaching profession.

Connecting with higher institute strategic positioning

Embedded within this consideration are two inextricably linked issues: the influence of research metrics in higher education institutes and aligning with the higher education institute's strategic positioning. Two recent teacher education initiatives in Ireland provide examples of how alignment can be encouraged and pursued.

One way in which many higher education institutes determine the visibility of individuals and/or discipline areas is the extent to which each contributes to the target research metrics of the specific institute (e.g., citations, funding submissions, publications). In a recent study that explored the challenges for Irish teacher educators in being active users and producers of research (MacPhail and O'Sullivan, 2019), it was evident that, for most, the expectation for promotion and career development demanded a research profile as teacher educators. Teacher educators were members of the university community and were keen to engage in research. While some noted they should be more active but struggled to manage the level of teaching required with the time to be research active, others described how they measured that engagement carefully while focussed on generating the right kind of research metrics.

Increasing exposure in higher education institutes of credible teacher educators who can connect with the university's strategic positioning is another way to strive towards a greater visibility for teacher education. This includes considering how teacher educators can best position themselves to contribute to the discussion of what constitutes 'research', as well as access, and contribute to, what is determined as meaningful knowledge and the dominant orientations of universities.

A realistic and feasible way in which teacher education is attempting to position itself strategically in higher education institutes in a specific region in Ireland has been the establishment of the National Institute for the Study of Education (NISE). This has entailed forming one integrated centre for teacher education across three institutes with a shared agreement to nurture a culture where staff involved in teacher education are research active, familiar with current educational research and programmes, and engage with schools and relevant stakeholders as research partners (NISE 2014). Teacher educators are encouraged to publish and/ or disseminate educational research focussed on national and international priority education needs and promote a culture of research-led teaching, inter-disciplinary research, and enhanced research-training.

There is evidence that teacher educators working in Ireland are clear about expectations for research productivity and building a national and international research profile, securing grants to support their research, yet without the necessary university and/or national level infrastructure for teacher education research (MacPhail and O'Sullivan, 2019). The necessity (posed by Sahlberg, Furlong, and Munn 2012) for a national research institution for educational research funded by the Irish government continues to be a hoped-for research infrastructure for teacher education and teacher educator research. The recent establishment of the National Teacher Education and Teacher Educator Forum in Ireland intends to support the professional development of teacher educators and contribute to a collective voice on shaping national teacher education and related research discourse. While this forum was established in the first instance by myself and two colleagues, we hope that once it gains momentum that it may provide evidence and impetus for the proposed government-funded national research institution for educational research.

Contributing to interdisciplinary and multidisciplinary agendas

Opportunities to contribute to interdisciplinary/multidisciplinary research illustrate how teacher educators, and by association their research identity, can complement research of other disciplines in a bid to contribute to specific knowledge bases as well as access more research (funding) opportunities.

In rethinking the significance of disciplines in higher education, Trowler, Saunders, and Bamber (2012) set out to address the significance, relevance, and power of disciplines in contemporary higher education across the world. They critique and develop the work of Becher and Trowler (2001) who enquired into the nature of the linkages between academic cultures/communities (the 'tribes') and disciplinary knowledge/academic ideas (their 'territories'). Trowler, Saunders, and Bamber (2012) encourage revisiting the disciplinary classificatory systems and suggest that such classifications have limitations in light of contextual changes and more expansive thinking. Regardless, there is merit in exploring how changing higher education landscapes have significant implications for academics, their various tribes, and disciplinary territories (in whatever way they are constituted). Contemplating the extent to which particular segments of the discipline can reap a mutual benefit from a related segment from another discipline – for example, teacher education – would encourage the consideration of 'adjoining territories' (Becher and Trowler 2001) with areas of common ground. Extending the groups/communities in which teacher education is represented increases the potential to access infrastructures within 'adjoining territories' that afford us access to opportunities that we would be unlikely to secure as a freestanding international teacher education / teacher educator community.

The success of teacher education aligning with other disciplines in a bid to connect with the institute's or university's strategic positioning is very much determined by the extent to which the university values such activity. My own university's strategic plan is clear in noting that the university has competitive challenges in terms of research performance and its international profile. The nature of each of these challenges is reinforced through the university's celebration of successful research income, research collaborations with industry, and commercialisation related to venture capital investment and spin-out companies sold. Such measures of success are more easily attained in specific disciplines and it is perhaps not surprising to note in the university's research strategy that the areas considered as research strengths are advanced manufacturing, software, applied mathematical sciences, health, and materials. To intensify critical mass in the identified areas of research strength, three formalised university-based institutes have been established: one to foster multidisciplinary research collaboration with health practitioners, one to build on significant strengths in applied sciences and engineering, and one in software engineering. If teacher education wishes to connect with the university's research priorities, then it appears that the only way to do this is to align itself with, and work with, discipline areas that allow teacher education to contribute to multidisciplinary research collaborations.

I have strived to expose teacher education as a valuable contributor to multidisciplinary research collaboration with health practitioners. This arises from my involvement in a national project tender that aims to improve health behaviours (increased physical activity, reduced sedentary behavior, and healthy eating) and health literacy in Irish post-primary school-aged children, aligned with a recently introduced well-being curriculum. This has entailed complementing the skill set of the project team, which includes a consultant endocrinologist, exercise psychologist, public health lawyer, and dietitian. The interest and advantage to including a teacher educator (albeit with a specialism in physical education) is the expertise in understanding the school and teaching context in which the proposed study is to take place, as well as interrogating the discourse of the well-being curricula to understand the potential for teachers, as well as school-aged children, to be health literate. In establishing this, it is imperative that Irish teacher education programmes begin to consider how best to embed the well-being curriculum to effectively prepare pre-service teachers to enact wellbeing.

Final comments and future research

I consider conducting research as significant to my professionalism as a teacher educator. This relates to undertaking and utilising research to inform my learning and practice as a teacher educator and, in turn, improving the experience of pre-service teachers. This also relates to educating others on the centrality and importance that teacher education has on understanding and improving learning and teaching in relation to ourselves and others (Livingston, McCall, and Morgado 2009). Appreciating that some teacher educators' research capacity is stifled by a limiting infrastructure of support, collaboration, and enquiry, it is imperative that we continue to establish and research professional learning communities for teacher educators. In researching such communities, we can explore how they can serve as a sounding board for teacher educators to make their own enquiry public and available to others' critiques (Hadar and Brody 2016). To this end, the recently formed National Teacher Education and Teacher Educator Forum in Ireland (discussed earlier) is a space in which this can be encouraged (and researched) in Ireland.

For those teacher educators who are well established in terms of research activity, it should be expected that they would mentor colleagues in professional learning communities for teacher educators. Researching (formal or informal) teacher educator research mentoring infrastructures would allow us to determine the most effective ways in which to encourage less-experienced teacher educators to engage with the ever-prevailing research culture. In addition to this, it would be prudent for more experienced teacher educator researchers to become members of interdisciplinary and multidisciplinary communities, where teacher education would be one of numerous disciplines looking to contribute to a common interest in a research topic. Teacher educators need to be proactive in ensuring their research skill set and area of interest and expertise are shared widely across all communities to increase the likelihood of being invited to contribute to already, or newly, established interdisciplinary and multidisciplinary communities.

If, in our teacher educator as researcher role, we genuinely wish for greater visibility for teacher education, we need to collectively embrace, and continually reinforce, that teachers are seen by many governments as central to educational, economic, and social reform (Cochran-Smith 2008). In order to increase the centrality of teacher educators in governmental considerations, it is imperative that the teacher education profession conduct evidence-based and practice-informed research that informs current and proposed policy reforms to the teaching and teacher education profession. In the Irish context, the teacher education contin-uum (including teacher recruitment, preparation, and retention) has more recently undertaken consultations and developments as part of national policy agendas. Once individual jurisdictions have had an opportunity to undertake sustained and systematic research on teacher education policy (Kennedy 2017), the challenge is to formalise teacher education connections across all jurisdictions in a bid to pro-duce coherent teacher education policies in the European Union (Sayer 2006). It appears there are more opportunities at the European level to secure funding to explore teacher education and teacher educators than for small-scale, nationally focussed teacher education studies. The previously mentioned International Forum for Teacher Educator Development (InFo-TED) is a European-funded project that brings together teacher educators from a range of jurisdictions to translate teacher educators' knowledge bases into an international professional development pro-gramme for teacher educators as well as explore how an enduring international supportive structure can be implemented (www.info-ted.eu).

The edited text *A Companion to Research in Teacher Education* forefronts the importance of global and internal connections in the three overlapping worlds of policy, practice, and research (Menter, Peters, and Cowie 2017). The importance of research as a central university activity and the urgency of obtaining exter-nal (to the university) research funding has increased significantly for all univer-sity departments and disciplines (Pring 2017). Tatto (2017, 633) proposes that we engage national and international networks in what she calls the "collaborative and reflective construction of policy knowledge in context" through comparative international research. She explains that this approach supersedes the notion of 'policy borrowing' by bringing about "the re-contextualisation of policy useable knowledge, an action that should not only explain what is, but must identify the factors within specific macro, meso and micro context that may lead to continuous educational improvement". It is to this end that the teacher educator as researcher needs to strive towards a greater visibility for teacher education.

Acknowledgements

To Professors Mary O'Sullivan and Paul Conway, who contributed to the text in conference papers from which the Irish context for this chapter draws.

References

Becher, T., and P. Trowler. 2001. *Academic Tribes and Territories*. Buckingham: Society for Research in Higher Education.

Christie, D., and I. Menter. 2009. "Research Capacity Building in Teacher Education: Scot-tish Collaborative Approaches." *Journal of Education for Teaching* 35 (4): 337–354.

Cochran-Smith, M. 2005. "The New Teacher Education: For Better or For Worse?" *Educational Researcher* 34 (7): 3–17.

Cochran-Smith, M. 2008. "The New Teacher Education in The United States: Directions Forward." *Teachers and Teaching: theory and practice* 14 (4): 271–282.

Conway, P. F., R. Murphy, A. Rath, and K. Hall. 2009. *Learning to Teach and Its Implications for the Continuum of Teacher Education: A Nine-Country Cross-National Study.* Report commissioned by the Teaching Council (Ireland), http://www.teachingcouncil.ie/en/Publications/Research/Documents/Learningto-Teach-and-its-Implications-for-the-Continuum-of-Teacher-Education.pdf.

Czerniawski, G., D. Gray, A. MacPhail, Y. Bain, P. Conway, and A. Guberman. 2018. "The Professional Learning Needs and Priorities of Higher-Education-Based Teacher Educators in England, Ireland and Scotland." *Journal of Education for Teaching* 44 (2): 133–148.

European Commission. 2015. "Strengthening Teaching in Europe: New Evidence from Teachers Compiled by Eurydice and CRELL." Accessed on 17 January 2019 at http://ec.europa.eu/assets/eac/education/library/policy/teaching-profession-practices_en.pdf.

Furlong, J. 2013. "Globalisation, Neoliberalism, and the Reform of Teacher Education in England." *The Educational Forum* 77 (1): 28–50.

Gleeson, J., R. Leitch, C. Sugrue, and J. O'Flaherty. 2012. "Understanding the Role and Potential For Research Capacity-Building in Initial Teacher Education (ITE) Programmes North-South Ireland: A Baseline and Comparative Study." Centre for Cross Border Studies for the Standing Conference on Teacher Education North and South (SCoTENS).

Hadar, L., and D. Brody. 2016. *Teacher Educators' Professional Learning in Communities.* London: Routledge.

Kane, R. 2007. "From Naïve Practitioner to Teacher Educator and Researcher: Constructing a Personal Pedagogy of Teacher Education." In *Enacting a Pedagogy of Teacher Education*, edited by T. Russell and J. Loughran, 70–86. London: Routledge.

Kelchtermans, G., K. Smith, and R. Vanderlinde. 2018. "Towards an 'International Forum for Teacher Educator Development': An Agenda for Research and Action." *European Journal of Teacher Education* 41 (1): 120–134.

Kennedy, A. 2017. "Researching Teacher Education Policy: A Case Study from Scotland." In *A Companion to Research in Teacher Education*, edited by M. Peters, B. Cowie and I. Menter, 569–581. Singapore: Springer.

Kosnik, C. 2007. "Still the Same but Different: Enduring Values and Commitments in My Work as a Teacher and Teacher Educator." In *Enacting a Pedagogy of Teacher Education*, edited by T. Russell and J. Loughran, 16–30. London: Routledge.

Livingston, K., J. McCall, and M. Morgado. 2009. "Teacher Educators as Researchers." In *Becoming a Teacher Educator*, edited by A. Swennen and M. van der Klink, 191–203. Dordrecht: Springer.

Lunenberg, M., E. White, A. MacPhail, J. Jarvis, M. O'Sullivan, and H. Guðjónsdóttir. In press. "Self-Study Methodology: An Emerging Approach for Practitioner Research in Europe." In *Second International Handbook of Self-Study of Teaching and Teacher Education*, edited by J. Kitchen, A. Berry, H. Guðjónsdóttir, S.M. Bullock, M. Taylor and A.R. Crowe.

MacPhail, A. 2011. "Professional Learning as a Physical Education Teacher Educator." *Physical Education and Sport Pedagogy* 16 (4): 435–451.

MacPhail, A. 2014. "Becoming a Teacher Educator: Legitimate Participation and the Reflexivity of Being Situated." In *Self-study in Physical Education Teacher Education*, edited by A. Ovens and T. Fletcher, 47–62. London: Springer.

MacPhail, A. 2017. " 'Physical Education and Sport Pedagogy 'and the Three 'A's: Apprenticeship, Academia and Administration." *Sport, Education and Society* 22 (5): 669–683.

MacPhail, A., and M. O'Sullivan. 2019. "Challenges for Irish Teacher Educators in Being Active Users and Producers of Research." *European Journal of Teacher Education* 42 (4): 492–506.

MacPhail, A., and F. Murphy. 2017. "Too Much Freedom and Autonomy in the Enactment of Assessment? Assessment in Physical Education in Ireland." *Irish Educational Studies* 36 (2): 237–252.

MacPhail, A., K. Patton, M. Parker, and D. Tannehill. 2014. "Leading by Example: Teacher Educators' Professional Learning Through Communities of Practice." *Quest* 66 (1): 39–56.

MacPhail, A., and D. Tannehill. 2012. "Helping Pre-service and Beginning Teachers Examine and Reframe Assumptions About Themselves as Teachers and Change Agents: 'Who is Going to Listen to you Anyway?'." *Quest* 64 (4): 299–312.

MacPhail, A., D. Tannehill, and G. Goc Karp. 2013. "Preparing physical Education preservice Teachers to Design Instructionally Aligned Lessons Through Constructivist Pedagogical Practices." *Teaching and Teacher Education* 33: 100–112.

Menter, I., M. Hulme, J. Murray, A. Campbell, I. Hextall, M. Jones, P. Mahony, R. Procter, and K. Wall. 2010. "Teacher Education Research in the UK: The State of the Art." *Schweizerische Zeitschrift für Bildungswissenschaften* 32 (1): 121–142.

Menter, I., and J. Murray. 2009. "Capacity Building in Teacher Education Research." *Journal of Education for Teaching* 35 (4): 315–319.

Menter, I., M. Peters, and B. Cowie. 2017. "A Companion to Research in Teacher Education." In *A Companion to Research in Teacher Education*, edited by M. Peters, B. Cowie and I. Menter, 1–15. Singapore: Springer.

Munn, P., and S. Baron. 2008. "Research and Practice." In *Scottish Education,* edited by T. Bryce and W. Humes, 3rd ed., 864–872. Edinburgh: University of Edinburgh.

NISE (National Institute for the Study of Education). 2014. *Framework Proposal Regarding the Establishment of a National Institute for the Study of Education (NISE).* Unpublished document. Limerick: University of Limerick.

Pring, R. 2017. "Research and the Undermining of Teacher Education." In *A Companion to Research in Teacher Education*, edited by M. Peters, B. Cowie and I. Menter, 609–620. Singapore: Springer.

Sahlberg, P., J. Furlong, and P. Munn. 2012. *Report of the International Review Panel on the Structure of Initial Teacher Education in Ireland: Review conducted on behalf of the Department of Education and Skills*, 1–36. Dublin: Department of Education and Skills.

Sayer, J. 2006. "European Perspectives of Teacher Education and Training." *Comparative Education* 42 (1): 63–75.

Stern, N. 2016. *Building on Success and Learning from Experience: An Independent Review of the Research Excellence Framework.* London: Department for Business, Energy and Industrial Strategy.

Tack, H., and R. Vanderlinde. 2014. "Teacher Educators' Professional Development: Towards a Typology of Teacher Educators' Researcherly Disposition." *British Journal of Educational Studies* 62 (3): 297–315.

Tannehill, D., and A. MacPhail. 2014. "What Examining Teaching Metaphors Tells us About Pre-service Teachers' Developing Beliefs About Teaching and Learning." *Physical Education and Sport Pedagogy* 19 (2): 149–163.

Tannehill, D., M. Parker, D. Tindall, B. Moody, and A. MacPhail. 2015. "Looking Across and Within: Studying Ourselves as Teacher Educators." *Asia-Pacific Journal of Health, Sport and Physical Education* 6 (3): 299–311.

Tatto, M. 2017. "The Role of Comparative and International Research in Developing Capacity to Study and Improve Teacher Education." In *A Companion to Research in Teacher Education*, edited by M. Peters, B. Cowie and I. Menter, 621–636. Singapore: Springer.

Teaching Council. 2017. *Initial Teacher Education: Criteria and Guidelines for Programme Providers*. Maynooth: Teaching Council.

Trowler, P., M. Saunders, and V. Bamber. 2012. *Tribes and Territories in the 21st Century*. Oxon: Routledge.

Waldron, F., J. Smith, M. Fitzpatrick, and T. Dooley, eds. 2012. *Re-imagining Initial Teacher Education: Perspectives on Transformation*. Dublin: Liffey Press. Accessed on 17 January 2019 at www.info-ted.eu/

12

BRAVE RESEARCH AS A MEANS TO TRANSFORM TEACHER EDUCATION

Anja Swennen and David Powell

Introduction

Lamott (1994) urges writers to embrace the complexity of real life and to write with passion about the biggest questions. This chapter seeks to introduce and develop the concept of Brave Research (Swennen 2018), a new idea for teacher educator research, and is our response, as teacher educators, to Lamott's invitation. Brave Research is an idea we are beginning to conceptualise as teacher educator research that contributes towards the much-needed transformation of teacher education and teacher educators (Ellis, Souto-Manning, and Turvey 2019; Kretchmar and Zeichner 2016), and the communities we serve. It puts our work and research as teacher educators at the very heart of this process. It seeks to use this research to make changes, however small, to our practices and to the knowledge base of teacher education. It is our ultimate goal to understand better the places where we practise so that we contribute to making this world a better place for our students to learn, for our teachers to teach, and for those we live alongside to live. By doing so, we are aiming to re-position teacher educator research so that it is seen as being of value to government and policy makers and those who fund educational research.

Influenced by the writing of Arao and Clemens (2013) about brave spaces, Anja first used the phrase 'Brave Research' in a Skype conversation with David in June 2017. Shortly afterwards, in July 2017, she shared her idea with a group of teacher educators in Huddersfield. Since then David and Anja have returned to the idea to discuss it and try to develop it. During these conversations it has become clear that Anja and David see Brave Research sometimes in the same way and sometimes in different ways. For instance, Anja sees Brave Research as "fighting for something that is worthwhile"; a response to the marginalised position of teacher educators' practitioner research within the field of educational research and an attempt to gain it some "recognition". David sees it as a way of teacher educators responding to the uncertain and troubled times we are living in. We do not see our sometimes different perspectives on Brave Research as problematic because we are united in our belief that teacher educators, including ourselves, need to be braver in the research we do if, together, we are to address the big questions of teacher education and how our research might address issues of equality and equity (Espinoza 2007), diversity, social justice, and sustainability. Nevertheless, our ideas about Brave Research are still forming. At times, we have found it a challenge to develop the phrase 'Brave Research' into a concept that others might use. It seems to us that by engaging in this activity, 'Brave Research' has invited us on a journey during which we are meeting new ideas and concepts that intrigue us and seem worthwhile.

However, this journey is not finished yet and this chapter stops somewhere in the middle of it. We know that there is still some way to go and recognising that, as we continue to think about Brave Research, our views may change. To date, our thinking has been informed by our own experiences as teacher educators and researchers – or more precisely as teacher educator researchers – by listening to our fellow teacher educators from the large and diverse community to which we belong, and what we have read about teacher educators' research over the past two decades. In this chapter we have drawn on all of these as we try to build the concept of Brave Research. We now feel ready to publicly share our ideas of Brave Research. To do this, we have structured the chapter into seven main sections:

1   What is Brave Research?
2   Why is Brave Research important?
3   David and Anja critically reflecting on some of their previous research to determine how Brave it was, what shaped it, and how it might have been Braver
4   Nine possible features of Brave Research's conceptual framework
5   What are the implications of Brave Research for teacher educator researchers?
6   What are the conditions that enable or constrain Brave Research?
7   What next for Brave Research?

Clearly, what we are presenting here is not a finished, neat definition of Brave Research and how it should be conducted. It is tentative and inquiring – we have not yet worked out all the questions or the answers yet. So, this is an invitation to you, as reader and colleague, to consider our ideas and determine their value to you and whether you want to join us in this discussion about Brave Research, what it means, and how together, as teacher educators, we can build it and make it happen. To summarise, this chapter invites teacher educators to be braver and reimagine why, how, and with whom they conduct their research; it proposes diverse and inclusive forms of research that positively change the world of teacher education, education, and the communities it serves.

What is Brave Research?

To help us develop our thinking about Brave Research, we have invited attendees at two different conferences to tell us what the term means to them. At the Association of Teacher Educators in Europe Annual Conference in Gävle, Sweden, we captured these ideas on a board and photographed them. They are presented in Figure 12.1.

Their suggestions were risk-taking, courage, open-mindedness, close to practice, passion, building mutual trust, creative, and vulnerability.

To these ideas we can add the voices of attendees at the ReimagineFE18 conference in Birmingham, England, where Participant A, a higher-education-based teacher and researcher, suggested that Brave Research would "challenge the orthodoxy that further education is for economic development or for employment". This suggests that Brave Research might resist dominant and dangerous narratives used by the powerful to label and control the powerless, what MacDonald (2019) calls 'Hunting Yetis'. Participant A added, "Brave Research is engaging 'outsiders'; the homeless, prisoners, asylum seekers, groups that we don't normally research, which aren't so well researched". We like this idea of researching with diverse and currently excluded groups in our communities, though we are less clear exactly

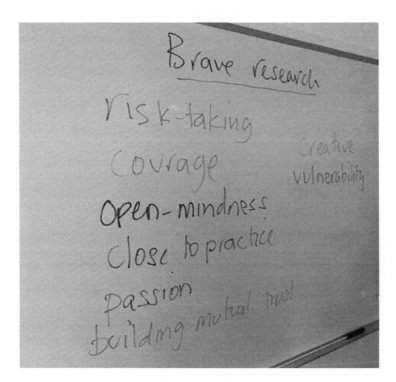

FIGURE 12.1   Teacher educators' suggestions about what Brave Research might mean

who, as teacher educators, we might do this research with. We tend to think about researching our own classrooms or the policies of our governments, though who else might we collaborate with?

Alongside these suggestions, we would like to adapt Arao and Clemens' (2013, 142) suggestion that "using the term *brave space* at the outset . . . has a positive impact in and of itself" to argue that the act of naming research as Brave Research makes a clear, positive statement about its intent. It is a commitment to being brave in our research. We argue that greater diversity and inclusivity is needed in educational research if we, as teacher educators, are to address issues of equality, diversity, social justice, and sustainability. Adopting a Brave Research approach aims to benefit researchers, educators, students, and the communities we serve. For this to happen, we argue that teacher educators may need to interrupt the way they currently see research as a practice if they are to braver in their choice of research topic, research design, and research partners. To be clear, Brave Research is not a specific strand of research with specific topics or methods. It is a way of thinking about teacher educator research; a way of doing it. As such, Brave Research is a way for teacher educators to understand and transform their own teaching practice, to develop teacher education, and to contribute to the formal knowledge about it. This, we hope, will raise its status, as it will better equip us to transform, for the better, education, the lives of those being educated, and the communities where they live.

Our proposal is that Brave Research should be about everything that concerns us as teacher educators; it is about everything that educates and develops the souls of teacher educators, their student teachers, and the communities they serve (Zeichner 2018). Thus, a focus of Brave Research should be on gaining a better understanding of teacher education and the practice of teacher educators. This can be done only by taking seriously teacher education and the practice of teacher educators and studying consistently and coherently. It seems we are a long way from understanding the practice of teacher education and transforming teacher education based on our understanding of its practice.

Why is Brave Research important?

We are worried by what seems to be the emerging dominance of scientific and evidence-based forms of educational research that have become popular with governments and policy makers who believe they are pursuing solutions to their country's perceived poor performance in international league tables like PISA. Compared with quantitative, scalable educational research, teacher educators' research is often seen to be of low status because it does not seem to give governments and policy makers the solutions they want and need to the policy problems they have. We know that our governments and the European Union recognise the role of teacher educators and teacher education in changing, for the better, our respective education systems (see http://ec.europa.eu/assets/eac/education/policy/school/doc/support-teacher-educators_en.pdf). Yet we feel that, for too long, teacher educators, and we include ourselves here, have been docile in our response to government policy initiatives. We have become too conservative in our research topics, research design, and research partners. The result of this has been that we often complain about what is happening without actually doing anything about it. How has it come to this?

There are many texts that promote and champion teacher educators' engagement with research (Cochran-Smith and Lytle 2009; Tack and Vanderlinde 2014). However, there seems to be – with perhaps the exception of self-study research by teacher educators – a scarcity of research publications available on teacher educators' research about their practice (Swennen, Geerdink, and Volman 2017). This is true, not only for teacher educators who work in higher education institutions like the Netherlands' Universities of Applied Sciences, but also for those who work in traditional research universities. Teacher educators' classrooms seem to have become almost private worlds which only their student teachers and perhaps an occasional colleague may enter.

Additionally, teacher educators' work is very different from that of our colleagues in other departments; the demands of teaching and supervising and observing student teachers during their practicum means that there is often limited time for our research and we find it difficult to attract funds to support it (Borg and Alshumaimeri 2012; Ellis et al. 2014). What Zeichner (1995, 153) wrote about research by teachers seems equally true of research by teacher educators: "Most academics who are involved in the teacher [education] research movement around the world have marginalized the process of school-based inquiry by teachers as a form of teacher [education] development but do not consider it as a form of knowledge production". For this to happen, teacher educator researchers need to be brave if we are to push, cross, change, and break down the boundaries between teacher educator research and traditional academic research (Zeichner 1995; Cochran-Smith 2005). Self-study by teacher educators offers us excellent and inspiring examples of how to achieve this dual goal of "learning about practice while simultaneously developing new opportunities for exploring scholarship in, and through, teaching" (Loughran 2007, ix). The same is true of action research, ethnography, and other research methodologies.

Participant B, a teacher educator at the ReimagineFE18 conference, told us why they thought Brave Research was important: "What it's suggesting is developing new ways of research, you will come across people that will churn out paper after paper after paper and have a strong focus on their research profile. But what impact does that have and where does that go? So we can be quite repetitive in research and what we do". There is a suggestion here that Brave Research can interrupt current ways of thinking about teacher educator research.

Teacher education plays a major role in the transformation of teachers and teaching. As teacher educators, we have a responsibility to undertake Brave Research that changes, for the better, its education practices, the sites of these practices, and the communities these sites serve. Major developments, such as the increasing diversity of students in schools, colleges, and universities – which we see as an opportunity and not as a problem – and a variety of scientific and technological changes, are already profoundly transforming education, the work of teachers, and that of teacher educators. Outside our classrooms, recent events in the world raise important questions about the role of educators, including teacher educators. We cannot and must not silently stand by. This is the "time to open up new spaces . . . [and] to explore new discourses" (Denzin and Lincoln 2018, x). It is a time to question the usefulness of traditional academic research, ask to what extent it is making the world a "better" place to "practise and live in" (Kemmis, McTaggart and Nixon 2014, 27); a time to reimagine how, as teacher educators, we do our research and with whom we do it.

Brave Research for us has its roots in the practice of teacher education and critical reflection on it. By engaging in Brave Research, we want to open up our classrooms and invite colleagues, school and college partners, and co-researchers to work with us to use the reflections and studies of others to improve our practice and share our practical and scientific knowledge about educating teachers. In doing this we hope to become more democratic teacher educators, allowing our student teachers to not only understand and experience what innovative practice may look like but also to influence and co-create teacher education. Teacher educators who are able to model Brave Research give student teachers a chance to see it in action, learn about it and benefit from it.

David and Anja critically reflecting on some of their previous research to determine how Brave it was, what shaped it, and how it might have been Braver

Whilst writing this chapter, Anja suggested that, if we are inviting teacher educators to undertake Brave Research, it is important, and perhaps valuable, for us to share some of our own research and critically reflect on to what extent it was brave and identify what, if anything, shaped this. David critically reflects on his professional doctorate research about modelling by teacher educators and its contribution to student teachers' learning, and Anja also starts her critical reflection by discussing her doctoral research about the development of the profession and identity of teacher educators.

How Brave am I? David's critical evaluation of his own research

My thesis involved working collaboratively with a team of further-education-based teacher educators from one English further-education college to explore their use of modelling with a university-approved in-service initial teacher education programme (Powell 2016). To do this, I adopted an action research approach called second-person practice (Chandler and Torbert 2003, 142). When recruiting potential teacher educators, I told them I wanted to film them using modelling in their teaching and afterwards conduct a stimulated recall interview with them so they could explain their pedagogical decision-making to me. I was surprised when some teacher educators told me they did not want to be filmed. Looking back on this now, my approach was rather undemocratic and non-participatory. Why had I not stepped out of my own comfort zone and invited my participants to suggest what data collections we could use to capture and learn more about how they were using modelling in their practice? Even though I had taught a module on action research, I actually did not really appreciate how different it was from other more traditional research methodologies. I wanted to be in control of my own doctorate and by doing so, I believed I was reducing the risk of something going wrong. This was the naïve research behaviour of a "research apprentice" (Murray 2012, 21). This resulted in a restrictive rather than expansive approach at the start of the study. It was far from brave.

However, as the study progressed, I become more confident about the data collection process and my relationship with the teacher educators and their student teachers, and I learned more about the philosophy of action research. This confidence helped me become more democratic and open to suggestions from my participants about what we might do in the study. For example, in the first cycle of data collection I had insisted on filming the classes and holding a focus group with the student teachers myself. At the start of the second cycle, one of the teacher educators expressed concern about the possible impact on the teacher educator and the student teachers of me filming the class. After some reflection and a discussion with my supervisor, I accepted their suggestion and agreed that we should invite one of the student teachers to film the class and that the teacher educator whose class was being filmed should hold the focus group afterwards. Was this brave? Probably not, though it was a sign of my growing confidence in the participants and the study that I agreed to this. Certainly I was moving away from my initial, overly cautious approach towards a braver approach.

As I began my data analysis I came across and was inspired by Segall's (2002, 152) idea of 'second text', a critical approach to presenting research findings that invites participants of a study to comment on how it was conducted, its findings, and the researcher's account of what happened. The participants do this by using "their own words . . . that are presented unedited and in full wherever participants chose to place them". I wanted to try this, as it seemed the right thing to do, though because of the time I had before submission and the amount of time my participants had to read the work, only two accepted my invitation and only then did they comment on small sections of the thesis. If I had known about Segall's work at the start of my thesis, I might not have opted for it, though by the end of the study I felt confident enough to try and use it. Was using second text a brave thing to do? Probably. I was opening up my study to peer review and comment by my participants and that is not something we routinely do (or see).

By undertaking this critical evaluation of my own research, I have realised how conservative my research approach was, and yet I am calling for colleagues to be brave researchers. What I also learned was that as I became more confident in my study, I became more adventurous in my approach, introducing elements of risk like allowing student teachers to film a class and collect data. It seems to me that our competence as researchers gives us the confidence to become more expansive in our approaches, creating the space for Brave Research to happen.

How Brave would I have liked to be? Anja's critical reflection on her research career

I always wanted to be a teacher educator and I was happy when I had a chance to become a teacher educator for primary education. I developed an identity as teacher educator and moved further into the community of teacher educators. I was also attracted to writing and researching, and in 1998 I was given the chance to move to the Vrije Universiteit, in Amsterdam. It was there that I started my doctoral studies. It was wonderful to be able to work on a study for a longer period and be (at least partly, as I still worked for the larger part of the week as a teacher educator) part of the academic world. It was also rewarding to become an expert in the field of the identity and professional development of teacher educators. This gave me the chance to go to conferences and meet people who were engaged in the same field. I began to collaborate and publish with colleagues in the Netherlands and internationally. I thrived as a practitioner researcher.

As a result of my deepened understanding of the profession of teacher education and teacher educators' position in the academic world, I became more aware of the political status of teacher educators in the Netherlands. While the government funded doctoral studies for teacher educators and promoted practice-based research in universities for applied sciences (in which Dutch teacher education is situated), I felt at the same time there was a chasm between the universities of applied sciences and the research universities. I noticed that teacher educators who had obtained their PhDs were rarely recognised as researchers. Their research developed their professional knowledge, but it seemed to have no impact beyond that. A colleague and I interviewed 16 Dutch teacher educators who had finished their doctoral studies between 2000 and 2014. We concluded that there was a big divide between educational research undertaken at the universities and the practice-based research conducted by teacher educators. Today, educational research in the Netherlands is dominated by technical-instrumental visions (Biesta 2007), such as cognitive psychology and neuropsychology. Researchers who have a more social or critical view on learning and teaching have a difficult time fighting for and securing funding for their research (Volman 2019; Klatter and Martens 2019). Interestingly enough, my fellow teacher educators and I recognise what is going on, but so far we have not taken any action.

During my doctoral study, I tried to understand why teacher educators did not – as individuals or as a professional group – resist the many and ever-changing policies over which they had no or only very little influence (Swennen 2012). In my most recent research, about teacher education in the Netherlands during the Second World War, I stumbled across the concept of compliance. To survive, it seems as if teachers and teacher educators allow themselves to be taken by the tide of government policies and comply or, perhaps better, they adapt the rules and regulations in a way they see as good for themselves and their students. An important reason for this adaptation strategy may be the fact that teacher educators mostly work individually. If I was 40 years old (and who over 65 would not want that?) and with my current knowledge, I would like to be brave enough to start a community of teacher educators that actively supported the development and use of Brave Research. I would like to follow more the examples of the self-study researchers or thinkers, like Michael Apple, who try to incorporate a sense of community and activism in their work (Apple 2014) and, more than I have done so far, create a platform for teacher educators who want to contribute to activist and transformative research for and about teacher educators.

Nine possible features of Brave Research's conceptual framework

Bain (1990, 9) suggested that "if we want to create a new world we must have new ways of seeing the world. We must have new visions and new voices". This section presents nine possible features of Brave Research's conceptual framework for your consideration.

1   Brave Research is close to practice research that seeks out new ways of doing research for diversity, inclusivity, social justice, and sustainability (see, for example, Burnett and McArdle 2011).
2   Brave Research adopts an insider perspective. We assert that adopting an insider perspective (Sikes and Potts 2008) takes courage for practitioners, teachers – and teacher educators, in our case – to engage in this kind of research. Our view is supported by one of the teachers we spoke to about Brave Research, who said, "Actually all of us here were Brave Researchers, being that we all came from organisations or cultures that maybe didn't particularly support practitioner research" (Participant F, ReimagineFE event, June 2018). The perspectives of insiders are, as Murray, Swennen, and Kosnik (2019, 8) argue, not only "valuable in their own right but they also contribute to better understanding of the field of teacher education". And we want to go one step further and argue that academics should not only value the insider perspective and incorporate it into their research, but that the insiders should 'bravely' and actively contribute to knowledge production, as fellow researchers or, even better, as members of research communities.
3   Brave Research focuses on what MacDonald (2019) calls "local wins"; forms of research that benefit the students, staff, and communities where it takes place.

4   Brave Research engages with diverse and excluded groups.
5   We assert that 'Brave Researchers' need to create a third space, a 'brave space', which is always an unknown space in which a new practice and new values need to be developed: "The non-synchronous temporality of school and academic cultures opens up a cultural space – a third space – where the negotiation of incommensurable differences creates a tension peculiar to borderline existences" (Babbha, 1994, 218). If different perspectives of insider and outsider researchers, teachers, teacher educators, university-based researchers, students, and other stakeholders are to be taken seriously, we all have to collaborate to foster this diversity and use it to understand better all aspects of teacher education and the work of teacher educators, improve it, and create public knowledge.
6   Brave Research is an idea, not a methodology.
7   Brave Research comes face to face with "human and contextual messiness" (Mockler 2017, xx) and works with it.
8   Brave Research is a form of activism that involves risk, courage, building trust, and vulnerability.
9   Brave Research is inclusive, co-operative, collaborative, and respectful (Denzin and Lincoln 2018), resulting in action that changes the world for the better. This action might be by a practitioner or by a policy maker who is responding to a piece of Brave Research.

These nine possible features are not a checklist for Brave Research; they are suggestions of what it might constitute. What do you think of them? Have we missed anything important? Are there contradictions in our ideas?

What are the implications of Brave Research for teacher educator researchers?

While this chapter focuses on teacher education and teacher educators, we believe that ultimately it is the student teachers who are educated by teacher educators, teachers and students in schools, and their communities who should benefit from the Brave Research efforts of teacher educator researchers. So what might this mean for teacher educators? We suggest there are two possible implications. First, teacher educators need to be role models for Brave Research. Second, they will need to be bricoleurs (Kincheloe 2004) as they do this. We will now explain what we mean by this.

One important aspect of teacher educators' pedagogy is their use of modelling (Loughran and Berry 2005; Lunenberg, Korthagen, and Swennen 2007). If we want our student teachers to go out and change the world from within their classrooms, is it not reasonable for teacher educators to model Brave Research in their research practice? Teacher educators who adopt Brave Research will need to be "bricoleurs" (Kincheloe 2004, 2), who creatively and skilfully use the site

FIGURE 12.2   Example ArtActivistBarbie

of their research, including the relationships that exist amongst the participants in the study, to make a study happen. They adopt a bricolage approach to methodology, methods, and data analysis to generate knowledge and action. Their aim is to use bricolage to progress "beyond describing, analysing and theorizing social practices" (Somekh 2006, 1) and search for praxis that changes practice(s) and the site where these practices take place (Kemmis, McTaggart, and Nixon 2014). One of the advantages of Brave Researchers being bricoleurs and adopting a bricolage approach is that it invites us to recognise and investigate difference and diversity in our research (Kincheloe 2004), and to discover and map new areas of practice and with new groups (Petrie 2015). An example of how this might happen is set out in Figure 12.2, in which the profile of ArtActivistBarbie is presented, a pedagogic and research intervention aimed at calling out the misrepresentations of women in art galleries and museum.

Sarah Williamson is a teacher educator and a feminist, and a qualitative researcher based at the University of Huddersfield; she describes her work as practitioner research. Sarah's commitment to feminist activism has led her to stage and pose Barbie dolls in art galleries and museums "to draw attention to, and ask questions about, gender representation, inequalities and injustices" (Williamson 2019). This intentionally political work is part of a research project, funded by the Canadian Social Sciences and Humanities Research Council, on how art galleries and museum spaces can be used to highlight injustices and inequalities, especially those relating to gender, and how these sites can be potentially "sites for change" (Williamson 2018). Sarah asserts that the staging and posing of the Barbie dolls in art galleries and museums is "an aesthetic and imaginative provocation, a public and performative critical practice that intervenes and disrupts" (Williamson 2019), though she says it takes courage to go into a gallery and then hold her nerve whilst doing this type of activist work. To make visible this work and explore the potential of social media to disseminate it to a wider audience, Sarah has used Twitter – the Twitter handle is @BarbieReports – to communicate her message and reach a diverse and eclectic range of followers, creating considerable international impact in a short space of time.

What are the conditions that enable or constrain Brave Research?

Any attempts to undertake Brave Research will be shaped by three factors: the availability of funding to sustain it; the site where it is undertaken; and ourselves. Here we set out how Brave Research might be funded and by whom, the conditions that might enable or constrain Brave Research at a site, and how we might become Brave Researchers.

We urge teacher educators to be brave and apply for types of funding that include practitioners, students, and their local community as full and equal partners. Because funding bodies tend to favour and fund traditional research by well-known professors, we call for governments and other funding bodies to be brave and fund diverse forms of teacher education research that promote inclusivity, community cohesion, and sustainability.

Pennanen et al. (2017, 203) would assert that the "practice architectures" of the site where the Brave Research takes place will also shape what happens, prefiguring it. "Practice architectures" are the "three kinds of arrangements" (ibid, 201) found at a site: cultural-discursive arrangements (ideas); material-economic (resources); and social-political (relationships). To illustrate this, let us listen to the voice of Participant L, a teacher at a further-education college in England:

> We were just slightly concerned about getting consent for some Brave Research because I know there's plenty of stuff I'd like to research within my college and I doubt very much if I'd get the consent to do it. The taboo subjects, you know, the bums on seats and the box ticking culture and stuff like that and college management just wouldn't agree to it.

This teachers' saying reflects their frustration with how the leaders and managers of education institutions seem preoccupied with filling courses and classes with students almost regardless of the quality of the students. It reflects the marketization of education, and many education leaders and managers are sensitive to the accusation from staff that they, as leaders and managers, are only interested in how many students' 'bums are on the seats in the class'. Here we can see how the differing ideas (cultural-discursive arrangements) of the teacher and manager about what constitutes suitable research are likely to stifle certain types of research at this site. Another example comes from Participant G, another teacher from a further-education college in England: "Research can be as brave as you want, but if the subjects [participants] are not brave, then the data is not forthcoming". Participant G's voice seems to be suggesting that the ideas (cultural-discursive) and relationships (social-cultural arrangements) might be shaping this instance of research. A further example comes from Participant A, a higher education-based teacher and researcher, who suggested that "to conduct Brave Research, perhaps you need the conditions such as collegial decision making, challenging the managerialist approach of many colleges and what is called often academic freedom. How can you do Brave Research unless you are protected by academic freedom?" We need to acknowledge that doing Brave Research may not be easy or even possible for some at present; there may not yet be the academic freedom for them to do it. However, we suggest that Brave Researchers will seek to change the conditions that prevent the research as a precursor to doing their Brave Research.

Finally, Brave Research will not happen unless we decide to be brave and take the first step. Perhaps the greatest barrier to Brave Research happening is ourselves, as teacher educators, and our own bravery. Cowley (2019), an English writer and former teacher, has written a book chapter called '#10% Braver: Feel the Fear and Do It Anyway'. The chapter is not about Brave Research; it is about women leaders in education. The point Cowley makes is that if we can actually be just a little braver, then small changes might actually happen that lead to further changes that then become significant changes. We like Cowley's idea and suggest that it might be a good starting place for us all; a 10% braver starting place.

To summarise, there are three sets of factors that might shape Brave Research: an ability to attract funding to support it; the place the research takes place and the participants involved in it; and our own bravery as teacher educators.

What next for Brave Research?

This chapter started with Lamott's (1994) call for us to write with passion about the big questions of our time. We hope we have done so, because we believe that Brave Research can contribute to answering the big questions of diversity, inclusion, social justice, and sustainability in teacher education and that this chapter suggests how it might be done. However, we are aware that this is just the beginning of an idea, and like all new propositions, it needs to be debated and built, however slowly. Then, if it is of value, it can be established in the curriculum for those learning how to conduct research. By doing so, we are hoping to develop new dispositions towards teacher educator research that imagine a better future for student teachers, their students, and their communities, and for ourselves as researchers – an approach that makes a difference and is valued by governments, offering hope and harmony for all. We argue that Brave Research means that practitioners and academic researchers have to accept each other's research as valuable contributions to understanding and improving various aspects of education. But acceptance is not enough. This could lead to the co-existence of researchers, each 'in their own world', with their own culture and language, but without any real understanding, appreciation, or connection to a wider research community (Swennen, Geerdink, and Volman 2017). To fully understand the diversity of cultures and languages in educational research, we need to not only learn about the various research traditions but also develop new ways of doing research.

To conclude, we invite you to do three things: first, to contact us by email and let us know what you think of the idea of Brave Research and if it might apply to your own research practice; second, if you believe that Brave Research has a place in teacher education and teacher educator research, we want you to imagine how you might employ it to address issues of power, social justice, inclusivity, democracy, and sustainability in your own professional context and let us know how you get on; and third, to identify who can help you do Brave Research.

David Powell, d.powell@hud.ac.uk

Anja Swennen, anjaswennen@xs4all.nl

References

Apple, M. 2014. *Official Knowledge: Democratic Education in a Conservative Age*. New York and London: Routledge, Kindle Edition.

Arao, B., and K. Clemens. 2013. "From Safe Spaces to Brave Spaces: A New Way to Frame Dialogue Around Diversity and Social Justice." In *The Art of Effective Facilitation: Reflections from Social Justice Educators*, edited by L. Landreman, 35–150. Sterling: Stylus Publishers.

Babbha, H. 1994. *The Location of Culture*. London and New York: Routledge.

Bain, L. 1990. "Visions and Voices." *Quest* 42 (2): 1–12.

Biesta, G. 2007. "Why 'What Works' Won't Work: Evidence-Based Practice and the Democratic Deficit in Educational Research." *Educational Theory* 57 (1): 1–22.

Borg, S., and Y. Alshumaimeri. 2012. "University Teacher Educators' Research Engagement: Perspectives from Saudi Arabia." *Teaching and Teacher Education* 28 (3): 347–356.

Burnett, B., and F. McArdle. 2011. "Multiculturalism, Education for Sustainable Development (ESD) and the Shifting Discursive Landscape of Social Inclusion." *Discourse: Studies in the Cultural Politics of Education* 32 (1): 43–56.

Chandler, D., and B. Torbert. 2003. "Transforming Inquiry and Action: Interweaving 27 Flavors of *Action Research.*" *Action Research* 1 (2): 133–152.

Cochran-Smith, M. 2005. "Teacher Educators as Researchers: Multiple Perspectives." *Teaching and Teacher Education* 21: 219–225.

Cochran-Smith, M., and M. Lytle. 2009. *Inquiry as Stance: Practitioner Research in the Next Generation.* New York: Teachers College Press.

Cowley, S. 2019. "#10% Braver: Feel the Fear and Do it Anyway." In *10% Braver: Inspiring Women to Lead Education,* edited by V. Porritt, and K. Featherstone, 5–24. London: Sage.

Denzin, N., and Y. Lincoln. 2018. "Preface." In *The Sage Handbook of Qualitative Research,* edited by N. Denzin, and Y. Lincoln, 5th ed., IX–XX. Thousand Oaks: Sage Publications Ltd.

Ellis, V., J. McNicholl, A. Blake, and J. McNally. 2014. "Academic Work and Proletarianisation: A Study of Higher Education-Based Teacher Educators." *Teaching and Teacher Education* 40: 33–43.

Ellis, V., M. Souto-Manning, and K. Turvey. 2019. "Innovation in Teacher Education: Towards a Critical Re-Examination." *Journal of Education for Teaching* 45 (1): 2–14.

Espinoza, O. 2007. "Solving the Equity-Equality Conceptual Dilemma: A New Model for Analysis of the Educational Process." *Educational Research* 49 (4): 343–363. doi: 10.1080/00131880701717198.

Kemmis, S., R. McTaggart, and R. Nixon. 2014. *The Action Research Planner: Doing Critical Participatory Action Research.* Dordrecht: Springer.

Kincheloe, J. 2004. "The Power of the Bricolage." In *Rigour and Complexity in Educational Research: Conceptualizing the Bricolage,* edited by J. Kincheloe, and K. Berry, 1–122. Maidenhead: Open University Press.

Klatter, E., and R. Martens. 2019. "Onderwijs Om (te) Vormen." *Didactief.* Accessed on 6 August 2019 at https://didactiefonline.nl/blog/blonz/onderwijs-om-te-vormen.

Kretchmar, K., and K. Zeichner. 2016. "Teacher Prep 3.0: A Vision for Teacher Education to Impact Social Transformation." *Journal of Education for Teaching* 42 (4): 417–433.

Lamott, A. 1994. *Bird By Bird: Some Instructions on Writing and Life.* New York: Anchor Books.

Loughran, J. 2007. "Preface." In *International Handbook of Self-Study of Teaching and Teacher Education Practices,* edited by J. Loughran, M-L. Hamilton, V. Laboskey, and T. Russell, ix–xii. Dordrecht: Springer.

Loughran, J., and A. Berry. 2005. "Modelling by Teacher Educators." *Teaching and Teacher Education* 21: 193–203.

Lunenberg, M., F. Korthagen, and A. Swennen. 2007. "The Teacher Educator as a Role Model." *Teaching and Teacher Education* 23 (5): 586–601.

MacDonald, R. 2019. *'Not Under Conditions of Their Own Choosing': Youth Transitions, Place, and History.* Inaugural Professorial Lecture. Thursday, 28 March 2019. University of Huddersfield.

Mockler, N. 2017. "Foreword Practical Theory for Complex Times." In *Exploring Education and Professional Practice Through the Lens of Practice Architectures,* edited by K. Mahon, S. Francisco, and S. Kemmis, xix–xxiv Singapore: Springer.

Murray, J. 2012. "Performativity Cultures and Their Effects on Teacher Educators' Work." *Research in Teacher Education* 22: 19–23.

Murray, J., A. Swennen, and C. Kosnik. 2019. "International Policy Perspectives on Change in Teacher Education." In *International Perspectives on Policy and Practice: The Insider Perspective*, edited by J. Murray, A. Swennen, and C. Kosnik, 1–13. Switzerland: Springer Nature.

Pennanen, M., L. Bristol, J. Wilkinson, and H. Heikinnen. 2017. "Articulating the Practice Architectures of Collaborative Practice Research." In *Exploring Education and Professional Practice Through the Lens of Practice Architectures*, edited by K. Mahon, S. Francisco, and S. Kemmis, 201–218. Singapore: Springer.

Petrie, J. 2015. "Introduction: How Grimm is FE." In *Further Education and the Twelve Dancing Princesses*, edited by M. Daley, K. Orr, and J. Petrie, 1–12. London: IOE/Trentham.

Powell, D. 2016. "'It's Not As Straightforward As It Sounds': An Action Research Study of a Team of Further Education-Based Teacher Educators and Their Use of Modelling During a Period of De-Regulation and Austerity." Unpublished EdD thesis. University of Huddersfield.

Segall, A. 2002. *Disturbing Practice: Reading Teacher Education As Text*. New York: Peter Lang.

Sikes, P., and A. Potts. 2008. *Researching Education From the Inside: Investigating Institutions From Within*. London: Routledge/Falmer.

Somekh, B. 2006. *Action Research: A Methodology for Change and Development*. Maidenhead: Open University Press.

Swennen, A. 2012. "Van Oppermeesters tot Docenten Hoger Onderwijs: De Ontwikkeling van het Beroep en de Identiteit van Lerarenopleiders" [The Development of the Profession and Identity of Teacher Educators]. Amsterdam: VU University Amsterdam. Accessed on 6 August 2019 at http://dare.ubvu.vu.nl/handle/1871/38045.

Swennen, A. 2018. "Brave Research as More Than Just Professional Development." *Professional Development in Education* 44 (2): 141–144.

Swennen, A., G. Geerdink, and M. Volman. 2017. "Developing a Researcher Identity as Teacher Educator." In *Teachers and Teacher Educators Learning Through Inquiry: Internal Perspectives*, edited by P. Boyd, and A. Szplit, 143–167. Prague: Jan Kochanowski University. Accessed on 5 August 2019 at https://atee1.org/wpcontent/uploads/2016/06/Teachers-and-teacher-educators-learningthrough-inquiry-international perspectives.pdf

Tack, H., and R. Vanderlinde. 2014. "Teacher Educators' Professional Development: Towards a Typology of Teacher Educators' Researcherly Disposition." *British Journal of Educational Studies* 62 (3): 297–315.

Volman, M. 2019. "Pleidooi voor een Onderwijskundige Visie op Gepersonaliseerd Leren." [Plea for an Educational Vision of Personalised Learning] *Pedagogische Studiën* 96: 64–75.

Williamson, S. 2018. "Challenging Gender Representation, Injustice and Inequality Through Art Gallery Interventions: Huddersfield Did It First!" Accessed on 5 August 2019 at http://blogs.hud.ac.uk/subject-areas/hudcres/2018/02/28/challenging-gender-representation/

Williamson, S. 2019. "'ArtActivistBarbie' – Promoting Social Justice and 'Wokeness'." Accessed on 5 August 2019 at https://blogs.hud.ac.uk/hudcres/2019/april/art-activist-barbie/

Zeichner, K. 1995. "Beyond the Divide of Teacher Research and Academic Research." *Teachers and Teaching: Theory and Practice* 1: 153–172.

Zeichner, K. 2018. *The Struggle for the Soul of Teacher Education*. Abingdon: Routledge.

13

EPILOGUE

Lessons from this book and next steps in developing the profession of teacher educators

Anja Swennen and Elizabeth White

Introduction

This book provides a collection of chapters with research by authors who for the most part know teacher education from within, as most of them work as both teacher educators and researchers. As a result, each of the chapters contributes in its own way to making research by and for teacher educators visible, and to understanding and improving the work of teacher educators. Because of the connectedness of the book with a larger community, the Association of Teacher Educators (ATEE), the book will, we hope, not only be read, but will also play a role in the further development and innovation of teacher education in Europe and beyond. In this epilogue we discuss the lessons that we believe can be learned from the book and we speculate about the future of the teacher educator profession. We start with a theme that was also prominent in the Epilogue of *Becoming a Teacher Educator*. We then discuss themes that emerged from this book that are crucial for teacher educators and are worth exploring in new research and books for teacher educators. Finally, we formulate recommendations for the future and we conclude the same way as *Becoming a Teacher Educator*: with the challenges for teacher educators in the coming ten years.

Reflection on teacher educators' research in this book

A critical lesson from the chapters is that more and more teacher educators are actively engaged in understanding and improving their own practice. Several chapters in the book pay attention to teacher educator research, sometimes as part of a chapter, sometimes as the subject of an entire chapter. These chapters provide insight into the nature of the research that is useful for teacher educators and the importance of research in the development of teacher education and teacher educators. However, the fact that four chapters in the book deal partly or entirely with teacher educator research means that doing research is not yet self-evident for all teacher educators in all contexts. Explicitly and implicitly, the authors ask questions about why research is important for teacher educators and what the benefits will be from being engaged (often in their own time) in research studies.

In the various chapters, six significant functions of research by – and also for and about – teacher educators emerge. The first function is to fulfil the expectations associated with their academic appointment. MacPhail describes in her chapter, 'Teacher educator as researcher: striving towards a greater visibility for teacher education', how teacher educators in research universities are expected to engage in research as part of their job. This is important for them and for their universities as research activities may lead to publications and contribute to the academic status of teacher education programmes and universities.

But MacPhail also claims that visibility alone is not a central function of research when it comes to teacher educators themselves. For her it is imperative that teacher educators make teacher education more visible through their research. This second function involves the search for opportunities for the teacher educator as a researcher to increase the visibility of teacher education at local, university, national, and international levels, as Shagrir does with her study about collaborative research of teacher educators in her chapter, titled 'International semi-collaborative research initiative: a critical reflection of the research process'.

The third function of teacher educator research is the improvement of the work of teacher educators. This function has received much attention in the research literature as it is a key goal of self-studies, and it is highlighted in the self-studies in this book: Attard's chapter, 'Understanding the reflective process through self-study: A teacher educator's journey towards continuous professional development', Beaton's chapter, 'Old learning, new learning: teacher educators as enquiring professionals', and the chapter by Russell and Flores, 'Developing as teacher educators: lessons learned from student voices during practice and research'. These chapters show how valuable self-studies and self-study-related studies are for improving the work of teacher educators.

Self-studies also contribute to the fourth function of research that becomes clear from this book: research by teacher educators contributes to the professional development of teacher educators. This applies not only to research conducted by teacher educators themselves but also to what they experience as participants, as in the studies of Leijgraaf, '"Are we doing the right thing?" Challenges teacher educators face when taking the risk of opening up possibilities for students', and Powell, 'Teacher educator collaboration and a pedagogy of teacher education: Practice architectures, professional learning, praxis, and production'. Teacher educator research underpins the development of resources that can support the professional development of teacher educators, as demonstrated in White, Timmermans, and Dickerson's chapter, 'Learning from stories about the practice of teacher educators in partnerships between schools and higher education institutions'.

The chapters of these books also make it clear that research by teacher educators and for teacher educators contributes to knowledge and understanding of the work of teacher educators, the fifth function we identified. The chapter by Holdsworth, 'Being a reflective teacher educator: professionalism or pipe-dream?', gives us insight into how reflection by teacher educators is not as obvious as prescriptive literature (publications about how it should be) makes us believe, and the chapter by Seifert and Bar-Tal, 'A professional social network as a platform for teacher educators' professional development', gives us insight into the experiences of teacher educators working in digital networks. The sharing of practical experiences and research is slowly but surely creating a research-based practice knowledge base for teacher educators.

Finally, there is a sixth function of research described in this book, which is related to, among other things, the visibility of teacher educators. This receives attention in the chapter by Swennen and Powell – emancipation of the profession of teacher educators. Signature research for teacher educators can contribute to strengthening the profession. As Swennen and Powell explain in their chapter, 'Brave Research as a means to transform teacher education', searching for ways to strengthen research is not always easy, but it is necessary for the further development of the research of teacher educators and their profession.

Reflection on the themes for research and development of teacher educators

The themes in this book are essential to, and characteristic of, being a teacher educator. The authors write about themes that touch upon the core of teacher educators' practice. Some of the themes in this book are part of the increasing research tradition in teacher education, such as modelling and school-based teacher education. Others are relatively new: reflection by teacher educators and the learning of teacher educators from student teachers.

Modelling

Various chapters, such as that of Russell and Flores, Attard, and Powell, deal with the pedagogy of teacher education. Since the 1990s, the study for a specific pedagogy for teacher education has been developed. Through works of people like Loughran (2006), Loughran and Berry (2005), and Russell (1997), and that of Murray (2002) on second-order practitioners, more thought is given to what distinguishes the pedagogy of teacher educators from that of teachers. One way of thinking about a specific pedagogy for teacher educators is the concept of 'signature pedagogies', introduced in 1989 by Shulman (2005). According to Shulman, signature pedagogies are "the forms of instruction that leap to mind when we first think about the preparation or members of particular professions" (p. 52). In the case of law, for example, that is the study of cases, and for medicine, walking with doctors in the hospital. For teacher educators, explicit modelling is undoubtedly a signature pedagogy. Various chapters show that modelling is not a simple form of demonstration. Three forms of modelling are applied in this book alone: making one's own education transparent, systematically reflecting for a long time on reflection (by student teachers and their teacher educator), and cooperation between teacher educators to explore modelling and learn from it for their own practice. Recent literature describes many more ways of explicit modelling that give teacher educators insight into what modelling is and how it works in different practices. However, research about pedagogies of teacher education as explicit modelling is not yet common, as Boyd (2014) states, and more research is needed to understand what explicit modelling is and how it could benefit the education of teachers (Lunenberg, Korthagen, and Swennen 2007). Thinking about explicit modelling as a signature pedagogy might help. Shulman (2005: 54–55) describes the structure of the signature pedagogies which may be useful in the research about explicit modelling:

> First, it has a surface structure, which consists of concrete, operational acts of teaching and learning, of showing and demonstrating, of questioning and answering, of interacting and withholding, of approaching and withdrawing. Any signature pedagogy also has a deep structure, a set of assumptions about how best to impart a certain body of knowledge and know-how. And it has an implicit structure, a moral dimension that comprises a set of beliefs about professional attitudes, values, and dispositions. Finally, each signature pedagogy can also be characterized by what it is not – by the way it is shaped by what it does not impart or exemplify.

School-based teacher education

Student teachers' learning in the workplace is facilitated by school- and institute-based teacher educators working in partnership. The complexity of partnerships for initial teacher education provides challenges for teacher educators that are explored in the chapters by White, Timmermans, and Dickerson, and by Beaton, considering the ways that school-based teacher educators work with institute-based teacher educators; and with student teachers and pupils, as they model their practice. By taking a magnifying glass to the issues in the workplace, we can understand better how student teachers learn in the workplace and how teacher educators can collaborate more effectively in partnerships to support student teacher learning. Listening to the actors 'on the ground' – whether pupils, student teachers, or teacher educators – we can bring to the surface hegemonic assumptions that can be detrimental to the development of teacher education, and to the professional learning and development of teacher educators, enabling us to work together to enhance our practice.

Reflection

The literature pays a lot of attention to reflection by student teachers, but interestingly enough, reflection by teacher educators is an explicit theme in three chapters. A quick search of the literature shows that 'reflection by teacher educators' is usually used in the sense that teacher educators must have knowledge about how to teach and support reflection or as a self-evident characteristic of teacher educators for professional development and enquiry skills (Beauchamp 2015; Nelson and Sadler 2013).

In this book, reflection is also seen as a means of modelling, as described in the preceding paragraph and a means of improving one's own work, individually and collaboratively. In this respect, the study by Holdsworth provides us with results that show that professional development in this field is needed. We would welcome more research about reflection by teacher educators.

Teacher educators learning from their students

A second and, in our eyes, fairly new and interesting topic in this book is teacher educators' learning to professionalise. In their study, Russell and Flores state that talking to and listening to students is one of the main ways to improve teacher education. Also, Attard writes about how teacher educators can learn about the learning of their students to improve their own teaching and support of teacher educators.

Collaboration

Cooperation between teacher educators, and between teacher educators and their students, is, of course, not a really new topic. However, we noticed that it plays a vital role in the chapters. It is a subject that hardly played a role in *Becoming a Teacher Educator*. It seems that ten years ago, teacher educators conducted research and developed much more often individually or in small and close groups of people who knew each other well. The collaboration can be found in authors working together on projects, collaborating on chapters, and collaborating in larger contexts, such as the research described by Shagrir or in the digital network researched by Seifert and Bar-Tal.

What was missing

Diversity

In *Becoming a Teacher Educator*, we explicitly demanded that each chapter be written by at least one author from Southern or Eastern Europe to guarantee diversity and geographical distribution. We received mixed responses to this: some thought that this forced diversity was not the answer to the lack of diversity among the authors, while others welcomed the fact that authors from very different countries contributed to a book. Our call for papers for *Being a Teacher Educator* was widely disseminated within the ATEE, but this time we have made no demands on the diversity of the authors. The result is that the authors mainly come from countries where the development of and research into teacher educators is traditionally strong.

When it comes to diversity, we miss having one or more chapters on diversity in teacher education in this book – chapters on diversity within the profession of teacher educators, teacher education for teaching diverse pupils (teaching for inclusion), and the way teacher educators work inclusively to prepare diverse students. We think that further research and publications about diversity in teacher education would be very welcome – that is, not only publications that emphasise the importance of diversity in teacher education, but especially studies into the current practice of diversity, the problems that teacher educators encounter and the education with which they come, and so on. In retrospect, we should have looked for teacher educators and researchers who write about diversity.

The use of technology in teacher education

One chapter is dedicated to the use of digital technologies, collaboration of teacher educators in a digital network. However, we miss in the book the way teacher educators may improve or enhance their pedagogy by using technologies. The question of what modern technology can mean specifically for teacher education is significant and interesting. What are best practices? How can teacher educators make use of diverse technology? How can they resist hype and at the same time process irreversible developments in the field of education and teaching, or are they at the forefront when it comes to applying them? Is the use of technology in teacher education not particularly useful or are teacher educators lagging behind in development? We don't know, but it seems apposite to determine this.

Next steps for the development of the profession of teacher educators

As research in all its functions, and the themes we mentioned – and more than those – are important, it is imperative to think about the future development of the profession of teacher educators. How can teacher educators be supported to teach, supervise students, develop themselves, use innovative practice, and engage in research within the limits of their working days? How can they improve their status as teacher educators? How can they improve their status as researchers and receive more funding for their research?

First of all, we think the profession of teacher educators needs to work on all of this themselves. Associations of teacher educators such as the ATEE are vital for this. Unfortunately, there are only two European countries with a national association of teacher educators: Belgium (VELOV) and the Netherlands (VELON).

It is time for other European teacher educators to unite and organise themselves nationally into associations to enhance the profession.

What is also needed is academic leadership for teacher education and teacher educators. As far as we know, there are currently no full academic professors who are specially appointed to promote the development of the teacher educator's profession, the professional development of teacher educators, and/or research by teacher educators.

The themes in this book – old and new ones – will undoubtedly remain important in the coming ten years, but how these themes will be interpreted depends on the political situation in a country. For example, we know only too well how different the interpretation of a concept such as school-based teacher education is in, for example, the Netherlands and England, and in other countries and regions such as Scotland, Norway, and Flanders. Whether school-based teacher education will be given such a focus that the development of new teachers becomes an even more practice-oriented and short training, or whether it will provide well-thought-out courses in which there is a good match between practice and theory and their inter-relationship, cannot be predicted. That is also one of the concerns we have, based on this book. A fairly optimistic attitude emerges from most chapters, but that optimism is often local and related to individual research or projects. Nationally and internationally, there are hardly any initiatives that promote the previously mentioned themes in terms of content and research. One initiative has been the International Forum for Teacher Educator Development (InFo-TED) which delivered a project from 2016 through 2019, funded by the European Union, with the aim of developing the professional knowledge base and guidelines for induction and professional learning programmes for teacher educators. Going forward, it will be necessary to face the challenge of how an enduring, international supportive structure can be implemented and sustained. Such initiatives and research will certainly have an impact on the renewal of teacher education, and the leadership of these initiatives and research will only increase that effect.

References

Beauchamp, C. 2015. "Reflection in Teacher Education: Issues Emerging From a Review of Current Literature." *Reflective Practice* 16 (1): 123–141.

Boyd, P. 2014. "Using 'Modelling' to Improve the Coherence of Initial Teacher Education." In *Teacher Educators and Teachers as Learners: International Perspectives*, edited by P. Boyd, A. Szplit, and Z. Zbróg (51–73). Kraków, Poland: Wydawnictwo Libron.

Loughran, J. 2006. *Developing a Pedagogy of Teacher Education: Understanding Teaching and Learning about Teaching*. Abingdon: Routledge.

Loughran, J. and A. Berry. 2005. "Modelling by Teacher Educators." *Teaching and Teacher Education* 21: 193–203.

Lunenberg, M., F. Korthagen, and A. Swennen. 2007. "The Teacher Educator as a Role Model." *Teaching and Teacher Education* 23: 586–601.

Murray, J. 2002. "Between the Chalkface and the Ivory Towers? A study of the Professionalism of Teacher Educators Working on Primary Initial Teacher Education Courses in the English Education System." *Collected Original Resources in Education (CORE)* 26 (3): 1–503.

Nelson, F., and T. Sadler. 2013. "A Third Space for Reflection by Teacher Educators: A Heuristic for Understanding Orientations to and Components of Reflection." *Reflective Practice* 14 (1): 43–57.

Russell, T. 1997. "How I Teach Is the Message." In *Teaching about Teaching: Purpose, Passion and Pedagogy in Teacher Education,* edited by J. Loughran and T. Russel, 32–47. Abingdon: Routledge.

Shulman, L. 2005. "Signature Pedagogies in the Professions." *Daedalus* 134 (3): 52–59.

INDEX

Printed in Great Britain
by Amazon